The BRICs and Emerging in Comparative Perspectiv

C000264723

In the past ten to twenty years the global political economy picture has dramatically changed with the emergence of the economies of Brazil, Russia, India and, notably, China (the BRICs) as big players and competitors of the advanced economies in the West and Eastern Asia.

This book examines the BRICs by analysing their institutional development, their main continuities and changes, and their differences. It provides a comparative analysis of the political economies of the BRICs, but also considers South Africa and Turkey. The contributors provide a systematic comparison of the state–economy and the capital–labour relationships and explore whether they liberalised or followed a specific trajectory. The book also addresses debates on the varieties of capitalism and explores whether the emerging economies fit into the dichotomous construction of liberal and coordinated capitalism or whether they require a more differentiated typological approach.

Moving away from rigid conceptions and the static classification of political economies as either liberal or coordinated and presenting a more open approach, *The BRICs and Emerging Economies in Comparative Perspective* will be vital reading for students and scholars of comparative political economy, international relations, capitalism, the BRICs, emerging markets and the role of the state in the economy.

Uwe Becker is Associate Professor of Political Science at the University of Amsterdam, The Netherlands.

The BRICs and Emerging Economies in Comparative Perspective

Political economy, liberalisation and institutional change

Edited by
Uwe Becker

Routledge
Taylor & Francis Group

LONDON AND NEW YORK

First published 2014
by Routledge
2 Park Square, Milton Park, Abingdon, Oxon OX14 4RN

and by Routledge
711 Third Avenue, New York, NY 10017

Routledge is an imprint of the Taylor & Francis Group, an informa business.

British Library Cataloguing in Publication Data
A catalogue record for this book is available from the British Library

Library of Congress Cataloging in Publication Data
The BRICs and emerging economies in comparative perspective : political economy, liberalisation and institutional change / [edited by] Uwe Becker.
    p. cm
    Summary: "In the past ten to twenty years the global political economy picture has dramatically changed with the emergence of the economies of Brazil, Russia, India and, notably, China (BRICs) as big players and competitors of the advanced economies in the West and Eastern Asia. The book comparatively analyses institutional change in the BRICs"– Provided by publisher.
    Includes bibliographical references and index.
    1. BRIC countries–Economic conditions–21st century. 2. Developing countries–Economic conditions–21st century. I. Becker, Uwe, 1951-
    HC59.7.B6872 2013
    338.9009172'4–dc23
                2013014454

ISBN: 978-0-415-84349-2 (hbk)
ISBN: 978-0-415-84350-8 (pbk)
ISBN: 978-1-315-88483-7 (ebk)

Typeset in Times New Roman
by Taylor & Francis Books

MIX
Paper from
responsible sources
FSC
www.fsc.org   FSC® C013056

Printed and bound in Great Britain by
TJ International Ltd, Padstow, Cornwall

Contents

8 Emerging on an illiberal path: the Turkish variety of capitalism

IŞIK ÖZEL

9 Prospects and politics: a sketch

UWE BECKER

Illustrations

Figures

Tables

Contributors

Uwe Becker is Associate Professor of Political Science at the University of Amsterdam, The Netherlands. He was a visiting scholar at the European University Institute, the Wissenschaftszentrum Berlin, the Center for European Studies at Harvard University, Uppsala University, the University of New South Wales and the State University of Rio de Janeiro. From 2003 to 2006, he was coordinator of an international research project on the political cultures and economies of the Benelux, Scandinavian and the Alpine countries. The main fields of his work are comparative politics and comparative political economy, recently with focus on the BRICs. He has published in journals such as *Politics & Society*, *Theory & Society*, *Journal of European Public Policy*, *New Political Economy*, *Socio-Economic Review* and *Review of International Political Economy*. Recent books have been *Employment 'Miracles'* (Amsterdam University Press 2005; ed. with Herman Schwartz), *Politicologie* (Het Spinhuis 2006; ed. with P. v. Praag), *Open Varieties of Capitalism* (Palgrave 2009), *Het Obama experiment* (Het Spinhuis 2010) and *The Changing Political Economies of Small West European Countries* (ed., Amsterdam University Press 2011).

Renato Raul Boschi, PhD in Political Science (University of Michigan 1978), is full Professor of Political Science at IESP/UERJ (Institute for Social and Political Studies of the University of the State of Rio de Janeiro, formerly IUPERJ). He is also retired full Professor at UFMG (Federal University of Minas Gerais). He was Senior Fulbright/CAPES Visiting Professor at CUNY (2006), Visiting Professor at the Institut d'Études Politiques de Toulouse (2006, 2007, 2008 and 2009), and Directeur de Recherche Associé at the Maison des Sciences de l'Homme, Paris (2009), in addition to teaching at Stanford, Duke and Michigan in previous years. He is the author of several books on entrepreneurs, interest representation, the state and capitalist development in Brazil. He is 1A top researcher and has a research grant from CNPQ (Brazilian National Research Council), and coordinates the research network INCT/PPED dedicated to studying varieties of capitalism and development perspectives in Brazil. His latest books include *Variedades de Capitalismo, Política e Desenvolvimento na América Latina* (Belo Horizonte, UFMG Editora

2011) and *Development and Semi-Periphery: Post Neoliberal Trajectories in South America and Central Eastern Europe* (New York: Anthem Press 2012; ed. with Carlos Henrique Santana).

Surajit Mazumdar is an Associate Professor in Economics at Ambedkar University, Delhi, India. Prior to this, he taught at Hindu College, University of Delhi, for fourteen years before moving to the Institute for Studies in Industrial Development, New Delhi, in 2007. He was also visiting scholar under the Erasmus Mundus European Global Studies Programme at the University of Wroclaw, Poland, in 2011. His research interests include the Indian corporate sector, the political economy of industrialisation, globalisation and the Indian economy, and growth and structural change in India. He has recently contributed papers to books including *Globalisation and Economic Nationalism in Asia* (Oxford University Press 2012), *Two Decades of Market Reforms in India: Some Dissenting Views* (Anthem Press 2013), and has published in journals including *Economic History of the Developing Regions*, *Economic and Political Weekly* and *Contemporary Perspectives/History and Sociology of South Asia*.

Christopher A. McNally is an Associate Professor of Political Economy at Chaminade University and Nonresident Fellow at the East-West Center in Honolulu, USA. His research focuses on comparative capitalisms, especially the nature and logic of China's capitalist transition. He is also working on a book project that studies the implications of China's international re-emergence in the form of Sino-capitalism on the global order. He has held fellowships conducting fieldwork and research at the Asia Research Centre in West Australia, the Institute of Asia Pacific Studies at the Chinese University of Hong Kong, and at the Shanghai Academy of Social Sciences. Recent books include a volume edited by him examining China's changing capitalism, *China's Emergent Political Economy – Capitalism in the Dragon's Lair* (Routledge 2008). He also has authored numerous book chapters, policy analyses, editorials, and articles in journals such as *World Politics*, *The China Quarterly*, *Business and Politics*, *Communist and Post-Communist Studies* and *Comparative Social Research*.

Nicoli Nattrass is Professor of Economics and Director of the AIDS and Society Research Unit at the University of Cape Town, South Africa. She is also a regular Visiting Professor at Yale and is on the World Bank/ UNAIDS/WHO Economics Reference Group. She has a DPhil from the University of Oxford and has published widely in the field of political economy, focusing recently on the international AIDS epidemic and on the relationship between class, inequality and growth in South Africa. Recent books include *Class, Race and Inequality in South Africa* (Yale University Press 2005; co-authored with Jeremy Seekings), *Mortal Combat: AIDS Denialism and the Struggle for Antiretroviral Treatment in South Africa* (KwaZulu-Natal University Press 2007) and *The AIDS Conspiracy: Science Fights Back* (Columbia University Press 2012).

Işık Özel is Assistant Professor of Political Science at Sabancı University (2007–), Istanbul. She received her PhD in political science from the University of Washington, Seattle, in 2006 and worked as a postdoctoral researcher at the Barcelona Institute of International Studies (2006–07) and Freie Universität Berlin. Her research and teaching focus on international and comparative political economy, and development. She is particularly interested in the politics of market transitions, institutional change and regulatory governance; varieties of capitalism in emerging countries; democratisation and its setbacks; and Europeanisation in the context of enlargement. She has published articles in the *Journal of European Public Policy*, *Regulation and Governance*, *Democratization*, the *Journal of International Studies* and *New Perspectives on Turkey*. She has a forthcoming book entitled *State-Business Coalitions and Economic Development, Comparative Perspectives from Mexico and Turkey* (Routledge 2014).

Alexandra Vasileva (MA in political science at the Freie Universität Berlin, April 2012) is a PhD student at the University of Amsterdam and researches the nexus between politics, economy and structural power relations in Russia. Her research interests include comparative political economy of the post-Soviet countries and China, as well as international relations. She has published on foreign policy discourses and EU–Russia relations in *Atlantic Community* and *Russlandanalysen*. Alexandra worked for the European Parliament in Brussels, German political foundations in China and Georgia, and made a documentary film about trade barriers in Central Asia on behalf of the German Development Cooperation (GIZ).

Preface

Who remembers Eyjafjallajökul? The eruption of this Icelandic volcano in late April 2010 was at the root of this volume, or to be precise the ash cloud that the eruption caused. As a consequence, transatlantic flights were put on the shelf for an indefinite period. The Europeans at the Conference of Europeanists in Montreal had to wait and think about what to do. Wi-Fi did not work in the conference hotel and therefore many of them each day went repeatedly to the computer room to check flight possibilities. Many participants who had never personally talked to each other met there, as I met Ana Maria Evans from Lisbon, Portugal.

Ana and Portugal have been very important for this volume. For a while, I had been thinking about switching my research focus from Western capitalism to emerging political economies, particularly the BRICs. I also knew that a small conference on the Revival of Political Economy was going to take place in the beautiful medieval capital of Portugal, Coimbra, in October 2010. As a start to collaboration, scholars from the BRICs or researchers specialised in them would be brought together at this meeting. So the scholars who later turned out to be the authors of the BRICs contributions to this volume were asked whether they would like to come to Coimbra to discuss the development of 'their' political economies. Moreover, they were asked to do so in terms of a critical 'varieties of capitalism' approach. Luckily, all of them approved, and, in case any of them could not manage the entire funding, Ana and I had to find a solution during the application process.

Ana's intention was to contribute on the former emerging economies of Southern Europe, and it became clear that, to complement this, we also needed someone covering Eastern Europe. Jan Drahokoupil took on this task. He participated in one of our BRICs+ panels at the Conference of Europeanists 2011 in Barcelona and in the subsequent meetings of the 'BRICs club' in Rio de Janeiro (October 2011) and Istanbul (early June 2012). In Rio de Janeiro, where the meeting was perfectly organised by Renato Boschi and Ana Celia Castro in the context of a big research programme (INCT-PPED), we furthermore welcomed Vivien Schmidt with a contribution on statism, Nicoli Nattrass with one on South Africa and Işık Özel with one on Turkey. Işık became enthusiastic about the project at the SASE conference in Madrid in

2011, and after Rio she immediately started to set up the meeting at Sabancı University in Istanbul, which, for the entire group, turned out to be a well-arranged finale. Some of us presented papers once more in late June at the SASE conference in Cambridge (Mass.).

For several reasons including health problems, deadlines and other priorities, not everybody could reach the finish line. In the case of China, we were fortunate that Christopher A. McNally, who also originally had been asked to participate, could quickly fill in the gap left by Michael Witt after Coimbra.

One big problem in the course of time has been the question of which countries and regions should be included. The second challenge was the improvement of the coherence of the individual contributions. Regarding the first issue, we discussed Latin America in its entirety as well as a separate chapter on Mexico as options, and there was an argument for looking for someone who would cover Indonesia. In the end, we stuck to just the BRICs plus South Africa, a member of the annually meeting BRICS countries since 2011, and Turkey, as a large, strongly growing economy in the vicinity of the European Union.

The second issue, coherence, is a thematic question and also one of approach. What always has to be balanced in an edited volume consisting of case studies is the individuality of the authors against a common denominator with respect to basic theoretical points of departure. It is up to the readers to decide whether and how we have accomplished this goal.

Collectively, we have to thank those who left the group for their contributions and their constructive participation in the discussion of the articles published here: Jan Drahokoupil, Ana Evans, Vivien Schmidt, Ben Schneider and Michael Witt. Thanks are also due to the organisations that made possible the exciting meetings in Rio de Janeiro and Istanbul, which reminded us what a privilege it is to work in an international scientific context. In Rio, the active role of Ilán Bizberg, Eduardo Conde, Eli Diniz, Daniel Friel, Flovio Gaitán, Anna Jaguaribe, Arnaldo Lanzara and Jaime Marques Pereira was essential for the success of the meeting; in Istanbul, the chairs and discussants Senem Aydin, Caner Bakir, Mine Eder, Ziya Önis, Sevket Pamuk, Sabri Sayari, Umut Türem and Osman Ulagay constructively contributed. We are furthermore grateful to the two anonymous reviewers and to Alexander Quayle of Routledge who always very quickly answered editorial questions. Finally, for editorial assistance we would like to thank Harm Hoksbergen, who helped with the bibliography and the index, as well as Emiel Bijlmakers whose skills were sometimes very useful in drawing figures.

Uwe Becker
Amsterdam/Rio de Janeiro
March 2013

1 Introduction[1]

Uwe Becker

The global political-economic scene is fundamentally on the move. In the past fifteen to twenty years of the most recent wave of globalisation, it has dramatically changed. The background of this wave and subsequently of the changing proportions of global wealth and influence has been the breakdown of Soviet socialism, the triumph of the liberal doctrine of open global markets and the growth of financial interdependence that was facilitated by the worldwide penetration of the internet. The main feature of the new global political-economic picture has become, notably in the 2000s, the emergence of the economies of Brazil, Russia, India and China – summarised as the 'BRICs' – as big players and, partially, serious competitors to the advanced economies in the West and Eastern Asia, which, in relative terms, have declined. The global business cycle has also become largely simultaneous. The rise of the BRICs – the countries that will get the main attention in this volume – is accompanied by that of a number of mid-size and smaller economies such as those of South Africa, Turkey and the Central and Eastern European countries. Indonesia, the Philippines, Angola, Nigeria and Vietnam could also be mentioned. High gross domestic product (GDP) growth in these countries is one indicator, while their increasing share of world production (see Figure 1.1) and trade is another one. Global trade relative to world GDP increased from 39 per cent in 1992 to 52 per cent in 2005, and the share of non-Organisation for Economic Co-operation and Development (OECD) countries went up from 27 per cent to 36 per cent (OECD 2008b: 10). Since then, this process has continued (cf. the country shares in world exports in Table 1.1).

There are considerable differences between these countries, in size, wealth, performance, global impact, institutional structure and politics. These differences will be addressed or, as in the case of politics, touched upon in this volume. Some of the countries feature true emerging economies, while others are experiencing a comeback. The most spectacular cases are the highly populated China (1.33 billion inhabitants) and India (1.24 billion), both of which departed thirty years ago from very low levels. Particularly China has also started to become a competitor of the advanced economies in the West and East Asia when it comes to technologically sophisticated goods, and with its exports of cheap consumer goods it helps to reduce inflation in the rich economies, while its hunger for basic materials

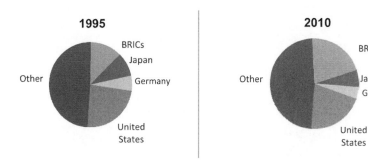

Figure 1.1 Shares of world GDP 1995 and 2010, selected countries
Source: (Schrooten 2011: 19)

Table 1.1 Annual GDP growth, exports and export shares in the BRICs+, 2004–10 (in %)★

	(2000)	2004	2005	2006	2007	2008	2009	2010
Brazil: GDP growth		5.7	3.2	4.0	6.1	5.2	0.6	7.6
Population growth		1.1	1.1	1.1	1.0	1.0	0.9	0.9
Exports as % GDP		14.6	13.4	12.7	11.8	12.1	9.6	9.7
Share in world exports	0.9/0.5	1.1/0.5	1.1/0.6	1.1/0.7	1.2/0.7	1.2/0.8	1.2/0.8	1.3/0.8
China GDP growth		10.1	11.3	12.7	14.2	9.1	9.2	10.3
Population growth		0.6	0.5	0.5	0.5	0.5	0.5	0.5
Exports as % GDP		34.0	37.1	39.1	38.4	35.0	26.7	
Share in world exports	3.5/1.8	6.5/2.9	7.3/3.1	8.0/3.3	8.7/3.7	8.9/3.9	9.6/3.8	10.4/4.6
India GDP growth		8.1	9.2	9.7	9.9	6.2	6.8	10.4
Population growth		1.5	1.5	1.5	1.5	1.4	1.4	1.4
Exports as % GDP				Estimates for 2011: 16				
Share in world exports	0.6/1.0	0.8/1.9	0.9/2.3	1.0/2.7	1.0/2.7	1.1/2.7	1.3/2.6	1.4/3.3
Russia GDP growth		7.2	6.4	8.2	8.5	5.2	-7.9	4.0
Population growth		-0.4	-0.3	-0.2	-0.2	-0.1	-0.1	-0.1
Exports as % GDP		34.4	35.2	33.7	30.2	31.2	27.5	
Share in world exports	1.3/ 0.7	2.0/ 0.9	2.3/1.0	2.5/1.1	2.5/1.2	2.9/1.3	2.4/1.2	2.6/1.2
South Africa GDP growth		4.6	5.3	5.6	5.5	3.6	-1.5	2.9
Population growth		1.3	1.3	1.2	1.1	1.0	0.9	0.8
Exports as % GDP		26.4	27.4	30.0	31.5	35.6	27.4	27.1
Share in world exports	0.5/0.4	0.5/0.4	0.5/0.3	0.5/0.4	0.5/0.4	0.5/0.4	0.5/0.4	0.5/0.3
Turkey GDP growth		9.4	8.4	6.9	4.7	0.7	-4.8	8.9
Population growth		1.3	1.3	1.2	1.2	1.2	1.2	1.1
Exports as % GDP		23.6	21.9	22.7	22.3	23.9	23.3	21.1
Share in world exports	0.7/1.1	0.7/1.1	0.7/1.1	0.7/0.9	0.8/0.9	0.8/0.9	0.8/1.0	0.7/0.9
Eastern EU average GDP★★ growth per capita		5.1	4.2	4.3	6.1	4.5	-5.1	1.7

Note: ★ The export shares are split into those of merchandise (on the left) and services (on the right).
★★ These are average percentages for Bulgaria, the Czech Republic, Hungary, Poland, Romania, Slovakia and Slovenia. The heavy ups and downs of the very small Estonia, Latvia and Lithuania (together 7 million of the 105 million inhabitants of the Eastern European EU members) would have skewed the averages.
Source: (OECD Statistics Portal; OECD 2012a; MDIF 2012; Wikipedia: *Indian Economy* n.d.; WTO 2000–11; EU Commission 2012)

and machinery imports has become a driving force of the world economy as a whole.

These processes have recently received much attention. This is also true for the discussion on the theory of Varieties of Capitalism (VoC) with its dichotomous construction of liberal and coordinated capitalism. However, whether the BRICs and the other emerging countries fit into this dichotomy, which sorts of possibly fundamentally different capitalism or political economy – concepts I want to use synonymously – they reveal, and what change they have undergone in the past fifteen to twenty years is under-researched and under-theorised. This volume addresses these questions with respect to the BRICs, South Africa and Turkey (together the six countries are here indicated as BRICs+), and the two introductory chapters also provide some information on a few representative Eastern European countries: Estonia as an early liberaliser, Slovakia as a late but strong one, the Czech Republic as a modest one, Slovenia as a host of significant corporatism and Poland, the biggest Eastern European Union (EU) member, as a careful liberaliser.

Why this selection? The choice of the BRICs is evident, but why South Africa, Turkey and even a few Eastern European countries but not Indonesia, Mexico, Egypt or some other countries that are also 'emerging'? South Africa is relatively small (52 million inhabitants) and its GDP growth is lower than that of the four BRICs, but it has been chosen because it has joined the club of the BRICs that annually meets as BRICS. It is nearly twice as rich as the more populous Egypt (90 million), while Nigeria, big (170 million) and only relying on oil, is still very poor. In Asia, something similar is true for Indonesia (237 million) and the Philippines (93 million) as a producer of cheap consumer goods. They are not emerging competitors. Just as Eastern Europe, Turkey (75 million), however, has become one, and its GDP has grown solidly in recent years. The latter is less true for the richer Mexico – a long-time OECD member.

The smaller Eastern European economies will only receive marginal attention in this and the next chapter. In part, they are very small: Estonia, with 1.35 million inhabitants, is 1,000 times less populated than China. Even Poland with about 40 million inhabitants is relatively small. It would be inappropriate to discuss them in direct comparison to the BRICs countries. As main contrast cases from the advanced economies, the USA and France or, in socio-economic matters, Sweden are chosen: the USA as the highly liberal leading world economy, Sweden as one of the relatively egalitarian Scandinavian countries, and France because its relatively high level of statism renders it best suited for the comparison to political economies where the state is also strongly present. Including their data in the statistics has to sharpen the view on the peculiarities of the BRICs+. The contrast cases will not be analysed, however.

The first goal of this volume is systematically and comparatively to inform about the selected political economies, to describe their institutional development and to identify the main changes in this respect, particularly concerning the state–economy and the capital–labour relations. We also want to contribute to the theoretical framework of this analysis by presenting a more open approach. We do not intend, however, to explain in depth the different trajectories of our selected political economies, as for example the high rise of China and the big problems of the Russian economy apart from oil and gas.

The volume is theory guided. We depart from the mainstream on capitalist varieties with its rigid conception of complementarities and its static classification of national political economies as either liberal or coordinated. We present a more open approach. Open means that institutional complementarities will be stressed much less and differently, and that the distinction between ideal types and empirical cases of capitalism will give space to grasp nuances and gradual change.

In this Introduction, I first summarise the socio-economic performances of the considered countries, notably of the BRICs+. The chapter also gives attention to social (inequality, poverty) and environmental (emissions, pollution) developments because these factors directly affect the conditions of daily life. Thereafter, I will discuss the topics of institutional complementarity and coherence. The question is how analytically to deal with economic expansion in a context where non-complementarity, as for example India demonstrates, is sometimes a foremost feature. The overview of the subsequent chapters is the closing part.

1.1 Socio-economic performances: an overview

On closer investigation, it is remarkable that some emerging economies do not really belong to this category. No doubt, China, India and to a lesser degree Turkey are 'emerging', but this holds less for the other countries discussed here (see Figure 1.2). Brazil, South Africa and notably Russia rather are making a

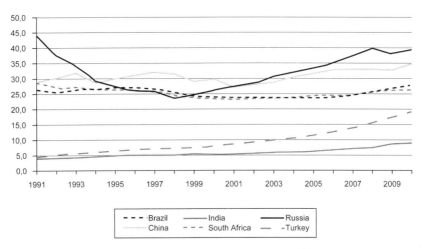

Figure 1.2 Gaps in GDP per capita: BRICs+ to the upper half of the OECD countries
Source: (IMF 2012; OECD 2010a)

'come-back'. Compared to the advanced economies, the Soviet Union in the 1980s had a higher GDP in PPP (purchasing power parity) per capita than Russia today. Thereafter, it sharply declined before growth returned in the late 1990s (the Eastern European countries did not experience this sharp decline). Figure 1.2 further shows still considerable income differences in PPP among the separate BRICs, South Africa and Turkey, as well as between them and the upper half of the OECD (the Anglo-Saxon countries, Japan, the Asian Tigers and north-west Europe). Russia is still the richest, India still a poor country and all of them have a long way to go to the level of the USA (or the slightly lower level of the north-western EU countries).

Comparing GDP per capita data (in PPP), one has to be aware of the enormous difference in the size of our countries. Particularly China has many provinces with a much higher GDP per capita than the national average, and these provinces are sometimes very large. Per head, in 2010, the provinces of Shanghai, Beijing and Tianjin (23 million, 20 million and 13 million inhabitants, respectively) were considerably richer than Russia and 2.5 times richer than China on average. Zhejiang and Guangdong (54 million and 104 million inhabitants; see Wikipedia on 'administrative provinces of the People's Republic of China') had a per head income comparable to that of South Africa and Brazil. In the city of Shanghai, still larger than most Eastern European EU states, Portugal, Greece or Belgium, per capita income is even higher. One has to add that Moscow, Bangalore or Rio de Janeiro are also considerably richer than their national averages.

Table 1.1 provides a more detailed look at recent developments. The table shows real GDP growth and population growth. Overall GDP data, the basis for many other calculations, might be misleading. In Russia and some Eastern European countries, for example, GDP per capita is rising more than GDP because of a declining population, while it is increasing less in most other countries, notably in Brazil, India, South Africa and Turkey, because their populations are growing. So, to put GDP figures into perspective, population growth data, an important indicator by itself, are added. China has a relatively stable population because of its (not strictly practised) one-child policy. It also has the highest GDP growth of all. India, Russia (140 million inhabitants) and Turkey (75 million) did not perform much worse, though the latter two show a strong decline in 2009, the year of the global, particularly Western, financial crisis. Growth in Brazil (nearly 200 million) and South Africa (nearly 50 million) has been lower.

Looking at exports, the most remarkable countries are perhaps Brazil with its low rate and Russia with its extreme dependence on oil and gas, while China appears to be the export economy par excellence. Its figures might be more misleading than those of other countries, however. China assembles many goods the components of which are imported and then re-exported as parts of the final goods. Mobile (cell) phones are an example. So, its enormously increasing share in global exports has to be taken with a pinch of salt. At a lower level, the Indian share in global exports has also grown strongly and its service exports consist probably of fewer imported components than Chinese merchandise. The Indian percentage of services in total exports is by far the highest (Table 1.2). This country's exports in the category of oil/gas and minerals are relatively high because it refines and re-exports oil (imported from Arab countries and Iran). Remarkably, this crowded country is a big agricultural exporter too. Brazil is also relatively strong in the agricultural market (among other things with basic materials for bio-fuel). China specialises in electronics, machinery and textiles; Turkish exports are spread across all sectors, with textiles and vehicles ahead (Toyota, for example, produces cars there); and South Africa heavily relies, but not as much as Russia, on basic materials and steel and iron, as well as pearls (diamonds).

Related to exports and imports, the inflow of foreign direct investment (FDI) (see Figure 1.3) has been high in Brazil and China in the period since 1999, and remarkably high – given its strong reliance on gas and oil – in Russia. The figure shows net percentages (inflow minus outflow). The picture changes when one looks separately at the percentages (of GDP) of inflows and outflows. In relative terms, China is losing its lead then to South Africa, Brazil (OECD 2010a: 20) and Russia (UNCTAD 2011: 4, 9). The reason for this is that China's FDI outflow is considerably lower than its inflow. Chinese FDI outflow is relatively modest and with 0.9 per cent of the global outflow in 2010 (India 0.4 per cent) it was about five times smaller than that of the USA. Fears of a Chinese take-over of the world economy appear somewhat exaggerated, therefore.

Considering growth data, the size of the population and the economy, economic specialisation and the impact on the world economy, it becomes clear that the story about emerging economies has first of all to be one on China. It is the most populated country on earth, its growth percentages are the highest of the economies discussed here, the same is true for its impact on international trade and its exported goods do not primarily consist of oil, gas, minerals and other basic materials, as is the case with Russia, South Africa and, less so, Brazil. China manufactures and exports middle- and high-tech goods and is increasingly becoming a real competitor of the advanced economies – even if the value added of its production of high-tech goods is still limited (OECD 2010c: 32). With different specialisations and on a lower level, India, Brazil and, to a much smaller extent, Turkey and the Eastern European countries also belong to this category of new competitors.

By and large, the picture is similar when we look at innovation. The innovation capacity of the advanced economies is still considerably higher than that of the BRICs and other countries discussed here. In Figure 1.4, this capacity is based on indicators such as the extent of tertiary education, the relative number of patents, cited publications, doctoral degrees, research and development (R&D) expenditure, and the volume of middle- and high-tech as well as knowledge exports (it excludes, however, spontaneous inventions on the work floor, which might be particularly relevant in emerging countries). In this figure, the BRICs+ and, for comparative reasons, the USA are put in relation to the average innovative capacity of the EU27. The figure reveals that the USA has a

Table 1.2 Export specialisations of the BRICs+ in 2010 in % of 'main goods': exclusive services, columns 2–9; services as % of total exports and main service exports as % of total services, columns 10–12

| | Oil, gas, minerals | Other basic materials | Electrical, electronic | Agricultural | Machinery | Vehicles | Steel, iron, aluminium | Pearls, precious stones | Textiles | Services (as % of total exports) | Of which mainly | |
											ICT services	Other business services
Brazil	8.9	9.5	2.3	14.4	5.3	8.0	2.5	1.1	0.1	13.9		49.6
China	–	–	24.5	1.2	20.2	2.3	2.8	0.6	8.4	9.8		35.8
India	13.5	4.4	5.4	13.0	4.1	5.9	2.5	18.0	3.5	36.1	45.8	12.1*
Russia	63.0	12.0	0.9	1.0	1.9	0.5	6.8	–	–	2.8		
S. Africa	22.2	11.8	2.3	3.0	7.5	9.3	12.6	15.7	–	15.2		25.7**
Turkey	3.8	1.9	6.5	2.7	8.0	11.8	8.9	5.8	11.0	23.2		scattered

Note: * 2001   ** 2008
Source: (Intracen 2012 (main goods); United Nations Service Trade Statistics Database)

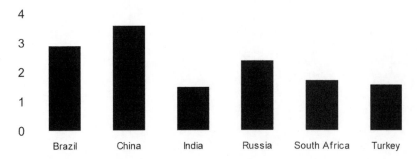

Figure 1.3 Net FDI inflow (inflow minus outflow) as percentage of GDP, 1999–2011
Source: (World Bank 2012b)

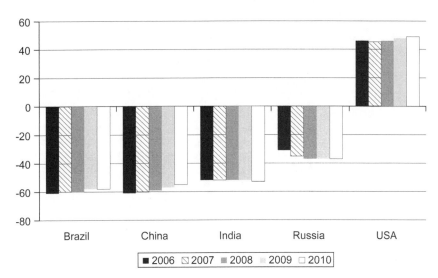

Figure 1.4 Innovation performance of the BRICs and the USA compared to the average of
          the EU27, 2006–10
Source: (Pro Inno Europe 2011)

considerably higher capacity than the average EU27 country (the same holds
for Japan, Switzerland, Denmark, Finland, Sweden and Germany).

Of the BRICs, Brazil – innovative in its field of agricultural materials –
China and India are 50 to 60 per cent below the EU level (just as Turkey; Pro Inno
Europe 2011: figure 8; no South African data), but only Brazil and notably China
are closing the gap, while India stagnates. Closing the gap is a slow process,
however, because most advanced economies continue to improve their innovative capacity. Particularly worth mentioning is Russia. Its innovation performance
is 'only' about 35 per cent below the average EU level (on average, the Eastern

European economies are comparable to Russia). In the 1950s, this country for the first time ever shot a human being into space, it still has many more researchers per 1,000 employed persons than China, India or Brazil (the respective figures are 6.7, 1.9, 0.2 and 1.3; cf. OECD 2009: 40f) and its population is still considerably higher educated (OECD 2010a: figure 7.8). In spite of high levels of GDP per capita growth, Russia does not use its potential, however, and is, apart from successfully selling oil and gas, in a process of serious decline.

1.2 The BRICs' increasing global importance

With their recent economic success, the BRICs' geo-political importance has increased. To emphasise this they established a political association, the *BRICs* (the name was coined in 2002) to discuss economic and political issues and to make their voice better heard. The first summit was held on 16 June 2009 in Yekaterinburg (Russia). There they called for an equitable, democratic and multi-polar world order with more say for themselves and emerging countries in general. In an interdependent world where on average both the advanced and the emerging countries go up and down together (as illustrated in Figure 1.5), the BRICs ask for more inclusion in relevant decision-making processes. Similar declarations have been issued at the subsequent meetings in Brasilia (2010), Sanyo (China, 2011) and Delhi (India, 2012). Since 2011, South Africa has also been a member and in this context the BRICs became the *BRICS*. The establishment of the G20, the first meeting of which was held in Washington in November 2008, reflects the demand of the BRICS for more inclusion that had been put forward before they organised as a bloc.

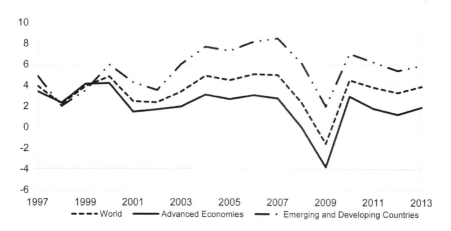

Figure 1.5 GDP growth 1997–2013 in advanced and emerging economies indicating interdependence

Source: (IMF 2012)

What they repeatedly ask for is better representation in the World Bank as well as a reform of the International Monetary Fund (IMF). They also criticise the status of the US dollar as world reserve currency. With respect to world politics, the BRICS time and again proclaim the principles of multi-polarity, peaceful negotiation and non-interference (Bergsten *et al.* 2009; Chellaney 2012; Grant 2012). In the West, the latter is regularly interpreted as self-protection. China is an authoritarian regime with human rights issues and the other four BRICS, though they meet most of the basic formal criteria of a representative democracy, are hardly accepted as full democracies because of their high level of corruption, restricted freedom of speech (Russia, Turkey; see Politkovskaya 2007; Turam 2012) and the dubious role of the police (Brazil; see Brinks 2010: 210–15). What unites the BRICS is being emerging, big (although South Africa is relatively small) and discontent with certain aspects of the current world order.

The BRICS do not have a common identity, however. What divides them are, as said, differences in size, economic power, political principles and ambition, but also of history and future prospects. Some of the BRIC+ countries have had a great past. The Chinese Empire lasted for more than 2,000 years, and technologically it was the most advanced part of the world until the 16th to 17th centuries (with inventions such as the windmill, mechanical clockwork, water-powered metallurgical engines and hemp-spinning machines; Kynge 2009: 35). India has a similarly long and impressive past, and economically it was also highly developed, particularly in textile manufacturing (Parthasarathi 2011), but its history was interrupted several times – for example by British colonialism – and it was never really as innovative as China. Turkey was the centre of the Ottoman Empire that in early modern times (until a few years after the First World War) dominated the Balkans and large parts of the Middle East and northern Africa. As opposed to the USA, the Soviet Union/Russia was one of the two powers that until the early 1990s dominated the post-war global order. Brazil and South Africa, by contrast, have a past of colonialism and domination by immigrants from Europe, although both countries reached independence relatively early.

Currently, the importance of the BRICs+ is unevenly spread. Brazil, South Africa, Turkey and the huge India are hardly visible on the international stage and have primarily regional political influence, although Brazil and India want to become members of the United Nations (UN) Security Council (Karackattu 2011: 7), and Brazil, while criticising the liberal Washington Consensus, managed to get more liberalised agricultural trade within the World Trade Organization (WTO) context in its own specific interests (Hopewell 2013). China and Russia, by contrast, are global players and permanent members of the Security Council (since 1971 and its foundation in 1946, respectively). This corresponds to their ambition to be eminent international powers. Russia is furthermore a member of the G8, the club of the richest countries, which attempts to guide global relations, while China, as Brazil and India, is a member of the G20, which discusses global financial and political issues (it appears to be in a process of upgrading). More important, however, China has gained informal power to a degree that no fundamental international decision can any longer be made against it (Bergsten *et al.* 2009: 210f). It also seems to be dominant in the BRICS, because all of this organisation's claims are separately and forcefully put forward by China.

Russia is doing the same but with less emphasis (MacFarlane 2006: 51). Its predecessor, the Russian-dominated Soviet Union, was one of the two powers dominating the post-war global order, while China was only a poor country with some nuclear military capacity. Today, Russia is still a foremost military power, on which China depends for much of its military equipment (Bergsten *et al.* 2009: 218), and economically and politically it is, based on its gas and oil, climbing back. Nonetheless, it has taken a pragmatic stance and, according to MacFarlane (2006: 49, 56), it has accepted the leading role of the USA in global affairs since the terrorist attacks of 11 September 2001. This could be exaggerated. The antagonism of the Cold War has vanished, but Russia's behaviour in the UN and with respect to Iran and Syria could also be interpreted as pointing in a different direction. Perhaps the critical stance towards US dominance that Gudkov and Zaslavsky (2011: 127f), as well as Roett (2010: 13), detected a few years later is a more adequate characterisation (cf. *The Economist*, 16 June 2012). Being aware, however, of its own economic decline in many fields and the conspicuous rise of China, it is perhaps a point of discussion when it is said (as by Grant 2012: II) that Russia has become anxious of China – though one has to add that the analysis of geo-political relations is highly interpretive.

China has become more assertive vis-à-vis the USA than is Russia. 'Let China sleep, for when she wakes, she will shake the world', Napoleon said more than 200 years ago (Kynge 2009: 7). Exaggerated or not, the times of Deng's maxim 'observe calmly, be good in maintaining a low profile and never claim leadership' (Bergsten *et al.* 2009: 208) are over. Among the emerging economies, China claims leadership, spends more than twice as much for military purposes as Russia (though still much less than the USA; SIPRI 2012), does not support membership of the long-time rival India in the Security Council (Chellaney 2012: 4) and wishes for a more important role for its national currency, the Renminbi (Yuan), in the international financial system (Karackattu 2011: 7). Fed by economic success (and by the often referred-to US bombing of the Chinese Embassy in Belgrade in 1999), Chinese nationalism has also grown (Bergsten *et al.* 2009: 46ff). Chinese separateness rooted in the Confucian tradition (Kynge 2009: 249f) is stressed today, and even mythical narratives of the Chinese as all descending from an ancient 'yellow emperor' do well in public opinion (ibid.: 241–49).

Anti-Americanism is the other side of the same coin. In a survey in 2006, 62 per cent of the Chinese respondents claimed to have a negative view of the USA (against 42 per cent in 2005; Bergsten *et al.* 2009: 47), while the political leadership distrusts the Americans, sees their rampant private spending as well as the alarming US household deficit as weakness, and views the USA as a declining power (Perlez 2012). To temper Chinese nationalism and to avoid open antagonism, a readjustment of the Chinese-US relationship seems to be urgently required. In this view, the liberal world order is principally flexible enough to integrate the more statist-authoritarian China (Ikenberry 2008: 24, 36), while Mearsheimer (2010, cited from McNally 2012: 742) argues that 'China cannot rise peacefully'.

Perhaps the BRICs will also serve as examples of an alternative view on economic development, or at least some of them. As we will see in Chapter 2, on balance, liberalisation has been less significant in the BRICs than in most advanced economies in the two decades up to 2010. The state's role is continuously significant in the BRICs; in Brazil and notably Russia, it even became strengthened. The 'Beijing Consensus', by assigning an important role to the state, often appears in the literature as opposed to the liberal 'Washington Consensus'. It may be that Brazil is more important in this ideological field than China, however (cf. Roett 2010: 9f). The statism of the Lula and Rousseff years has not been authoritarian but, by tendency, social democratic.

1.3 The social face of the BRICs+: do they have one?

To look at performances only in terms of GDP, exports and FDI is a restricted view. The social dimension has to be included. By this, we have to think of employment levels, the extent of inequality and poverty as well as the environmental dimension that to a considerable degree determines the quality of life. In these fields, the BRICs+ perform worse than in the narrowly economic area. The environmental indicator most referred to, CO_2 emissions per capita, is still (much) lower in India, Brazil and Turkey than in the advanced economies, but this is no longer the case in Russia, South Africa and China (though the USA still has a much higher level). The Chinese increase is particularly alarming (Table 1.3). Russian emissions have already been nearly twice as high in 1990 as those of the EU member states, but declined thereafter and in the 2000s increased again. At a lower level, something similar holds for Eastern Europe, which in the table is indicated by Poland and the EU12 (including Cyprus and Malta).

The problem with CO_2 emissions in the BRICs+ is that with continuing increases the level of Western countries, being in decline, will be surpassed – very soon in China. At the same time, CO_2 is only one aspect of the environmental story in emerging countries, for daily life perhaps not even the most relevant one. More important for the quality of air and water are gases – notably nitrogen dioxide (NO_2) and sulphur dioxide (SO_2, poisonous), which are the basis of acid rain and the generation of low-level or ground ozone – as well as particulate matter (PM) and toxic matter like lead. In this respect, the BRICs (least of them Brazil) and generally most emerging economies are already more polluted than most advanced economies (except the USA and Australia, for which some values are also very high). Most BRICs+ (except South Africa) share in the global trend of PM reduction, but the overall environmental picture is alarmingly worsening.

Table 1.3 Emissions of CO_2, sulphur dioxide (SO_2), particulate matter (PM), plus population density (recent data)

	CO_2, tons per capita			SO_2, kg per capita 2010	PM in μg per m^3		Population density 2007
	1990	2000	2011		2001	2010	
Brazil	1.5	2.0	2.3		33	19	22
China	2.2	5.9	7.2	16	87	60	140★★★
India	0.8	1.0	1.6		89	57	368
Russia	16.5	11.3	12.8	31	26	16	8★★★
South Africa	7.3	6.9	7.2		24	26	41
Turkey	1.7	–	3.6★★	23	54	37	90
Poland	8.2	7.5	9.1	32	44	34	122
EU12★	9.3	6.9	7.4	16	22	12	110
EU15	9.1	8.8	7.6	4	15	10	20
USA	19.7	20.8	17.3	41	25	18	32

Note: ★ New member states   ★★ 2007   ★★★ 2010
Source: (OECD 2009: 7.46ff; EDGAR 2012; BRICS 2012: 78; World Bank 2003, 2012a)

Combined, CO_2 omissions, low-level ozone, PM, lead and other toxic metals in the air produce the widely known pictures of cities like Beijing (which moreover is unfavourably located near a desert) in dust and smog, with people who do not leave their houses without breathing protection (there was much news coverage of this in early 2013). Notably in China and India, this is a disastrous development because these countries have a very high population density. Many emissions are measured per head, but the more people who live together on a small surface area, the more polluted each unit of area is. China's and India's average population densities are mentioned in Table 1.3, but in certain highly populated regions they are much higher. Along the Ganges river in India about 400 million inhabitants live on an area of about the size of France (60 million), and the connected Chinese provinces of Shanghai, Jiangsu, Shandong and Zhejiang together have the area of Germany but are inhabited by 250 million people (Germany: 80 million), resulting in a population density of almost $1,000/km^2$.

In the megacities (more than 10 million inhabitants) in emerging economies, air pollution reaches its climax. This is not only true for Chinese and Indian cities like Beijing, Chongqing, Shanghai, Linfen (with 4 million inhabitants not 'mega', but often called the most polluted city in the world), Delhi, Mumbai and Kolkata (according to Dicken 2011: 465, they are ahead, however). It is also true for Buenos Aires, Mexico City, São Paulo and, somewhat less, Istanbul (Incecik and Im 2012) or cities in poor African and Asian countries such as Cairo (like Beijing, also influenced by a nearby desert), Luanda, Karachi, Dhaka, Lagos and similar places that are regularly mentioned in rankings of the most polluted megacities on earth.

A main source of extreme air pollution in China and India appears to be, leaving aside factories in typical industrial cities like Linfen, coal-powered energy plants. In

2004, the proportion of coal-powered energy was 69 per cent in China, 54 per cent in India, but only 16 per cent in Russia (Naughton 2007: 336). In India (and other poor countries), the burning of fuel wood and biomass in households is an additional cause of air pollution. In Brazil, 40 per cent of all fuel comes from ethanol, which is causing the chemical reaction of surface ozone and as a result dense smog (Wikipedia). Everywhere (increasing) traffic by car, truck and motorbike is a central polluter (in Delhi, 67 per cent of air pollution comes from vehicles; Incecik and Im 2012: 89). In cities, such as those in India or inland China, where roads are often not the best, traffic is very slow. This raises fuel consumption by up to 100 per cent and most vehicles, particularly trucks and partially oil-powered motorcycles, do not have a catalytic converter.

Water pollution is at least as serious as air pollution. It is produced by industry and city sewage of all sorts. Brazil has its toxic Tietê River in São Paulo, 75 per cent of Russian surface water is polluted, but, again, extreme water pollution is notably a Chinese and Indian phenomenon. Some 75 per cent of Chinese rivers are affected by pollution, 28 per cent are in the worst, in fact toxic, category (Shapiro 2012: 8; *People's Daily Online* from 17 February 2012 even reports 40 per cent for 2011). It is unsuitable for irrigation. Half of the length of the Hai, Huai and Liao rivers, and one third of the Yellow River have this toxic quality (Naughton 2007: 492; his percentages are, where comparable, somewhat lower than Shapiro's, but referring to 2003, a few years older). Industry-caused persistent heavy metals and chlorinated hydrocarbon build up in the water. In India, city sewage is at least as relevant a polluter as industry. Only 13 per cent of the towns and cities have partial sewage treatment facilities (*The Economist*, 17 July 2008), while 700 million Indian people do not have a toilet. Rivers such as the Ganges and Yamuna are sacred: where the Ganges enters the holy city of Varanasi (Benares), it contains 120 times as many faecal coliform bacteria as is considered safe; when the river leaves the city, the value is 3,000 times the safe level (cf. Agoramoorthy 2012). In part, this is not capitalist pollution, but pollution in a still economically underdeveloped country.

According to the *Kuznets curve* as described by Naughton (2007: 487), pollution is increasing in the early stages of industrialisation/modernisation, but will decrease when countries reach higher levels of development and wealth. Then, people start to care about the environment, pollution becomes a political issue and the countries at stake can afford more advanced technologies. Does this hold? The Western experience is mixed. New technologies for vehicles, industry and energy production have reduced the emission of toxic gases and materials, but in Australia, Canada and the USA the values for NO_2, SO_2 and PM are still higher than in the emerging economies, while – indeed! – CO_2 emissions have started to decline in the EU and very recently even in the USA,[2] from a very high level. Rivers are cleaner today than they were a few decades ago, in part because dirty production has been outsourced to emerging economies. Perhaps, rivers will in the longer run also become cleaner in the latter. Could it be that figures for Beijing, indicating that not only PM pollution is decreasing (cf.

Table 1.3 for the overall Chinese trend) but also SO_2 and CO_2 (but not NO_2) emissions, point to a general trend (Incecik and Im 2012: 85, 101)? Naughton (2007: 488) some years ago tended to be optimistic and compared Chinese urban centres with major Western cities in the 1950s, and the World Bank is positive on India's environmental prospects. The *OECD Environmental Outlook to 2030* (OECD 2008a: 5) does not share this view and forecasts a drastically rising number of deaths from urban ozone exposure in 2030, in the advanced as well as the emerging economies. Recent news, particularly from Beijing, rather supports this latter view. Time will show.

Moving to traditional social issues, we observe extremely different employment rates in our countries. Brazil, China and Russia have high rates, while in Eastern Europe, with Poland as a deviant case, the situation is similar, but India and particularly South Africa as well as Turkey have lower or much lower rates. This could point to a very big black economy in the latter two countries. An open question, however, is how reliable these employment data are, notably with respect to India with its huge agrarian population. The data for non-agrarian informal employment underline this with estimates differing by 30 to 100 per cent per country. In this context, it does not make sense to look for more specific data such as part-time and female employment. Reliably official data on child labour – which is widespread in India (cf. www.tagesschau.de of 11 June 2012) – do not exist. Interestingly, the employment rate of the Brazilian statistical office includes juveniles from 10 to 14 years old (see Chapter 6).

Inequality is rising in most BRICs+ economies. Brazil is the exception. There it has decreased from a very high level. Even higher and still increasing is the inequality level in post-apartheid South Africa, where it is about three times as high as in some Eastern European countries and Scandinavia (in Table 1.4 exemplified by Sweden). In between, India, China and Russia have reached or already exceeded the level of the USA, the most unequal Western economy. Given that the Chinese urban Gini index was calculated as 0.166 in 1983, Naughton (2007: 217f) talks of an 'inexorable' and 'unprecedented' increase of inequality in China. He also reports values higher than those from the OECD in Table 1.4. As the generator of this rise, he identifies *inter alia* the self-enrichment of managers (of all grades) in the process of company privatisation (ibid.: 323f). This feature is also relevant in Russia (see Vasileva, this volume), where a recent study estimates that the 'real' Gini in Russia might have risen to 0.6 (OECD 2011c: 111). When we obviously do not know the 'real' levels of inequality in China and Russia, what then should be said about survey results (upon which the Gini index is based) from India with its large illiterate population living in a poor peasant economy?

Special aspects briefly to be touched upon are the strongly unequal gender relations in South Africa, (rural) China and (rural) India (a very brutal case of public rape in late 2012 shed light on this). It is not clear how far this affects employment and income differences, but it should in any case be mentioned. Regarding the extent of gender inequality, a clear divide appears to exist between European/European-influenced societies on the one hand and

Table 1.4 Employment, formal and informal, plus social indicators

| | Employment rates | | | Public social expenditure, % of GDP | Gini coefficient | | Poverty rate [*][**] | |
| | Formal, of population (15–64) | Informal (non-agricultural; estimates) | | | | | | |
	2008	Low late 2000	High late 2000s	2007	mid-1990s	mid-2000s	mid-1990s	late 2000s
Brazil	68.2	36.5	50.6	16.3	0.61	0.55	35.0/14.9	16.0/5.4
China	71.0	13.5	30.7	6.5	0.33	0.41	7.7/23.7	1.6/15.9
India	58.2[***]	54.1	84.9	4.6	0.32	0.38	30.7/53.7	21.8/34.7
South Africa	41.5	26.2	35.8	8.1	0.67	0.70	54.0/20.7	54.5/17.7
Russia	68.0	–	8.6	15.5	–	0.47	–	15.5
Turkey	44.9	–	33.2	10.5	0.49	0.43	15.2	17.0
Czech Rep.	66.6	–	–	18.8	0.26	0.27	4.5	5.4
Estonia	69.7	–	–	13.0	–	0.35	–	13.9
Poland	59.2	–	–	20.0	0.32[****]	0.37	–	10.1
Slovakia	62.3	–	–	15.7	–	0.27	–	6.7
Slovenia	68.6	–	–	20.3	–	0.25	–	7.8
Sweden	75.8	–	–	27.3	0.21	0.23	7.0	8.4
USA	70.9	–	–	16.2	0.36	0.38	17.3	17.3

[*] First value: persons below the national poverty line in the BICS as reported by the OECD (on the basis of the same criterion the World Bank *World Development Indicators* reports different data; for South Africa the difference is huge: 31% and 23%, respectively, instead of 54% and 54.5% for India (45.3% to 29.8% in the *WDI*) and Brazil (30.8% to 21.8%) the difference is big); < 50% median income in the other countries.

[**] The second value for the BICS counts the percentage of people living on less than US$1.25 a day.

[***] 2007

[****] 2000

Source: (OECD 2008a: 25, 135; OECD 2010b: 24, 30, 33, 35, 37; OECD 2010c: 130; OECD 2011a: 239; OECD 2011b: 69; World Bank 2012b)

societies with a different background on the other hand. In South Africa, the status of women is so low that raping them is institutionally widely accepted as bringing health and strength to men (25 per cent of men claim to have raped someone; one third of 4,000 surveyed women said they had been raped in the past year (Wikipedia)), while in China and India female babies are so little valued that sex-selective abortion or even infanticide takes place (Miller 1997). A male–female ratio at birth of 117–100 in China and 109–100 in India is the result (Wikipedia).

Poverty is declining in most countries under consideration, though it still has a high level in many of them, most of all in India and South Africa. However, the data mentioned first in Table 1.4 (*poverty) on the BICS have only a limited comparative value since they depend on national poverty lines. In China, this line is very low (Naughton 2007: 212) and so is the poverty percentage. The high South African percentages could reflect a higher poverty line but they could also correspond to the extremely high inequality in this country. The social system is still underdeveloped in most BRICs+. Low public social spending illustrates this (Table 1.4; the richer Brazil, Russia and Eastern European countries fall apart), as do minimum wages: 21.2 per cent of the average wage in South Africa, 25.1 in India, 34.9 in Brazil and 37.5 in China; the top half of the OECD member countries score 51.6 per cent. Replacement rates in case of unemployment are also low (OECD 2010b: 272).

A final consideration regards the level of capitalism of these countries. Particularly in the case of India, one is justified in asking to what degree its economy is capitalist at all. A very large part of it consists of agricultural village production at the subsistence level that is only marginally integrated in the national, let alone international, market. Besides lacking sanitary facilities, one third (400 million) of the Indian population does not have access to electricity (*The Economist*, 25 September 2010) and extreme poverty is very high. Despite this, the Indian economy has capitalist characteristics: private firms exist and are exposed to competition and a labour market also exists, even if it includes only a part of the labour force. Capitalism is not fully developed, but clearly present. On a continuum from ideal-typical non-capitalism (no capitalism at all) to full-grown ideal-typical capitalism (Figure 1.6), the Indian political economy would have to be located somewhere in the middle – still at a considerable distance from advanced economies that closely approximate complete capitalism. For other countries, for example China with its huge state sector, similar considerations can be made.

1.4 Performance by complementarity?

After the preceding comparative consideration, we can ask whether top-growth economies such as the BRICs feature high levels of complementarity of its parts. I want to discuss this question briefly because complementarity is a specific topic in the literature on capitalist varieties (VoC theory) on the basis of which one would have to think that the BRICs are high-complementarity economies. Hall and Soskice (2001: 28ff) put forward a liberal and a coordinated market

Non-Capitalism |_____ ▬   ▬   ▬ | *Capitalism*

Figure 1.6 Continuum from non-capitalism to capitalism with cases in between
Note: The bloc on the left illustrates a highly non-capitalist position (e.g. Nepal), the one in the centre could represent India, and on the right side is an advanced capitalist economy

economy (LME and CME) and mention seven main institutions that, in order to maintain and enhance competitiveness of the two types, have to be in a relation of (mutual) functional complementarity: 1) industrial relations; 2) corporate governance; 3) inter-firm relations; 4) employer–employee relations within firms; 5) training and education systems; 6) the level of social protection; and 7) product market regulation. Complementarity supposed, the LME is supposed to be better in mass production and radical innovation, while the CME stands out in flexible specialisation and incremental innovation.

The good thing about this approach is its understanding of the requirements of a functioning economy which (implicitly) is conceived as a system. The workings of a capitalist economy are seriously hampered when education does not include maths and writing, when occupational training does not exist, when the financial system is nothing more than a casino, when capital and labour permanently clash and so on. However, Hall and Soskice's approach is rigid and static, and has been criticised (cf. Becker 2009 for a summary). The rigid construction is that political economies (= cases) are positioned as *belonging* to types and presented as LMEs and CMEs (plural). To these classified cases belong specifically complementary components: the liberal and coordinated varieties of the seven components just mentioned: for example, stock market reliance (LME) versus bank reliance (CME), stress on general skills versus stress on specific skills, unlimited versus regulated competition, and residual social security and easy hiring and firing versus generous social security and high employment protection. Space for gradual differences does not exist here. The systems are closed – either liberal or coordinated in all their components. Equi-functionality also does not exist. As a consequence, change is only possible in a complete overhaul (Thelen 2004: 3).

The closed has to be opened up. Types as analytical constructions and cases as changing empirical realities have to be distinguished clearly, the concept of complementarity should be replaced by that of functionality, and of functionality it has to be clear that pointing to its requirements does not say anything about their fulfilment. A list of functional requirements of competitiveness, somewhat more detailed than the seven components of VoC theory, looks like this:

- a culture of basically peaceful social and economic (capital-labour) interaction;
- high valuation of economic individualism;
- a state structure and bureaucracy enabling politics to accomplish envisaged policies;

- the rule of law;
- functional competition legislation, inheritance legislation and licensing procedures for start-ups;
- an adequate physical infrastructure;
- a wage structure that enhances worker performance;
- labour force availability;
- performance-facilitating education and training, formal as well as informal;
- suitable social security arrangements and employment protection; and
- functional tax and financial systems.

Furthermore, functional requirements should be conceived looser than Hall and Soskice do with their complementarities. Components of a political economy are required to have a certain level of functionality for the economy as a whole, for survival and competitiveness. This level cannot be specified *a priori*, though one can say that the more functional an economy's components, the better it performs. 'Loose' means that the possibility of equi-functionality has to be taken into account. Certain industrial relations can combine with training and education systems from different backgrounds (for example, specific skills are stressed in the USA, but also in France with its considerably less liberal industrial relations), and one sort of education and training system can combine with different industrial specialisations.

From the VoC literature, one gets the impression that mass production and Taylorism are limited to political economies approximating the liberal type. Does this mean that China, with very widespread mass production, or Germany and Scandinavia, where it is prominent, are highly liberal? In all countries, whether they facilitate general (as China (Li and Sheldon 2011) or the USA) or specific skills (like Germany and the Scandinavian countries), much manufacturing – tyres, bricks, furniture, bottles and other technically simple things, but also machine and electronic components – is operated by workers at assembly lines who for their job are not required to be skilled (even if they are). Or take technical services, where task specialisation is increasing. In car repair, for example, firms working with well-educated all-round mechanics generally lose ground against firms employing briefly trained specialists for tyres, clutches, brakes and so on. Here, division of labour is equi-functional to all-round qualification. On the other hand, so-called quality goods such as German and Japanese cars are also produced in countries with no highly developed apprenticeship system: Brazil, China, India, South Africa, Turkey and the USA. Many different configurations of components are possible: there is not only one way to Rome! So, *instead of rigid systems we receive open and relatively loosely ordered social configurations revealing some degree of systemness*.

Importantly, I want to stress once more, there is no guarantee that the level of systemness required for survival and competitiveness will be reached. That capitalist political economies are 'open' implies openness to failure. They are full of conflict about goals such as wage levels, employment, equality and environmental care, and policy makers, union and employer representatives and economists disagree or do not know what is required. Effective overall coordination does not exist or is limited even when it is attempted, as in China. The main players are relatively autonomous; they cannot anticipate accidental circumstances and their actions bring about unintended consequences. Add to this that national political economies evolve in the context of different historical traditions and that borders are open.

This openness is the basis of institutional change, different trajectories of hybridisation and of (partially) lacking functionality (see Chapter 2 for this). Empirical political economies (cases) are more or less liberal or coordinated or, leaving the mainstream dichotomy, more or less statist and they only more or less meet functional requirements. This is true for advanced and (because of their stronger pre-capitalist legacies) particularly for emerging countries.

Looking around in our countries, we can identify different hybrid combinations of components (with respect to China, McNally (2012: 748) talks of 'even contradictory sets of institutions'). With the exception of Russia and Eastern Europe (in Figure 1.7 represented by Estonia), they all have strongly increasing but still relatively low levels of education, notably of tertiary education. Something similar is true for the infrastructure. It is developing, but much has still to be done before Russian levels, let alone those of the advanced economies, are reached. Russia still has a higher level of education than the other BRICs, South Africa and Turkey, but it hardly has comparative advantages in fields where high levels of education are required (something similar was already said with respect to innovation).

The product market in China, India and Russia is still highly regulated, while Brazil, South Africa and Turkey approximate the European level in this respect. Labour markets are considerably liberalised in all BRICs+ – in South Africa even more so (cf. Chapter 2, Table 2.2). South African social spending is also low, as it is in most BRICs+. Does this make the South African economy or the Chinese, Indian and Turkish economies predominantly liberal ones? Is Russia rather coordinated?

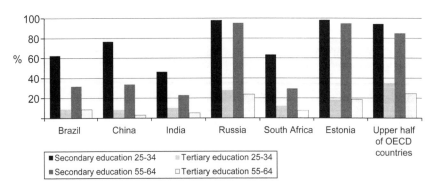

Figure 1.7 Population that has attained secondary and tertiary education, respectively, by age group, 2005 (in %)

Source: (OECD 2010a: 224)

Because of its decline in most non-oil/gas fields, Russia is a specific case. Are the parts of its political economy less functional for progressive development? Regarding cultural requirements, Russia lacks a tradition of entrepreneurialism (before the revolution of 1917 it was largely agrarian) and Russian politics rather seem to enhance this lack (300,000 businessmen are in jail; *NRC Handelsblad*, 26 March 2011). Combined with the strongly deficient rule of law and increasing corruption and clientelism, and the limited capacity of the state to get things done effectively, this seems to be a partial explanation of the Russian decline. In the other BRICs, the situation is not so deficient with respect to the rule of law, and in South Africa and Turkey it is even relatively high. Corruption has a similar level (cf. Chapter 2, Tables 2.1 and 2.4), but a (nonetheless) more facilitating government and stronger economic individualism seem to compensate for this. Comparing Russia and the other BRICs+, one could hypothesise that, apart from lucky circumstances like oil or minerals in a country's ground, the levels of economic individualism and state facilitation belong to the most important explanations of the divergences in economic development of the BRIC countries.

Corruption is a phenomenon that in this context deserves a few additional sentences. As the next chapter will show, it is strongly present in the BRICs and did not seriously decline in the decade under consideration. In Russia it even increased and the same is true for China when we take the past two decades. Corruption has different forms, however, and might not be non-complementary/non-functional in any case. Accounts of the losses corruption brings about in GDP terms circulate in the media (cf. *Newsweek Magazine*, 30 July 2012 on China; *The Economist*, 24 March 2011 on India, and 22 December 2012 on Brazil; Barry 2009 on Russia), but it is difficult exactly to determine these losses. For, in spite of corruption, growth has still been high in these countries. Corruption undermines predictability and increases insecurity, but bribing politicians in democracies might help business reforms easing investment or trade get done. Wedeman (2012: 4ff) calls this 'developmental corruption' and says it has been important in Japan and South Korea. Could this be true for India and Brazil too? Think about the 'Mensalao scandal' in Brazil, where in 2003 oppositional parliamentarians had been bribed to support reforms of the ruling Labour Party (prosecution of the persons involved, with much news coverage, started in 2012). Research is lacking. Wedeman calls the Chinese business-state corruption 'predatory', but hypothesises that even there it could have facilitated economic development in periods of reform when it bought space for entrepreneurial initiative (ibid.: 8 and 13; cf. Gregory and Zhou 2009: 5). Again, for Russia no productive role of corruption is mentioned in the literature.

1.5 What the chapters say

The next chapter discusses typological questions and the theory of institutional change. To avoid static analysis, it pleads for strict distinction between ideal types and empirical cases, presents a typology that is suitable to cover the BRICs and asks whether an actor-centred or a context-centred approach is most suitable to understand change. Subsequently, the chapter is a quantified overview of the institutional development of the political economies considered in this volume from 1998 to 2008. This period is determined by the availability of data from the OECD on product market regulation and employment protection legislation. Other databases are the World Bank's *Worldwide Governance Indicators* and the *Index of Economic Freedom* of the Heritage Foundation. The chapter stresses the need to attempt quantification because we have to look for as much precision as possible, but at the same time points to its limits. The results of the quantification largely support the findings of the country chapters.

All country contributions share the view that empirical cases have to be strictly distinguished from ideal types. The types with which they work are mostly but not always the same as those presented in this Introduction. As far as the concept of complementarities is relevant in these contributions, it is used in a loose form pointing to elementary institutional coherence but allowing for contradictions and equi-functionality. Thematically, all country studies investigate the state–economy and capital–labour relationships. The attention each of these relationships receives differs, however. In most studies, the state–economy nexus consumes more pages than that of capital and labour, but sometimes the amount of difference varies. Furthermore, the country studies have a profile of their own: they feature individual ways of systematising the material they present. Overall, the contributions concentrate on institutional analyses, but most of them also contain additional economic and statistical information.

Christopher A. McNally opens the country studies with his contribution on what he terms Sino-capitalism. We start with China because this country is the biggest one in our sample and economically the fastest growing. For this reason and its global aspirations, it gets more attention in international discussions than the other BRICs. Sino-capitalism in McNally's conception is first and foremost a hybrid. It combines liberal and statist elements, as well as a form of network capitalism based on *guanxi* ('making good friends') – a variety of clientelism/ patrimonialism. Sino-capitalism ultimately relies on a 'unique duality' that combines state-led, top-down development with bottom-up entrepreneurial networks of capitalists. Under this structural duality, *guanxi* calibrates state–capital ties, but also creates a 'deliberate ambiguity' in Chinese capitalism. Legal certainty and predictability – the rule of law – remain underdeveloped.

Historically, the start of liberalisation in 1979 predates our period of investigation by about a decade. After three decades of Maoist political economic experimentation that emphasised heavy industry in a centrally planned economy and shut China off from global commerce, liberalisation first of all meant allowing quasi-private businesses to grow, opening up markets and letting in some international competition. It was the beginning of decades of institutional experimentation. As McNally explains, neither did the state sector fully retreat in favour of markets and private capital, nor was the private sector smothered by the full reassertion of statist forces after initial liberalisation. Rather, Sino-capitalism's evolution enabled private-sector development while simultaneously strengthening the ability of the state to govern and guide an increasingly sophisticated and internationally integrated capitalist political economy. This evolution generated the conditions for the unique structural duality of Sino-capitalism to materialise, enabling compensating institutional arrangements of global integration, bottom-up networks of entrepreneurs and top-down state guidance to coexist and meld.

The contribution of Surajit Mazumdar on Indian capitalism differs from McNally's chapter by the bigger role given to historiography. Mazumdar explores the elements of continuity and change associated with Indian capitalism's transition to its so-called liberal phase after 1991 – starting more than a decade later than in rival China. While acknowledging the significant changes since then, he argues that the origins, nature and consequences of Indian liberalisation cannot be understood without recognising the important continuities between the pre- and post-liberalisation phases. Its colonial origins and the absence of a thoroughgoing agrarian transformation remain crucial for explaining the key outcomes being generated by the change from 'dirigisme' to liberalisation. Mazumdar stresses that Indian capitalism after liberalisation is less different from the dirigisme period than the term liberalisation might suggest.

The continuity of the preponderance of agriculture is crucial for understanding India. The same is true for the huge informal sector that produces half of GDP and strongly influences the capital–labour relationship. The state still plays a central role in economic life, too. According to Mazumdar, important changes after the liberalisation of the 1990s have, however, been the rise of inequality and the shift from import substitution industrialisation to the facilitation of the service sector. Industry remained relatively small and domestically oriented. The chapter concludes with some reflections on difficulties to localise the Indian political economy in the field between ideal-typical capitalist varieties.

Alexandra Vasileva analyses change of Russian capitalism after the fall of communism in the context of continuity and distinguishes the political, legal and economic dimensions of this development. She describes the 1990s to the early 2000s (Yeltsin's presidency and the early years of Putin's presidency) as a period of liberalisation and the subsequent period from 2003 to the present day (the Putin/Medvedev years) as a process of re-etatisation. Liberalisation started with 'shock therapy' and the rapid privatisation of most state-owned companies. This period saw the rise of the 'oligarchs' – billionaires who thanks to political connections became the owners of huge conglomerates. The decisive role of such connections points to the continuity of corruption and patrimonialism in the new Russia. Stressing continuity that accompanies change is the central aspect of Vasileva's account.

President Putin started to reverse the liberalisation process in 2003–04, re-centralising the state and gaining control of the firms in the strategic economic sectors. In the context of 're-etatisation', the oligarchs had to accommodate (if they refused they got into trouble, like Khodorkovsky) but did not cease to exist and were joined by the *siloviki* – the military and security service elites who gained influence under Putin. This illustrates that patrimonialism remained characteristic for Russian capitalism. Despite some liberalisation, Russian capital–labour relations demonstrate a remarkable continuity, having arguably undergone 'adaptation without restructuring'. The capital–labour relations are marked by a relatively stable level of employment, achieved through flexible wages and working hours, by weak trade unions, low strike activity and a spread of informal, paternalistic relations between management and workers, reminiscent of the Soviet labour model.

In his chapter on Brazil, Renato Boschi draws a sharp demarcation line between the pre-1990s and the time since then. Until the 1980s, Brazil was politically unstable and often subjected to authoritarian rule. Economically, it subscribed to the development model of import substitution industrialisation (ISI). The 1990s, then, have been the years of 'critical transition' involving the continuation of the democratisation that had begun a decade earlier, and economic liberalisation starting with the opening of the market and, to fight inflation, the *plano real* (1994) under Finance Minister and later President Cardoso. This cheapened imports, forced Brazilian producers under the pressure of foreign competitors to look for innovation and marked the beginning of the turn from ISI to a domestic demand-based model of GDP growth.

The period thereafter receives the most attention in Boschi's analysis. This is the period of Brazilian-style social democratisation and the age of Lula, the first president of the Labour Party (in 2011 succeeded by Rousseff). Boschi stresses that remnants of authoritarian state control of the unions made way for labour involvement and gave a new character to Brazilian etatism. Labour involvement also radically changed Brazilian corporatism. An element of continuity in the country's political-economic development since the 1930s, it then changed its face and moved in the direction of a more democratic, neo-corporatist capital–labour–state relationship. Boschi puts it in comparative perspective and points to the adoption of the social policies reducing inequality for which the changes he described had created room.

South Africa, the country presented by Nicoli Nattrass, is a very specific case because there economic change coincided with democratisation and the socio-political transformation into the post-apartheid era (in formal terms starting in April 1994). Nattrass analyses the peculiar results that the intermingling of these three processes brought about. Import substitution industrialisation did not simply make space for liberalisation, but was followed up by a decade of struggle between forces of liberalisation versus forces of social democratisation. In the context of very high unemployment and one of the highest (racial) inequality levels in the world, the original intention of the African National Congress (ANC) and its partners in the Tripartite Alliance, the unions and the communist party (SACP), was to set up a mixed economy to be fostered by a high-wage, high-productivity strategy and 'regulated flexibility' of the labour market. In Nattrass's words, they had a vision of a coordinated market economy.

There have even been some corporatist experiments with deals where wage increases were exchanged for jobs. In the end, however, no more has been realised than a few protective labour market measures and a more active industrial policy as concessions to the SACP and the socialists in the unions. The liberal forces inside and outside the ANC largely succeeded. Attempts to nationalise the mines and to overall social-democratisation petered out, the unions could not really come to terms with corporatism, employers became divided and the Black Economic Empowerment (BEE) strategy polarised society. Thus, unemployment is still intractable and, contrasting with Brazil, the high inequality rate has even increased. BEE has also triggered patrimonialism: by the governing ANC that since 1994 has attracted almost two thirds of the vote, BEE has caused clientelism and nepotism to flourish more than ever.

Turkey, Işık Özel's case, is a country that in 1960 was largely based on agriculture, which accounted for 38 per cent of GDP. Industrialisation had already begun in the 1930s, accompanied by protectionism and nationalist noise, but had not been particularly effective. It took until the 1960s for Turkish economic modernisation to move into gear. As in Brazil, India and many other countries, it was again the way of import substitution industrialisation that was chosen, as Özel shows in her highly comparative study. A large portion of statism is an implication of this choice, although Turkey was highly statist in those decades anyway, with more than half of the formal workforce in public employment. The success of ISI was only modest, however. Change came in the form of a liberal move in the 1990s – Turkey was one of the first emerging economies to liberalise – and notably in the 2000s by an acceleration of privatisation and the increasing opening of the economy to international competition.

Overall, Turkish liberalisation in the age of liberal hegemony was selective and limited, however. Statism, long combined with authoritarianism, remained strong and the government still tried to regulate capitalism, although Özel considers its capacity to accomplish this effectively as rather low. In part, this was due to the continuous impact of patrimonialism on economic policy, for another part, to the huge size of the informal economy with its millions of unregistered workers. The latter, together with the authoritarian tradition, also greatly determined the character of the capital–labour relationship in Turkey. Labour's rights are restricted, unions are weak and in decline, though, to compensate for this (and for electoral gains), the ruling Justice and Development Party (AKP) party after 2002 began to advance the welfare system.

In the brief final chapter, I want to address the prospects of the BRICs+ in the years to come. Will economic growth slow down? To mention a few exemplary questions, will China become an even fiercer competitor of the advanced economies than it already is, India reduce its enormous poverty, Russia's non-oil/gas industries re-emerge? What about these countries' environmental record: will the growth of emissions stop? These questions will be touched upon, because it is important to get a rough idea of possible developments in the next ten to twenty years.

The topic of political change will also only be touched upon, as serious analysis would require a separate book. Politics is, however, very relevant to economic progress or decline. Brazil and India are democracies, but highly corrupt. Could this change in the foreseeable future? Russia in very abstract terms is also democratic, but, having drifted towards authoritarianism for about a decade, will it turn back to a lived democracy? This question is important because Russia is still a leading world power. China is the rising world power, yet is still overtly authoritarian. In the old Leninist tradition, the Chinese Communist Party (CCP) always knows best. Is there any chance of a 'democratisation with Chinese characteristics', with Leninist as well as Confucian ingredients? These questions must be posed in the context of the description and tentative analysis of the current situation.

Notes

1 For comments I would like to thank all participants and the members of the PETGOV research group at the University of Amsterdam, where this chapter and Chapter 2 have been discussed at regular meetings. Thanks also to Alexandra Vasileva, who drew Figures 1.1–1.5 and 1.7, and collected some literature for section 1.2.
2 At least according to the EDGAR (2012) data. OECD (2009: 46f) data for 1990 and 2007 still report an increase in the USA, while EDGAR indicates higher emissions for 1990 than for 2008.

2 Institutional change in the BRICs, Eastern Europe, South Africa and Turkey, 1998–2008

Uwe Becker

What is more appropriate to understand change: a context-centred approach or a rational choice-based, actor-centred one? This is the first question I briefly want to deal with here. In the subsequent sections, I will provide statistical information on the institutional change the selected countries underwent between 1998 and 2008 and map this change. Did they liberalise to the degree that most advanced economies did? The answer is 'no', at least on the basis of the available data. At the start of the comparative section, I address the methodological question of what typological method and what types should be used. The choice is to distinguish liberal, statist, patrimonial, corporatist and (here not relevant) meso-communitarian types.

2.1 Conceiving change

In the Introduction, I discussed openness of capitalist varieties. As main factors of openness I identified:

- Open borders rendering national economies *fictitious* (less so *political* economies) to the degree that they are embedded in and depend on the international division of labour.
- The relative autonomy of the components of a political economy (for example, firms, stock markets, state units).
- The uncertainty among and the limited knowledge of relevant actors about functional action.
- Accidental circumstances and unintended consequences of action.
- The struggle over power and privilege as well as the related contention between the main politico-ideological forces on the overall direction of the political economy.

Openness results in institutional change by pressures and incentives such as capitalist competition, social-structural individualisation and the related emergence of new interest constellations. Economic crises or relatively autonomous ideological development might also trigger change: think about the slow decline or rise of state influence, the flexibilisation of dismissal rules and its effects on industrial relations, new monetary arrangements such as those in the European Union (EU), the adjustment of vocational training because of new technical requirements or of company financing because certain sources are no longer accessible. Or take international company mergers, the outsourcing of production processes and services, new management practices, new political ideas and strands, the redirection of aspects of public policy, possibly its correction after a while and so on. This is the order of the day and it does not pose any theoretical problem for an approach stressing openness.

Openness is the basis of institutional change. Forces of path continuity – transformation costs, habits like clientelist practices, inertia of action because bureaucratic machines in state departments and (big) companies routinely work according to established rules and insights, disagreement among policy makers on appropriate action and the power of status quo interests – limit the scope of change. Partially, path continuity may also stem from awareness of the exigencies of systemness. It does not necessarily involve path *dependence*, however.

For the mainstream of the Varieties of Capitalism theory, change is a difficult subject. This is a consequence of the static as well as rigid conceptualisation of capitalist varieties. The 'analysis of comparative statics' dominates the discussion and the theory of institutional change is in a state of 'underdevelopment' (Thelen 2009: 473). The attempts to change this situation contain helpful elements such as, for example, the identification of mechanisms of change such as defection, reinterpretation and reform (Hall and Thelen 2009). Notable also are the forms of gradual change as put forward by Thelen in several writings (cf. Streeck and Thelen 2005: 31): displacement (formerly marginal elements gradually rising to dominance), layering (adjustment by adding new elements to existing components), drift (slippage in institutional practice), conversion (new purposes for old structures) and exhaustion (gradual breakdown). These forms are interconnected and overlap each other. With respect to the BRICs+, we can think about the market successively gaining importance (displacement), the extension of existing arrangements in the welfare or tax system (layering), Chinese Township and Village Enterprises, set up as Commune and Brigade Enterprises around 1960 for limited purposes, evolving into or being reformed as capitalist enterprises (drift and conversion), and the rise of the market that implied the relative decline of the subsistence and socialist economies in India and Eastern Europe (exhaustion).

Despite Thelen's efforts, the progress from the 'state of underdevelopment' remains rather modest. Admittedly, there are multiple actors, they 'enact' change and change has different forms, but the question of where change originates is not even seriously posed. This limitation is due to the actor-centric approach (Hall and Thelen 2009: 9, 27). The context- or structure-centric approach, which I prefer (and which is also thinly present in Mahoney and Thelen 2009, and earlier in Steinmo *et al.* 1992), by contrast, concentrates on structural movers, pressures and constraints as well as on accidental circumstances. It situates action in this context. The focus on macro-configurations, which I want to understand largely as unintended consequences of action, moreover requires the context-centric approach.

There is some discussion of whether change is caused endogenously or exogenously. What is the difference in a globalised world? Is there something outside and not directly related to capitalism that could bring about change: a war, demographic change or a natural disaster? Does endogenous change come from actors triggered by themselves? The latter seems to be impossible. Perhaps the endogenous–exogenous distinction does not make any sense at all. There are always actors, whether they are individuals or organisations, and outside these are the contexts in which they operate and which compel them to action. This is the constellation behind adjustment processes ('layering') that, from very small to large, are the order of the day. A more important distinction is the one between contexts and (non-)action, that is between structural features, specific events, circumstances and developments like wars, demographic change and economic crises on the one hand, and structural and accidental movers on the other.

Of the latter, capitalist dynamism is the crucial force that since its origin in the 17th to 19th centuries has been revolutionising the human way of life. As the engine of this unique dynamic competition of relatively autonomous companies, has been identified that whoever owns them operate in largely anonymous markets. The productive force of competition is a point that liberals since Adam Smith never get tired of repeating. A current liberal author stressing it is Baumol (2002: 1ff, 10). Perhaps nobody, however, has formulated it as aptly as Marx and Engels in their *Communist Manifesto* (Marx and Engels 1966: 62): capitalism 'cannot exist without permanently revolutionising the instruments of production ... and all social relations ... The permanent revolution of production, the continuous convulsion of all social conditions ... distinguishes the bourgeois epoch from all the previous ones.' In *Capital* this theme returns and is central. Here Marx (1970: 618) stresses that competition forces companies to raise productivity (and to push down wages, which is the basis of class conflict): 'Competition compels every individual capitalist ... permanently to expand his capital for maintaining it.' This is a structural 'law of the capitalist mode of production'.

Until the emergence of capitalism, the pace of economic growth and social change was slow or even very slow. Before the 18th century, annual economic growth in the Western world was only 0.05 per cent and it took 1,400 years to double per capita income in Europe (Madison 2001). It is only with the emergence of capitalism thereafter that modern, systematic science developed and that competition (sports competitions are an example) and meritocracy evolved towards generalised principles. Today competition has become global competition, firms have become global players and change also has become a global affair. Society in all its components is under pressure to adapt to the more or less permanent change of its productive basis and the corresponding consumerist way of life. Society can regulate it if it has the political power to do so, and it can even fight it by raising restrictions and by combating cultural implications and threats of economic change such as individualisation and secularisation. Much conflict between capitalist modernisation and traditionalism stems from this.

Before capitalism can deploy its dynamism it has to exist, of course. Western capitalism did not originate from design, but, once it was there, it was not only under pressure from its own dynamism, but also the subject of more or less continuous re-modelling by policy makers who attempted to liberalise or to de-liberalise, to build up or cut down welfare arrangements, to legislate environmental protection and so on. In their own proportions this has also been true for the evolutionary economic development in Japan, the 'Asian Tiger economies' and the recently re-emerging economies of Brazil and Southern Africa as well as the truly emerging economies of Turkey and, coming from very far, India.

Russia, Eastern Europe and, to a lesser extent, China are different in this respect. China still has a communist regime and its capitalism, starting with the successive opening of its market to international competition in 1979 (after the so-called Deng reforms in late 1978; Lin 2011: 3f), developed with speed but nonetheless rather gradually. In the latter sense it is comparable to India. In the former communist countries of Russia and Eastern Europe, by contrast, communism broke down and policy makers had to redirect economic development towards the market by design, 'shopping' for advanced models and by trial and error. This might indicate that, in their entirety, the currently given political economies in Russia and Eastern Europe can hardly be understood as emanations of design. Some design, for example the regaining of control over the Russian oil and gas industry by Putin (which he already described as a necessity in his 1997 dissertation; Goldman 2010: 97ff), is always part of historical processes. However, design is only one of the factors that shaped them, and efforts to design, modernise, catch up and adjust always take place in contexts of specific pressures, formal-institutional frameworks such as the structure of the state, power relations, routines and prevalent ideas. There are always unintended consequences of action, too, which means that the course of development can never be completely anticipated (Pierson 2004: 15).

Russian development is a good example of a process that involved design but unavoidably turned out to take a largely non-anticipated trajectory. The Yeltsin administrations in the 1990s envisaged commercialisation, privatisation and preferred 'shock therapy' above gradual change, but did not have any coherent concept of reform. They had no idea which economic model was most suitable to realise the new post-totalitarian society (Gudkov and Zaslavsky 2011: 60). Moreover, these administrations did not have sufficient parliamentary support – in fact, there was permanent conflict between the reform-oriented government and the predominantly anti-reform parliament; the executive apparatus did not work as was required, decentralisation weakened the state's capacity to act coherently even more, corruption was endemic, Russian society was not prepared for a new, liberal mode of economic activity, and financial resources to pay the transformation costs were not available. As a result, decisions have often been taken by improvising and compromising (ibid.: 61ff). Given the specific circumstances, this was not a surprise.

Or take China, the more gradual trajectory. The 1978 reforms, a top-down event involving design, are regularly presented as a starting point of Chinese capitalist development. Does this hold? Nee and Opper (2012: 1) at the start of their book on Chinese institutional development assert that capitalist development was 'neither envisaged nor anticipated' by the political elites. Their intention was 'to address failures of central planning within the institutional framework of state socialism'. The reforms were 'committed to restoration rather than transformative change'. Change came from below: bottom-up. This is not news (see Tsai 2007; and Huang 2008), but what is original is the way Nee and Opper explicitly describe change towards capitalism as a non-designed process – even as a process running against governmental design.

There was a gradual liberalisation of agricultural markets (Nee and Opper 2012: 2), but no explicit policy to facilitate the founding of private firms (ibid.: 6). On the contrary, the political elite attempted to contain any capitalism by 'rules restricting the size of private firms to individual household production' (ibid.: 5f). Nonetheless, and unanticipated, after 1978 large numbers of sizeable enterprises developed (ibid.). Registration of larger private firms was only acknowledged in 1988, but even then legal uncertainty remained. What happened was a 'trial-and-error' process where the Chinese Communist Party (CCP) sometimes restricted bottom-up marketisation processes and at other times hesitantly followed them in piecemeal fashion (cf. Gregory and Zhou 2009).

The Russian and Chinese development seem to point to a general pattern in contexts where (radical) change and design is required but where various forces and factors resist change or shift its course in a direction that nobody anticipated. Because of this – the myriad of action, divergent interests and ideas, power relations and limited human cognitive capacities – the institutional configuration of capitalist variety can only partially be understood as a matter of design. At the macro level of political economies, we are, Hodgson and Knudsen (2006: 2f, 11) write, in the realm of 'undesigned social orders' that in their development are governed by the '"blindness" of Darwinian evolution', which 'assumes that organisms, including humans, act as if they are fumbling in the dark with little conception of what they are doing or where they are going'. This could be exaggerated, but by replacing 'blindness' with 'a considerable degree of blindness', and by conceding chances of successful design in sections of society, for example in technical projects such as the railways or, less technical, the judicial system, as well as incidentally at the macro level, we are still in an undesigned social order.

To find out what is functional has in this context to be understood as a medium- to long-term process of incremental evolution. This evolution can probably best be described as a permanent process of *societal* trial and error (cf. Becker 1988). The notion of trial and error reflects the 'fumbling in the dark' character of this process, the concept of 'societal' that conflict of interests and normative ideas are outstanding features. It is a process that is quite different from one situated in an experimental setting where all participants search together to solve a puzzle. It is also different from a process *determined* by strategic policy action. Strategic policy making is in the game, but as part of the trial-and-error process.

Processes of societal trial and error are the social form of natural selection. Individuals, organisations, firms and governments react to changes in their environments and frames of reference by adjusting and struggling to adjust their setting and rules. These processes are, to borrow an apt description from Herrigel (2005: 560), processes of 'piecemeal re-composition and re-articulation of institutional rules and ties'. Corresponding to their particular interests, depending on their knowledge of social reality and related to paradigmatic ideas, people and organisations formulate plans and strategies and try to realise them in contexts of ongoing social conflict and given power relations. Originally independent structures (think about a traditional education system and modern, highly electronic banking) become converted into related ones, supplemented by new elements and put together as is thought to be functional for a goal such as economic performance. This process takes place in a context of rival goals and institutional limitations (see also Boyer 2005a: 367; and Jackson 2005: 379f).

The process of 'radical' change in Russia during the 1990s is an example of such a constellation. Leaving the BRICs, one of the best examples one can find seems to be the enduring efforts of the eurozone managers to find a solution to the crisis of European monetary integration, and particularly of the Mediterranean members. These efforts have been societal trial and error par excellence. There has been a contest of answers to the urgent questions, with only temporary agreement (if at all), conflict of interest cross-cutting attempts at rational action, and actions of financial agents ('the markets', rating agencies), governments as well as protesters in the concerned countries repeatedly inducing unanticipated developments (for example the worsening instead of the improvement of the economic situation in Greece, a new, 'technocratic', government in Italy, new elections in Greece, then in Italy with its resulting stalemate). Policy efforts in this context have a high degree of 'fumbling in the dark'.

As a rule, the actors involved – politicians and policy makers at different levels, interest group representatives, advisory agencies and managers – do not act on the basis of grand visions and encompassing knowledge. They will probably produce some story, pack up their policies in ideological terms and point to necessities. Largely, they act within a given culture and given paradigms, the framework of their routines and, caused by uncertainty and the danger of high costs, with a high level of caution regarding new steps. The process of adjustment involves learning, accommodation and compromise. It slows or shuts down (for the time being) when the involved actors, or at least the dominant group of actors, are satisfied with the state they have reached. When error prevails over success these processes fail, however. The same is true when there is too much conflict. We are talking about open processes here, even if this openness is restricted by the structure of the paths where the processes take place.

2.2 Ideal types versus empirical cases

To illustrate gradual change, we must distinguish strictly between types as ideal types and empirical cases (Becker 2009: 44–50; cf. Crouch 2005a, 61f; similar argument in Schmidt 2002: 107f; and Bohle and Greskovits 2007; a basic reference is Thompson *et al.* 1990). Ideal types are fixed entities, while empirical cases are moving entities that more or less approximate a number of types. Remarkably, the mainstream of the literature on varieties of capitalism does not distinguish ideal types and empirical cases but classifies empirical cases. This way, it is impossible to capture gradual change. Classified cases *belong* to the types: capitalism A is liberal, capitalism B is coordinated. Gradual differences between the cases A and B (or C, D ... N) do not exist. Studies identifying all national capitalisms in Anglo-Saxon countries as liberal market economies (LMEs) and almost all national capitalisms in continental Western Europe, Eastern Europe, Latin America and East Asia as coordinated market economies (CMEs) in fact do not even define the demarcation line between the two market economies, and therefore classify cases arbitrarily. LMEs and CMEs illustrate an approach that does not leave any space for 'more or less' liberal or coordinated. The complete overhaul from the liberal to the coordinated type is the only change possible.

Ideal types are based on comparative empirical knowledge and analytically idealise reality. They are not normative ideals. Cases, by contrast, are entities such as countries or regions. Here the cases are national political economies (they are interwoven in the global division of labour, but national by their economic specialisation and their specific institutional mix). Complex cases such as political economies or democracies *never represent* ideal types. They *approximate* them more or less and contain elements of more than one type. A purely liberal empirical capitalism does not exist. The USA does not represent a liberal capitalism. It only features a highly liberal capitalism, but at the same time reveals statist elements. A similar story could be told about, for example, Sweden. It is highly corporatist, but its political economy also contains liberal elements (otherwise it would not be capitalist).

Ideal types may be reformulated, but in principle they are fixed constructions, while empirical cases are historical entities that, as a rule, change their character over time. They might liberalise or de-liberalise. Plotted into a figure, these national political economies have to be located somewhere in between the ideal types. In a dichotomous typology we have a continuum or axis from A to B – for example, from liberal to embedded market economies – with the empirical cases located somewhere on this continuum. The principle of this has already been illustrated in Figure 1.6. Institutional change is the movement of the cases in one of the two directions on the continuum, either to the liberal or to the embedded liberal pole.

Working with more than two ideal types, the empirical cases are located in the space between the types and approximate them more or less. Empirical diversity is a good reason for constructing more types, but a typology has only to reduce this diversity. This implies that the number of types has to be limited. Keeping this in mind, in Figure 2.1 five types and one case are chosen to illustrate the distinction between ideal types and empirical cases in a multi-type typology. At time T_1 the case is a hybrid of A, B, D and E plus some ingredients of C, while at T_2 (thin lined) it contains strong elements of types C and E, while D is almost absent.

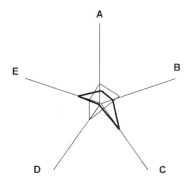

Figure 2.1 Illustration of the distinction between ideal-typical capitalist varieties and changing empirical cases as five-dimensional spider webs at T_1 (fat line) and T_2 (thin line)*

* In this figure, each of the five rays starts at a value of 0 at the centre of the web and has a maximum value of 100. The total of the spider web must add up to 100%. So at T_1 the illustrated imaginary case would roughly be 30% C, 25% E, 20% each of A and B, and 5% D.

2.3 Criteria and types

The criteria for the typology to be developed point to *fundamental features* of a political economy. They resemble those of Schmidt (2002: 107f) and cover most of Hall and Soskice's (2001) components of a capitalist variety. The criteria are:

I *The relationship between capital and labour:* involves the relations between unions and employers as well as management and employees. Corporate governance is related to this relationship which is also connected to stakeholder– shareholder relations.

II *The relationship between politics and economy:* includes employment protection and the welfare dimension, product-market regulation, privatisation/nationalisation of firms, the (non-)regulation of wages, supply and demand, and the character of economic policy.

What are the types to be constructed with these criteria? For the 'advanced' economies, the embedded/coordinated type – in the tradition of Polanyi (1957) I prefer the first term – could be split into statist, corporatist and meso-communitarian. These types cover crucial aspects of empirical realities where the state strongly complements or even rivals the market as traditionally in France (statism), where capital and labour cooperate with respect to macroeconomic policy as in Austria, Norway and the Netherlands (corporatism), and where workers and management of huge conglomerations of companies form a sort of family as in Japan and South Korea (meso-communitarianism). Boyer (2005a) has launched a similar proposal.

However, then do we have to add one or more types to integrate the emerging political economies into the comparative analysis? Do the BRICs and other emerging economies provide the empirical basis for a separate ideal type? State ownership is still considerable in Eastern Europe, and market capitalisation rather low (Lane 2006: 23), and the same is true in China and Russia. This feature can be covered by the statist type. Or does the hierarchical character of the capital–labour relationship within Latin American firms, as pointed out by Schneider (2009), qualify as the basis for a fifth type? He sees hierarchy within firms facilitated by business associations and reinforced by national governments, labour courts, the low-skilled labour force and atomistic labour relations. Hierarchy is only a single aspect of the capital–labour relationship, however, and can probably be subsumed under the elements of statism.

The dependent market economy (DME), which Nölke and Vliegenthart (2009) propose as an additional type, points to a very significant dimension in global capitalism, but this dimension is separate and based on a criterion of its own. All national capitalisms, whether they are strongly liberal, statist or whatever, are also located somewhere on the axis between autonomy and dependency. The dependent type could be best understood as a sub-type therefore. This might also be true for the 'foreign direct investment-based', 'peripheral' and 'remittance/aid-based' types of economic development that Myant and Drahokoupil (2010) present in their study of Central and Eastern Europe. Their 'oligarchic-clientelist' type resembles the patrimonial type (see below) and the 'order states' type resembles the statist type.

What about a patrimonial type? With patrimonial capitalism, a form of capitalism with an important role for political leadership is meant which is structured along the lines of patron–client relationships between political centre, local politicians and the top of businesses (see Brinkerhoff and Goldsmith 2002). Patrimonialism penetrates capitalism strongly in almost all emerging political economies. This is true for Eastern European, particularly Russian, political economies (King 2007: 316; Hale 2007), India (Mazumdar 2008c), Latin America (Levitsky 2007) and Africa (Arriola 2009). In the context of a legal system that is still dependent on the CCP, patrimonialism is also prominent in China (Nee and Opper 2007). When a legal system is weak, not universal rules but personal connections and power are decisive.

Patrimonial capitalism is sometimes called 'crony capitalism', which is described as 'an allegedly capitalist economy in which success in business depends on close relationships between businessmen and government officials. It may be exhibited by favouritism in the distribution of legal permits, government grants, special tax breaks, and so forth' (Wikipedia). Patrimonialism can be understood as a form of clientelism the basic aspect of which is the patron–client relationship at the individual level (among individuals and groups and between state or party officials and citizens/groups). The bonds between them are founded on mutual advantage: the patron furnishes excludable resources (jobs, welfare benefits) to dependants and accomplices in return for their support and cooperation (votes, services; cf. Brinkerhoff and Goldsmith 2002: 3). Clientelist exchanges, for example in the field of the allocation of permits and orders, undermine competition and meritocratic principles and therefore the efficacy of the market and of general administrative rules in the distribution of work, investment and other assets. A bit of clientelism might sometimes shortcut long bureaucratic procedures, but it becomes detrimental when it seriously undermines competition (see Chapter 1).

The relationship between state and economy, one of the two criteria to construct ideal-typical capitalisms, is clearly affected by patrimonialism in a particular way, and it also affects the employer–labour relationship. Patrimonialism seems to qualify for a separate ideal-typical variety of capitalism because it involves not only a culture denoting clientelist patterns of interaction among individuals and between the state and individuals, but also, and unlike societal clientelism, a structural relationship between state and economy. With respect to the capital–labour criterion, patrimonialism is somewhat weaker, but indirectly it relates to matters such as employment as it may undermine or circumvent dismissal legislation, giving access to jobs by family or clan ties, or rescue jobs by keeping alive uncompetitive companies.

The result of the preceding considerations is a typology consisting of five ideal types. It drastically simplifies reality yet attempts to cover the entire field of the main features of the world's political economies. One by one the types are characterised by these aspects:

1   *The liberal type*: here the market governs every aspect of the economy and politics unrestrictedly facilitates private property and the market – apart from basic legal and social regulations. State interventionism is limited; industrial relations tend to be individualised. Labour and companies are highly commodified. The Anglo-Saxon political economies most approximate this type.

2   *The statist type*: where the market is restricted by political regulation to determine the course of the economy. State-owned firms might be prominent. A hierarchical organisation of firms fits best, though social democratic statism is not impossible. France has traditionally been the case most approximating this type, but it is also strongly present in emerging political economies.

3   *The patrimonial type* (also named 'crony' capitalism): points to an important role for political leadership based on patron–client relationships between state and economy. It is related to corruption and involves a specific interaction pattern between political centre, local politicians and the top of business firms. It exhibits favouritism in the distribution of privileges. It is strongly present in non-Western economies.

4   *The corporatist type*: defines institutionalised capital–labour cooperation. Peak organisations and, directly or indirectly, the state negotiate on long-term socio-economic targets. Commitment to pragmatism and the common good, however contested, underlies corporatism. This type is most approximated in Scandinavia, Austria and the Netherlands, but to a lesser degree it is also present in Latin America.

5   *The meso-communitarian type*: distinctive is the organisation of networks of firms as communities. Managers and workers are expected to act cooperatively on behalf of the community. The networks also act as welfare agency. Next to

basic tasks politics is limited to enhance the firms' global competitiveness. This type is most approximated in Japan. (Anchordoguy 2005)

All political economies contain features of all five types. This is particularly true for the liberal and statist types. Without a considerable degree of liberal market relations, an economy is not capitalist, for capitalism is market and competition based. And without a certain politically guaranteed framework, that is a certain level of statism, an economy cannot function.

A point made in the previous chapter has to be remembered here. This point is that the countries under consideration here are not as fully capitalist as, for example, the USA and France or Germany. Large parts of the Indian economy take place at the subsistence level of agricultural village production. In China, these parts are smaller but still present, and China, as well as Russia, has a considerable state sector where competition is (almost) eliminated. In these segments we rather have a statist economy instead of statist capitalism, although the line of demarcation is difficult to trace. However, there are many private firms in these economies as well as some state companies that are exposed to competition; prices are, even if not completely, determined by supply and demand, and there exists a labour *market*, even if it does not include the entire labour force. Capitalism is not fully developed there, but it is present.

2.4 Indicators for the localisation of (changing) cases

The mapping of empirical capitalist varieties and their change from one location in the field between the ideal types at time T_1 to another location at T_2 has to be based on data and features that indicate these locations. Such indicators can be split into quantitative and qualitative ones. Examples of *quantitative indicators* are the level of:

- private versus state ownership of production assets;
- tax progression and welfare benefits (eligibility, level and duration);
- public expenditure;
- price control;
- infrastructure privatisation;
- market capitalisation;
- wage bargaining coverage; and
- the time it takes and cost to open a business.

Qualitative indicators that for many countries have already been quantified by the Organisation for Economic Co-operation and Development (OECD), the World Bank or Transparency International are:

- the level of state control;
- the freedom of trade, investment and establishing a company;

- the levels of employment protection and product market regulation; and
- the level of corruption.

These indicators do not inform whether or not a political economy is highly corporatist, statist or patrimonial. They are suitable, however, for determining with some precision the changing locations of political economies on the dichotomous axis between liberal and embedded ideal types (as is done for Western countries by Becker 2011: 32–35).

It has to be stressed that 'some precision' is all that is possible in such exercises. The empirical basis is not as hard as in (most of) the natural sciences. The localisation of cases on the axis between ideal types is not possible without the transformation of quality into quantity, and often data are deficient. This situation is regularly given in comparative political economy. With respect to OECD countries, this is, for example, the case when comparisons are lopsided and basic data are only crude approximations to the relevant reality (gross instead of net unemployment benefits is an example), when data are survey based and therefore to some degree 'subjective', when not all data are available for all years, and when a number of factors possibly relevant for estimating overall institutional change have to be neglected because of the lack of comparative data. With respect to emerging economies, the data situation is much worse. They have only recently attracted the attention of comparative data collectors, and for many years and fields no data are collected. When data are survey based, one has to consider that in a country such as India large parts of the population are illiterate.

The precision problems increase if we want to locate empirical political economies in the field between the liberal type and the four types (statist, patrimonial, corporatist and meso-communitarian) of embedded capitalism (Crouch 2005b: 53, makes a similar point). To perform this operation perfectly, we would need data on additional *qualitative* indicators such as the strength or relevance of planning agencies (indicating statism) and socio-economic councils (indicating corporatism). Employee influence within firms is another indicator of corporatism as the character of the political system (centralised or de-centralised, presidential or parliamentary) might be an indicator of the state–economy relationship in terms of liberalism and statism. How could such indicators be measured?

Principally, we have to recognise that in the multi-dimensional cartography of political economies we are in the realm of imprecision (cf. Crouch 2005b: 40, 53), not only because of the quality of the data, but particularly because the *qualitative* indicators of the capital–labour and state–market relations will have to be *quantified* and both the qualitative as well as the quantitative ones will have to be *weighted*. Do all indicators have the same weight, and, if not, what is the logic of differentiation? Quantification of quality and weighting (attaching scores to) every indicator is not possible without some degree of arbitrariness, and therefore not without violating the principle of precision. Something similar is true for the range we give to the quantitative indices. The larger the range and the empty field (for example all values between 0 and 50 in a range to 100), the more the relative difference between the scores will shrink.

2.5 Tentative indication of movements between liberal and embedded capitalism

The available data only partially contain the indicators just mentioned and are complementary to the analyses in the country chapters. They are based on surveys and law texts and collected by the Heritage Foundation in collaboration with the *Wall Street Journal* (*WSJ*) (Index of Economic Freedom, IEF), the OECD (indices of Product Market Regulation, or PMR, and Employment Protection Legislation, or EPL), and the World Bank (Worldwide Governance Indicators, or WGI). These organisations have a liberal bias, but this does not necessarily distort the data. The *WSJ*, for example, applauds high liberal scores but one does not need to share the applause.

The indices have different ranking and scoring systems (IEF: 0–100; PMR/EPL: 0–6; WGI: -2.5–2.5). For rendering them comparable, I will convert all data in a scale from 0 to 100. This way all scores can be understood as percentages. I also made a selection of indicators that have to be weighted. The chosen years T_1 and T_2 are 1998 and 2008. The year 2008 is the latest for which we have PMR and EPL data for all countries under consideration, while for 1998 we have at least PMR/EPL data for the OECD member states, which, regarding the BRICs, are completed by EPL data for 2003 and a few PMR estimates. Once again, we are in the realm of imprecision and missing data here. Claiming knowledge of the character and development of political economies implies the obligation to be as precise as possible, however.

Three of the indices reveal a dichotomous order: market and freedom respectively versus regulation (PMR and EPL), and effective political and judicial regulation versus clientelist corruption (WGI) respectively. The fourth, the IEF, relates corruption as a third dimension to the dichotomy of market versus regulation. Together they make possible the rough localisation of political economies in the field between liberalism, statism and patrimonialism, just the types that are relevant for the study of emerging political economies. Except Brazil and tiny Slovenia, which have a significant corporatist component, corporatism and meso-communitarianism are only of negligible relevance in the emerging political economies, and quantitative or quantifiable data required to map these two dimensions do not exist for the emerging economies.

Let us start with the Index of Economic Freedom. It is the broadest index and it works with a scale of 0 to 100 of 'freedom'/liberalism. Thereafter, we turn to the OECD's Product Market Regulation and Employment Protection Legislation indices, where 0 is the highest liberal value and 6 the lowest. The scores will be converted into the 0–100 scale. Put together, the IEF, PMR and EPL indices can be used to localise national political economies on an axis between liberal and embedded. Subsequently, the embedded scores will be divided into statist and patrimonial on the basis of the values of the Worldwide Governance Indicators.

The IEF is composed of ten single indicators, each of which has the same weight: 1) business freedom, 2) trade freedom, 3) fiscal freedom (taxation level), 4) government spending, 5) monetary freedom (how much inflation and political price distortion?), 6) investment freedom, 7) financial freedom, 8) property rights (the legal framework and judicial protection of private property), 9) freedom from corruption, and 10) labour freedom. Labour data do not exist for the years before 2008, and monetary freedom is too much bound to a certain idea of the causes of inflation and price distortion. I will neither include these indicators nor property rights, which are an aspect of the rule of law and accounted for in the WGI. Furthermore, I have combined the freedom of trade and investment, because separately they would count too much as compared to, for example, business or labour freedom. I also merged the related fiscal freedom and government spending. So, the selected indicators of the IEF are these:

- business freedom (level of regulation of business operations);
- trade freedom (level of trade restrictions) combined with investment freedom (ease of investment; level of equality of opportunity);
- fiscal freedom (the taxation level) combined with government spending;
- financial freedom (the business freedom of the financial sector); and
- freedom from corruption.

Table 2.1 shows the scores of these indicators. A general feature of the IEF is that the average country scores are relatively close to each other. China, India and Russia (2008) are about half as liberal ('free') as the USA (the same is true for Belarus, Burma, Venezuela and Libya). This is due to the entire systematic of the IEF. Worth mentioning are the high scores that low-developed and emerging economies have with respect to the indicators of fiscal freedom and government spending, because taxes and spending are low there. In their stage of economic development and level of social individualisation, this is quite normal, however, and not (mainly) a result of liberal policy. Therefore, in Table 2.1 the combined scores of these indicators in the BRICs and Turkey only count for 50 per cent.

What does the table show? The 1990s and 2000s were characterised as an era of liberalisation (Simmons *et al.* 2006). This characterisation is true for France, the USA and almost all advanced capitalist economies (and the picture would not be different when all IEF indicators are counted or when all years from 1991 until 2011 are considered). It also holds for most Eastern European economies, although Poland is an exception.[1] It de-liberalised somewhat, just as Turkey.

The BRICs experienced a differentiated development. India has liberalised (also in the years preceding 1998), Brazil looks relatively stable (though year-by-year data show it liberalising until 2003 and then de-liberalising again),

Table 2.1 Index of Economic Freedom, 1998 and 2008 (selected indicators, range 0–100)

	Average*		Business		Average of fiscal F & public spending**		Financial		Average investment & trade F		Freedom from corruption	
	1998	2008	1998	2008	1998	2008	1998	2008	1998	2008	1998	2008
Brazil	45.5	44.1	70	54.0	81.6	62.0	33	40	53.9	65.6	30	33
China	39.6	40.5	55	50.3	88.2	78.1	33	30	42.0	50.1	24	33
India	36.4	42.3	55	50.9	78.5	74.6	30	30	31.6	60.5	26	33
Russia	48.1	38.6	55	53.7	70.8	74.4	70	40	54.3	37.1	26	25
South Africa	57.7	60.9	85	71.4	64.3	73.2	50	60	65.5	62.1	57	46
Turkey	55.7	52.2	70	68.3	63.5	73.0	70	50	71.9	68.4	35	38
Czech Rep.	61.5	65.7	85	64.2	47.0	58.5	48	80	73.7	78.0	54	48
Estonia	74.4	78.9	85	85.3	63.7	74.0	67	80	86.5	88.0	70	67
Poland	58.0	56.1	70	54.2	42.4	56.1	50	60	71.5	73.0	56	37
Slovakia	58.8	75.4	70	69.5	50.9	71.7	50	80	61.5	78.0	50	47
Slovenia	59.8	65.8	70	74.1	44.6	47.8	70	60	64.5	73.0	50	64
France	58.5	66.9	85	88.0	23.4	32.2	50	70	63.9	70.5	70	74
USA	73.7	82.1	85	92.6	62.3	81.3	70	80	74.2	83.4	77	73

Note: * Average of 7 of 10 indicators (monetary freedom, property rights and labour (only data for 2008) are excluded).
** Regarding the BRICs and Turkey this indicator only counts for 50% in the calculation of the average.
Source: (Heritage Foundation database, *Wall Street Journal* 2012)

China appears hardly to have changed, while Russia has de-liberalised. In South Africa, the reverse development took place. The South African level of liberalisation is higher than that of the BRICs, however, and comparable to that of Eastern Europe. Looking at the single indicators, the most striking development took place in Brazil, where, due to the aspirations of the Labour government of President Lula, taxes and public spending rose and made the economy more embedded, thus less 'free' in terms of the IEF. Taxes and public spending also rose in China and India, but more than in the richer Brazil this has probably been the result of the fast modernisation related to industrialisation and urbanisation. Furthermore, in both countries, corruption somewhat declined and investment and trade became, notably in India, liberalised. In Russia, the financial markets as well as trade and investment conditions became de-liberalised, while corruption remained stable.[2] In South Africa, corruption is considerably lower than in the BRICs and Turkey, a feature that is confirmed by WGI data (see Table 2.4).

Table 2.2 shows whether the OECD's scores for Product Market Regulation and Employment Protection Legislation confirm or correct the IEF data. EPL is a monolithic indicator. It informs about the commodification of labour, and in this text it is the main indicator of the capital–labour relationship. PMR is more complex and consists of many sub-indicators. The first layer contains

Table 2.2 Product Market Regulation and Employment Protection Legislation

	Product Market Regulation*		Converted PMR***		Employment Protection* **		Converted EPL***	
	1998	2008	1998	2008	1998	2008	1998	2008
Brazil	(2.00)	1.94	66.7	67.7	2.6**** 2.3		58.4	61.7
China	(3.40)	3.30	43.3	45.0	3.0**** 2.7		50.0	55.0
India	(3.71)	2.75	47.5	54.1	2.8**** 2.3		53.3	61.7
Russia	(2.34)	3.09	61.0	48.5	1.9**** 1.9		68.2	68.2
South Africa	(2.51)	2.38	58.2	60.3	(1.5)	1.4	75.0	76.7
Turkey	3.25	2.17	45.1	63.2	3.4	3.5	43.3	41.7
Czech Rep.	2.99	1.62	50.2	73.0	1.9	2.0	68.2	66.7
Estonia	(1.31)	1.31	78.1	78.1	2.3**** 2.3		61.7	61.7
Poland	3.97	2.26	38.4	62.3	1.9	2.2	68.2	63.3
Slovakia	(2.50)	1.63	58.3	72.9	2.2	1.8	63.3	70.0
Slovenia	(1.52)	1.38	74.7	77.0	2.6**** 2.6		56.7	56.7
France	2.45	1.39	59.2	76.8	2.8	2.9	53.3	51.7
USA	1.28	0.84	78.7	86.0	0.7	0.7	80.0	83.0

Note: * Scale 0 (no regulation/protection) – 6 (fully regulated/protected); the scores for the BRICs in 1998 are estimated on the basis of their development in the IEF.
** version 2
*** 6 minus PMR/EPL score multiplied by 100/6 (0 = total regulation, 100 = no regulation)
**** 2003
Source: (EPL: OECD Library n.d.; OECD 2010c: 171; Tonin 2009: 479; PMR: OECD Statistics Portal n.d.)

'state control', 'barriers of entrepreneurship' and 'barriers to trade and invest-ment', which all count for one third in the overall PMR index. While the last two sub-indicators are also part of the IEF and might balance the IEF data, state control is specific to the PMR index. Sub-indicators of state control are public ownership and 'involvement in business operations', which at a lower level are sub-divided into 'scope of public enterprise' and price control (Wolf *et al.* 2010: 8). As in the IEF, the differences between the country scores are smaller than one might expect. The USA is not even twice as liberal as China.[3]

On average, liberalisation of PMR was stronger than liberalisation in the IEF, although, taken separately, this is not true for Brazil, China, Russia and South Africa. For these countries plus India, the scores for 1998 have, however, been estimated on the basis of their development in the IEF (indicated by the brackets). Notably due to EU legislation, PMR has declined in Eastern Europe, including Poland which somewhat de-liberalised in IEF terms. Eastern European PMR now approaches Western European levels, but in China, India and Russia PMR is still much more rigid, with Brazil, South Africa and Turkey in between. A look at the sub-domain of state control (the extent to which govern-ments influence firm decisions – an indicator determining the PMR index for one third) reveals a similar picture, though Poland here only slightly liberalised to a score of 3.35 in 2008 (put in perspective: the USA scored 1.1). China (4.63),

India (3.58), Russia (4.39), Turkey (3.79) and, somewhat less, South Africa (3.10) still had high levels of state control, while Brazil (2.69) was similar to France (2.62).

Contrasting PMR, the level of EPL changed only slightly from 1998 (2003 in the case of the BRICs) to 2008. In some cases – the Czech Republic, Poland and France – it even de-liberalised a little, while in Slovenia it kept its high level. Leaving apart the USA, we see South Africa as liberal outlier and Turkey (resembling France) as the opposite; in between, the differences are not particularly large. One has to be cautious with the data, however. Russia, for example, has a relatively liberal EPL, but a practice of easy hiring and firing has not yet been established (see Vasileva, this volume) and in Turkey, triggered by pressures from the large informal sector, the rigid EPL is regularly bypassed (see Özel, this volume).

We can now combine the IEF, PMR and EPL scores to calculate overall scores of economic liberalism and, by subtracting this score from 100, overall scores of embeddedness (statism/patrimonialism of which we do not yet know the proportions). Depending on the level of corruption, reality might differ, however, from the intentions of law texts and other codified regulations upon which the PMR and EPL indices are based. So, it makes sense to adjust the PMR and EPL figures for corruption. It will be done by using the corruption data of the Index of Economic Freedom. In Table 2.1, corruption determined the average scores for 20 per cent. Giving corruption with respect to PMR and the EPL the same weight as in Table 2.1, the formula to be applied in Table 2.3 is: $([2 \times \text{PMR}] + [2 \times \text{EPL}] + \text{IEF-corruption}) / 5$.

On the basis of Table 2.3, we can draw a figure roughly localising the considered political economies on the axis between ideal-typical liberal capitalism

Table 2.3 Overall liberal scores, 1998 and 2008

	Adjusted economic freedom average		Average of PMR and EPL adjusted for corruption		Overall liberal score		Extent of embeddedness (statism and patrimonialism)	
	1998	2008	1998	2008	1998	2008	1998	2008
Brazil	45.5	44.1	56.0	57.8	50.8	50.9	49.2	49.1
China	39.6	40.5	42.1	46.6	40.9	43.6	59.1	56.4
India	36.4	42.3	45.5	52.9	41.0	47.6	59.0	52.4
Russia	48.1	38.6	56.9	51.7	52.5	45.1	47.5	54.9
South Africa	57.7	60.9	64.7	64.0	61.2	62.5	38.8	37.5
Turkey	55.7	52.2	42.4	49.6	49.0	50.9	51.0	49.1
Czech Rep.	61.5	65.7	58.2	65.5	59.8	65.6	40.2	34.4
Estonia	74.4	78.9	69.9	69.3	72.2	74.1	27.8	25.9
Poland	58.0	56.1	53.8	57.6	55.9	56.9	44.1	43.1
Slovakia	58.8	75.4	58.6	66.6	58.7	71.0	41.3	29.0
Slovenia	59.8	65.8	62.7	66.3	61.3	66.1	38.7	33.9
France	58.5	66.9	59.0	66.2	58.8	66.6	41.2	33.4
USA	73.7	82.1	78.9	82.2	76.3	82.2	23.7	17.8

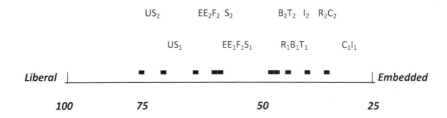

Figure 2.2 Location of selected political economies on the axis between the ideal types of liberal and embedded (here statist and patrimonial) capitalism, 1998 (T_1 grey) and 2008 (T_2 black)

B = Brazil, C = China, EE = average of the four Eastern European countries, F = France, I = India, R = Russia, S = South Africa, T = Turkey, US = USA

and ideal-typical embedded capitalism (here in the meaning of statism and/or patrimonialism). This is done in Figure 2.2. Slight differences, digits after the comma, cannot be shown in the figure and to avoid an unclear picture and to underline the focus on the BRICs, the five Eastern European political economies are averaged. For the same reason and since there are no scores below 40, the visible axis starts at level 25.

2.6 Indicating change in the field between liberalism, statism and patrimonialism

The intention of this chapter is, however, to localise the national political economies in the space of a five-dimensional typology. As two of the five types are almost negligible in the countries considered (except corporatism in Brazil and Slovenia), and as we already know the liberal scores, we have to fix the extent of the two remaining: statism and patrimonialism. This will be done on the basis of the Worldwide Governance Indicators. The WGI provides the possibility tentatively to determine the level of statism – tentatively because the WGI data are not exhaustive and because, once again, we are in the realm of imprecision here. The assumption is that the higher the WGI scores for 'government effectiveness', 'regulatory quality' and 'rule of law', the higher the level of statism. The fourth indicator – 'control of corruption' – will be left aside because corruption has already been an ingredient of the assessment of the levels of liberalism and, as a residual category, statism/patrimonialism. Now, with statism to be quantified, patrimonialism will be left in the basket as a residual category.

Table 2.4 shows the scores of the WGI. In the WGI scale, the highest score is 2.5 and the lowest -2.5. What is remarkable in Table 2.4? Again, at first sight it seems that the differences between notably the BRICs and the advanced economies are large. Yet the differences shrink when the WGI scores are converted to a scale from 0 to 100 (as in column four of the table). Worth mentioning is that the differences between Eastern European and the Western

Table 2.4 Worldwide Governance Indicators, 1998 and 2008 (scaled -2.5 to 2.5 and converted)

	1 government effectiveness *		*2 regulatory quality* *		*3 rule of law* *		*Converted average of 1, 2 and 3* **		*Control of corruption* * ***	
	1998	*2008*	*1998*	*2008*	*1998*	*2008*	*1998*	*2008*	*1998*	*2008*
Brazil	-0.13	0.00	0.44	0.07	-0.32	-0.37	50.0	48.0	0.00	-0.02
China	-0.14	0.19	-.026	-0.16	-0.37	-0.34	44.8	48.0	-0.25	-0.44
India	-0.06	-0.02	-0.36	-0.33	-0.28	-0.08	45.4	47.2	-0.29	-0.40
Russia	-0.76	-0.37	-0.47	-0.45	-0.94	-0.96	35.6	37.8	-0.94	-1.01
South Africa	0.58	0.52	0.32	0.51	0.14	0.02	57.0	57.0	0.65	0.15
Turkey	0.28	0.24	0.48	0.28	-0.10	0.07	54.4	54.0	-0.59	0.07
Czech Rep.	0.64	1.00	0.89	1.15	0.83	0.88	66.4	70.2	0.54	0.27
Estonia	0.53	1.19	1.28	1.47	0.55	1.17	65.8	75.4	0.57	0.92
Poland	0.60	0.50	0.61	0.80	0.76	0.52	63.2	62.2	0.66	0.33
Slovakia	0.52	0.84	0.44	1.12	0.20	0.57	57.8	66.8	0.25	0.31
Slovenia	0.79	1.20	1.05	0.83	1.22	0.97	70.4	70.0	1.30	0.90
France	1.55	1.58	0.87	1.29	1.36	1.46	75.2	78.2	1.40	1.40
USA	1.76	1.52	1.62	1.55	1.59	1.66	83.1	81.6	1.55	1.45

Note: * Scaled from -2.5 to 2.5
** -2.5 is converted into 0, the original 0 into a converted 2.5, the original 2.5 into the converted 5 and all scores are multiplied by 20.
*** Only implicitly included in the further calculations.
Source: (World Bank 2012b)

economies are larger than in the IEF, PMR and EPL indices (and would become even more pronounced if the Scandinavian countries, the Netherlands, Germany and Australia/New Zealand were included in the table). The most striking feature is perhaps that the Russian scores in both 1998 and 2008 are clearly below the level of the other BRIC countries. Government effectiveness has somewhat improved but the strong 'Putin state' is less strong and effective than it might seem on the basis of media news. Finally, one can observe that, according to this index, corruption has increased not only in Russia but in all of the BRICs because the measured 'control of corruption' has declined (supposing that this causal nexus is given). This differs from both the IEF and the Corruption Perception Index from Transparency International.

On the basis of the preceding tables, we can determine the level of statism (S). It will be done by calculating the average converted score of 'government effectiveness' (WGI_1), 'regulatory quality' (WGI_2) and 'rule of law' (WGI_3) as a percentage of the extent of (statist/patrimonial) embeddedness (E) as fixed in Table 2.3. The formula is: $S = (WGI_{1+2+3}) \times E/100$. Subsequently, the level of patrimonialism can simply be established by subtracting S from E ($P = E - S$). Table 2.5 shows the results.

One might twist whether the average of WGI 1, 2 and 3 is an appropriate indicator of statism and whether the residual value for corruption truly reflects

Table 2.5 Establishment of rough levels of statism and patrimonialism

	Level of liberal capitalism		Average of WGI₁ ₂ ₃ (as %)	of extent of embeddedness	= level of statism	Average of WGI₁ ₂ ₃ (as %)	of extent of embeddedness	= level of statism	Relative level of 'patrimonialism'	
	1998	2008	1998	1998	1998	2008	2008	2008	1998	2008
Brazil	50.8	50.9	50.0	49.2	24.6	48.0	49.1	23.6	24.6	25.6
China	40.9	43.6	44.8	59.1	26.5	48.0	56.4	27.1	32.6	29.3
India	41.0	47.6	45.4	59.0	26.8	47.2	52.4	24.7	32.2	27.7
Russia	52.5	45.1	35.6	47.5	16.9	37.8	54.9	20.8	30.6	34.1
South Africa	61.2	62.5	57.0	38.8	22.1	57.0	37.5	21.4	16.7	16.1
Turkey	49.0	50.9	54.4	51.0	27.7	54.0	49.1	26.5	23.3	22.6
Czech Rep.	59.8	65.6	66.4	40.2	26.7	70.2	34.4	24.1	13.5	10.3
Estonia	72.2	74.1	65.8	27.8	18.3	75.4	25.9	19.5	9.5	6.4
Poland	55.9	56.9	63.2	44.1	27.9	62.2	43.1	26.8	16.2	16.3
Slovakia	58.7	71.0	57.8	41.3	23.9	66.8	29.0	19.4	17.4	9.6
Slovenia	61.3	66.1	70.4	38.7	27.2	70.0	33.9	23.7	11.5	10.2
France	58.8	66.6	75.2	41.2	31.0	78.2	33.4	26.1	10.2	7.3
USA	76.3	82.2	83.1	23.7	19.7	81.6	17.8	14.5	4.0	3.3

the level of patrimonialism, but what is done here on the basis of IEF, PMR, EPL and WGI data is at this moment the only coherent way to determine with some precision the respective levels of liberalism, statism and patrimonialism in emerging economies and the extent of their development in these terms. The limits of precision do not only stem from a lack or the restricted range of data (is state effectiveness only limited by corruption?), but first of all because we have to transform quality into quantity. This is a process where interpretative judgements over the relevance and weight of single indicators have a huge impact, and so has some arbitrariness, even when the judgements are sophisticated.

There is not so much specifically worth mentioning in Table 2.5. Most striking is probably that statism is not higher in the BRICs than in Eastern Europe and France. The biggest difference between the (groups of) countries is in the levels of liberalism and patrimonialism. The BRICs and Turkey are still considerably less liberal and much more patrimonial than Western economies, with South Africa and most Eastern European economies in between (though some of them, such as Estonia, Slovakia and Slovenia, are quickly approaching the West). The differences between the three blocs did not change significantly between 1998 and 2008, although some single political economies did so. Russia de-liberalised, India, the Czech Republic, Slovakia and, slightly, China liberalised, and the same is true for France and the USA.

The data presented in the tables are fairly detailed. To enhance precision, statistical information is needed that is directly relevant to statism (instead of state efficiency) and patrimonialism (instead of corruption) – and to corporatism and meso-communitarianism in cases where these types are ad rem. Data with respect to the capital–labour relationship are also needed. Currently, comparative information on, for example, union density, social security benefits and tax progression in emerging economies is fragmentary or very soft. The existing data also reflect, however, the just mentioned fundamental difficulties of scientific precision in the field of institutional change. To avoid the suggestion of complete precision, these fundamental difficulties must always be indicated.

2.7 Mapping institutional change in the three- and four-dimensional field

Now the statistical data can be transformed into multi-dimensional spider webs. Before doing this (for the BRICs, South Africa, Turkey and, as a contrast, the USA), I have to point to some features of the exercise. As said, of the five ideal types I will only use the three (and once four) types that are relevant here. Furthermore, in drawing the figures, digits after the point and even single percentage points will be ignored. The drawing instruments are not sensible for millimetre differences.[4] Very small differences like those between the Chinese and Indian political economies in 1998 cannot be shown. The intention of the figures, however, is to give an impression at a glance of in what direction change developed. For the small differences we have the tables.

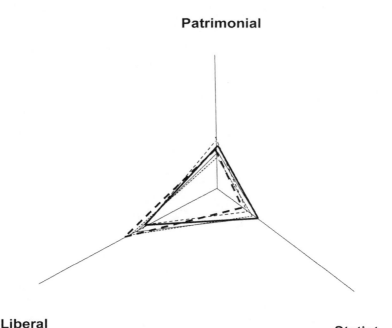

Patrimonial

Liberal

Statist

Figure 2.3 China, India and Russia comparatively mapped in the field between three ideal
        types, 1998 (fat) and 2008 (thin)★
Note: China = steady line;
India = short dashes;
Russia = long dashes.
★ Each ray starts at zero in the centre of the figure and has a value of 100. This is also true for
each spider wire over the three dimensions.

In Figure 2.3, the BRICs exclusive of Brazil (Figure 2.4) are mapped. It
visualises that China and India in 1998 featured the same configuration of liberalism, statism and patrimonialism and that thereafter India liberalised a bit
more. This result of statistical research fits with parts of the literature, but there
is also controversy. According to the influential book of Yasheng Huang
(2008), China's economy became liberalised after the 1978 reforms, but since
the 1990s, influenced by the bloody suppressed protest on Tiananmen Square
in June 1989, a process of re-etatisation took place. The mostly small and privately controlled Township and Village Enterprises seem to tell a different
story. They are still prominently present and increasingly contributing to
China's continuing economic growth (OECD 2010c: 106), though one has to
add that it is not always clear what private means in China and whether communist officials have decisive influence on the management. Naughton (2007:
chap. 4.6.1) concedes this in his standard work on the Chinese economy, but
nonetheless describes the institutional development as a process of slight privatisation

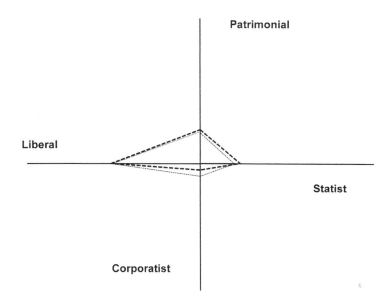

Figure 2.4 Brazil mapped in the field between four ideal types, 1998 (fat) and 2008 (thin)★
Note: ★ each ray starts at zero in the centre of the figure and has a value of 100. This is also
true for each spider wire over the four dimensions.

and liberalisation (ibid.: 106; see also McNally in this volume) – a view fitting
with the Chinese spider web in Figure 2.3.

India is sometimes – regularly by *The Economist* (as on 2 October 2010: 62;
cf. Huang 2008: 266–75) – presented as a liberal counterexample to China.
Kohli (2006), however, holds that India already in the 1980s moved towards a
statist course of GDP growth that was not disturbed by later liberal reforms.
The modest liberalisation that Figure 2.3 suggests seems somewhat to support
The Economist, but the figure comprises more components than state-led economic growth. In this volume, Mazumdar emphasises continuity in this large
country with its immense agricultural sector, where change by definition
appears to be very slow, and with its federal structure that renders possible
pronounced uneven development. He argues that the liberalisation of Indian
capitalism has to be put into the context of Indian traditions, among others that
of 'dirigisme'. His message of continuity does not contradict the Indian spider
in Figure 2.3. India has only modestly liberalised, meaning that continuity has
been strong.

Russian development has been different, but there is less controversy about
the trajectory. The country experienced a complete overhaul of its economy
by 'shock therapy' in the early 1990s under President Yeltsin. It gave rise to the
'oligarchs' who, based on clientelist relations with the bureaucracy and the

president, gained control of the oil and banking sectors. The 1990s brought about sharp economic as well as social decline and political 'chaos'. According to the dominant view (see Myant and Drahokoupil 2010: 143–58), Putin, elected president in 2000, strengthened the presidency, drew back local and regional autonomy, expropriated and prosecuted a number of the oligarchs, nationalised their companies, and generally tried to subordinate private businesses. As reflected in Figure 2.3, this process de-liberalised Russia. It was supported by popular demand for a strong state and relied on Putin's clientelist networks. It created the image of the strong Putin state, but in fact strengthened patrimonialism and gave way to a new generation of oligarchs or oligarch-bureaucrats (see Vasileva in this volume).

Brazil differs from the other BRICs in that it featured no change at all between 1998 and 2008. It was more liberal than China and India in 1998 and in 2008 it was more liberal than all of the other BRICs, even though it did not liberalise. Its level of statism and patrimonialism is somewhat lower, therefore. As Boschi in this volume describes, Brazil liberalised in the 1990s, but thereafter came a reversal during the Lula presidency.

On balance, there was no change worth mentioning, at least in terms of liberalism and statism, while patrimonialism slightly declined. The biggest difference between Brazil and the other BRICs is the existence of a significant corporatism. It is a legacy from the dictatorship in the 1930s when it was modelled after Mediterranean examples. Recently, during the presidencies of Cardoso and particularly Lula, it became stronger and developed from an authoritarian form into a more democratic one. This process was facilitated by the unions. Brazil is the only BRICs country where organised labour was an important player in recent processes of change (but, on the shop floor, labour is still weak). Lula even spoke of 'labour capitalism'.

It is difficult to estimate the extent of Brazilian corporatism. Data on corporatism in emerging economies do not exist (as they exist on advanced economies and are summarised by Siaroff 1999: 185). In Siaroff's index of indices (scaled 1–5) the USA and France score a bit more than 1, while highly corporatist countries (Austria, Netherland, Norway, Sweden) score higher than 4. Based on the guess that Brazil would score between 1.5 and 2, I have given it a few millimetres in Figure 2.4 and supposed an increasing corporatisation from 1998 to 2008.

Leaving the BRICs, we arrive at South Africa and Turkey. Their spider webs are drawn in Figure 2.5, which also includes the considerably more liberal contrast case of the USA. The most striking aspect of Figure 2.5 is that institutional change in the South African and Turkish political economies between 1998 and 2008 has been so small that it cartographically cannot be shown (both liberalised between 1 and 2 per cent; see Tables 2.3 and 2.5). We can only see that South Africa, perhaps reflecting an Anglo-Saxon legacy, has been more liberal and Turkey a bit more statist and patrimonial.

To some extent, the development of both countries is comparable to the Brazilian trajectory of the past two decades. In the 1990s, real GDP growth was low because inflation was high and overall liberalisation has been very limited.

Patrimonial

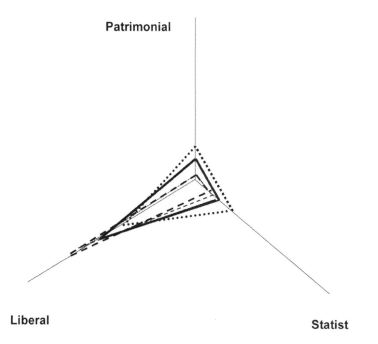

Liberal   **Statist**

Figure 2.5 South Africa, Turkey and the USA comparatively mapped in the field between
    three ideal types, 1998 (thin line) and 2008 (fat)
Note: South Africa = steady line; Turkey = short dashes; USA = long dashes

Neither country embraced pure market liberalism, but instead deliberately
chose an embedded variety. In 'post-apartheid' South Africa, this started, as the
Nattras's chapter describes, with the presidency of Mandela in 1994, who had
already pleaded for a 'mixed economy' that follows the examples of France and
Germany. Some discussion of nationalising the mining industry, contributing
nearly a fifth to South African GDP, has also taken place. However, neither
poverty (in terms of the national poverty line) nor inequality has declined in
the period under consideration (absolute poverty has slightly declined; see
Table 1.4). Therefore, regarding South Africa, there can be no talk of social
democratisation as it occurred in Brazil in the 2000s. The power of the African
National Congress (ANC) to change apartheid seems to have been limited.

   In Turkey, the conservative government of the Justice and Development
Party (AKP) was at least more successful in fighting inequality (poverty
increased somewhat), rendering Turkey comparable to Brazil in this respect.
The high and unchanged Turkish employment protection is also remarkable
(but probably explains the extreme low formal employment rate). There was
liberalisation in the sense of privatisation and some opening-up of the Turkish
market (which also is a requirement of the intended EU membership), but by
its 'social and regulatory neo-liberalism' the government at the same time founded a

sort of Turkish 'third way' response to neoliberal globalisation (Öniş 2012: 141f). The strong particularism (ibid.) and, related, hardly changing patrimonialism as described in Özel's chapter undermined this third way, however. On balance, there is little change in the Turkish political economy therefore.

Overall, as Figures 2.3–2.5 show at a glance and the preceding tables with more precision, the institutional differences between the BRICs have decreased in the ten years considered and only India has liberalised to a degree worth mentioning. Russia de-liberalised, Brazil neither liberalised nor de-liberalised overall (though it liberalised until 2004 and then de-liberalised), and China, just as South Africa and Turkey, marginally moved in a liberal direction (the small movement could not even be mapped). Statism was relatively stable, while patrimonialism in most cases slightly decreased. The trends shown in the figures and tables fit the tenor of the descriptions in the subsequent country chapters, where change is indicated by specific developments.

To enhance precision, data are needed that are directly relevant to statism (instead of state efficiency) and patrimonialism (instead of corruption) – and to corporatism and meso-communitarianism in cases where these types are ad rem – as well as data with respect to the capital–labour relationship. At this moment comparable data on, for example, union density, social security benefits and tax progression in emerging economies are fragmentary. Apart from the lack of data, we should not forget to mention, however, the fundamental difficulties of scientific precision in the field of institutional change. The relevance of potential factors to be considered cannot experimentally be tested, criteria have to be chosen, quality has to be transformed into quantity and factors have to be weighted. There is no 'objective' way to do this.

Notes

1 Taking all ten IEF indicators with each one counting for one tenth and 1995 instead of 1998 at T_1, Poland is a pronounced liberaliser, however.

2 The scores of the Corruption Perception Index from Transparency International in many cases deviate from those of the IEF. In Russia, corruption has increased relatively more in the CPI than in the IEF, but the Chinese, Turkish, Czech, Polish and Slovakian scores differ considerably.

3 At first sight, one could think, for example, that the Chinese product market in 2008 was four times as regulated as that of the USA (see the second column of Table 2.2), but the OECD scale runs from 0 to 6 (total regulation) and converted into scores from 0 (total regulation) to 100 the difference between China and the USA is only one between 45 and 86 (column four in Table 2.2; if the maximum PMR score were fixed at, for example, 4 or 5 instead of 6, the differences in the converted scores would increase).

4 On a ray of 10 centimetres, one index/percentage point would be 1 millimetre. In the space available, one index point is the equivalent of almost nothing, however, and 1 centimetre is, depending on the size of the figure, the equivalent of 20 to 25 index or percentage points.

3 The evolution and contemporary manifestations of Sino-capitalism

Christopher A. McNally

3.1 China and the BRICs

The emergence of new economic powers has begun to alter the geo-economic landscape of globalisation. Their increasing influence indicates a shift in economic power away from the advanced economies of Europe, the USA and Japan. Already the BRICs (Brazil, Russia, India and China) are key drivers of global economic growth. China and India in particular surfaced as the top two contributors to global growth starting in 2006 (Virmani 2011: 12). This trend has now further accelerated after the global financial crisis of 2008 and the European debt crisis. The BRICs plus other emerging market economies have become vital drivers of global growth for the first time since the end of the Second World War.

Among the BRICs, China stands out. It represents by far the biggest economy among this grouping. China's gross domestic product (GDP) in 2011 at over US $7 trillion was almost three times larger than Brazil's, the next largest member of the BRICs, with $2.5 trillion GDP in 2011 (World Bank 2012b). China also has been the fastest-growing, hence most dynamic economy among the BRICs, and it possesses a highly diversified industrial sector that has become the globe's largest exporter. For these reasons, China is often perceived as somewhat apart from the other BRICs. It garners more global attention and has truly global aspirations of its own by now.

As the introductory chapters to this volume illustrate, emerging market economies are a rather heterogeneous grouping. Just looking at the BRICs, the largest emerging market economies, one finds profound divergences in terms of geography, wealth, economic dynamism, global impact, and political, cultural and historical legacies. As Uwe Becker notes in the Introduction, 'what unites the BRICS is being emerging, big ... and discontent with certain aspects of the current world order'.

Despite their differences, however, emerging market economies represent a new global force. Any thorough understanding of this new force must first seriously tackle the nature and logic of China's global re-emergence. China's seemingly insatiable appetite for resources has already reshaped global commodities markets. It is likely to do the same to global geo-economic and geo-political arrangements in the next decade. Indeed, China is gaining increasing techno-logical sophistication, thus becoming a serious competitor to the advanced industrial economies of Europe, North America and Japan.

As all other late developers who attempted an industrial catch-up with the already advanced economies, China has undertaken a form of state-guided capitalist development (McNally 2008a). The mention of capitalism within China, though, is to this day frowned upon by the Chinese Communist Party (CCP). Con-ferences and workshops at universities in the People's Republic that aim to discuss China's emergent capitalism have to replace the term 'capitalism' with something like 'China's development model'. Officially, therefore, China is not capitalist but rather a 'socialist market economy with Chinese characteristics'.

This generates the question of how capitalist China really is. Certainly, China incorporates all the capitalist characteristics mentioned in the introductory chapter by Uwe Becker. China has a large, highly entrepreneurial private sector, firms are to varying extents exposed to intense market competition, and the economy is now based on endless capital accumulation in most of its realms. Conversely, China possesses a large state sector, issues five-year plans, employs a wide array of regulatory and industrial policy tools, and conducts monetary policy less via interest rate measures and more via administrative rules on credit allocation.

In China, a form of capitalism, albeit developing and evolving, is visibly present. This capitalism, however, is of a hybrid nature – a fact that has generated much conceptual confusion. For instance, China's emergent capitalism has gener-ated a proliferation of new terms, ranging from 'incomplete state socialism' to 'capitalism with Chinese characteristics', 'Confucian Leninism', 'capital social-ism', 'bureaupreneurialism' and 'nomenclature capitalism' (Baum and Shev-chenko 1999: 333–34). These concepts often obscure more in comparative terms than they elucidate. Yet they express the paradoxical nature of China's political economy, including processes of rapid institutional change and pro-found regional differences that China's vast size covers.

To cut through this conceptual confusion and its attendant difficulties in analysing China's emergent capitalism, an open approach is necessary. An open approach here implies an emphasis on comparative institutional analysis that does not fall into the rigid confines of certain ideal types. It follows Becker (2009) in emphasising an empirically oriented analysis of China's emergent capitalism that allows for space to grasp nuances, dynamic changes, and the panoply of characteristics that emanate from China's long historical legacy. Therefore, the approach taken here consciously eschews the binary conceptualisation of types of capitalism in the Varieties of Capitalism (VoC) literature (cf. Hall and Soskice 2001).

Certainly, the VoC approach has contributed much to the study of comparative capitalisms. However, its rather narrow conceptual framework has faced consider-able criticism (Pontusson 2005; Becker 2009). The approach focuses, for example, exclusively on the nature and sources of variation in the institutionally more stable political economies of advanced industrial nations (Streeck and Yamamura 2001). Especially with regard to emerging market economies like the BRICs, it fails to capture their dynamic institutional arrangements, particularly new forms of refurbished state capitalism as well as transnational influences (Nölke and Vliegenthart 2009). Philippe Schmitter in this context suggests that the dichotomy between liberal and coordinated market economies in the Varieties of Capitalism approach is too primitive in its attempt to capture capitalist variety in its entirety. At a minimum, greater attention needs to be paid to the degree of stateness permeating any given form of capitalism (Schmitter 2012).

The closed analytical framework of the VoC approach has to be opened. Many different configurations of capitalist institutions are possible. Therefore, I draw on the comparative capitalisms literature, but open it up analytically to capture the often paradoxical facets of China's emergent capitalism. I understand China as a mixture of ideal types proposed in this volume and refined by several of the country chapters. China encompasses aspects of the liberal, statist and certainly the patrimonial ideal types of capitalism. It also has seen applications of corporatist and meso-communitarian elements of capitalism, though these are less prominent. Finally, China's economy is highly open internationally, constantly absorbing global influences.

How to integrate the hybrid, even at times contradictory sets of institutions present in China into a conceptual whole? Indeed, how to capture empirical realities on the ground in China while paying heed to the conceptual insights of comparative capitalism approaches? I propose to conceive of China as generating a new and truly global capitalist force – Sino-capitalism.

Sino-capitalism is first and foremost a hybrid, combining liberal and statist elements plus a variety of clientelism/patrimonialism based on *guanxi* (the Chinese art of cultivating long-term personal reciprocal relationships that build enduring trust). Sino-capitalism hence relies on informal business networks rather than on legal codes and transparent rules (McNally 2011). It also assigns the state a leading role in fostering and guiding capitalist accumulation. China, ultimately, is a large developing economy with a distinct socialist and imperial legacy.

Evidently, Sino-capitalism differs both from the Anglo-American liberal free-market model and the continental European coordinated model of capitalism in important respects. Central to Sino-capitalism's institutional structure is a unique duality that combines state-led development top-down with entrepreneurial private capital accumulation bottom-up. Private capital accumulation in China has for the most part exhibited highly networked formal and informal institutional characteristics that tend to utilise the aforementioned cultivation of *guanxi*. Although informal, *guanxi* business networks are a central component of the Chinese political economy. The cultivation of *guanxi* has enabled entrepreneurs to overcome initial hostility from the state and to forge close cooperative relations on the local level with state officials. It is therefore at the local level where the two processes of state-led development from above and network-based development from below tend to meet (McNally 2008b, 2012).

The result is a profound dualism that integrates state-led development top-down with entrepreneurial and networked business activities bottom-up. *Guanxi* also introduces a deliberate ambiguity to Chinese capitalism, since a reliance on informal networks rather than transparent codes and rules leaves considerable discretion to local officials. According to Western standards, therefore, the rule of law is not fully developed.

As a further consequence of this dynamic, state–capital relations have been localised and engendered considerable variation within China. The highly networked character of private capital accumulation in China, moreover, has integrated Chinese firms into local, national and often globally linked production and knowledge networks. Considerable influences emanating from the global capitalist system have shaped Sino-capitalism outside-in.

What emerges is a unique form of capitalism that is not so much characterised by internal institutional arrangements that reinforce each other, as by institutional forces that are often juxtaposed in compensatory, even seemingly conflicting fashion (McNally 2012). Sino-capitalism has emerged as the result of medium- to long-term incremental evolution, a permanent process of socio-economic trial and error. Its institutional arrangements are, as a result, quite heterogeneous, exhibiting a jumble of authority relations and considerable incremental institutional adaptation that tends to make formal institutional structures appear incongruent with informal arrangements.

Seen from a global macro-perspective, the ascent of Sino-capitalism represents the first time since 1850 that the world capitalist system is experiencing the rise of a massive capitalist power that espouses domestic institutional arrangements and international viewpoints fundamentally different from those characterising the dominant liberal free-market model of capitalism. Sino-capitalism is, in fact, based on what could potentially become the globe's largest political economy. To stress this point, China is not just Germany or Japan. With 1.3 billion people, its population is four times the size of the USA, creating enormous economic potential on a continental, even global scale. China's rise thus represents the first time historically that the Anglo-American liberal model of capitalism could be challenged on the global level.

This analysis is intended as a qualitative case study of the evolution and contemporary manifestations of Sino-capitalism. I take an open approach that attempts to integrate conceptually the rather paradoxical nature of China's political economy. The objective is to create a conceptual whole that can tackle the complexity of China's emergent capitalism to elucidate its nature and logic. Since the policy of reform and opening began in 1979, my analysis predates the period of investigation in this volume by about a decade, covering the period from around 1980 to the present. I first review the evolution of Sino-capitalism by focusing on how the development of private capital accumulation put pressure on the state to reform. State reform in turn enabled further private-sector development while strengthening the ability of the state to govern and guide an increasingly sophisticated and internationally integrated capitalist political economy. This created the conditions for the unique institutional dualism of Sino-capitalism to materialise.

The second part then precisely conceptualises the institutional manifestations of contemporary Sino-capitalism. The major emphasis here lies on analysing China's state–capital dynamics. Less space is available to review the nature of capital–labour relations in China. I end the chapter with several analytical implications of the case of Sino-capitalism for the study of comparative capitalisms, the BRICs' emerging market economies and the globe's changing political economic order.

3.2 The evolution of Sino-capitalism

At the start of economic liberalisation in 1979, China had experienced a long period of emphasis on heavy industry in a cloistered centrally planned economy modelled primarily on the Soviet Union. Liberalisation began in the 1980s and involved enabling small-scale quasi-private businesses to grow, the gradual introduction of market forces and international competition, and various waves of reforms aimed at state enterprises and the state bureaucracy. These reforms ushered in decades of institutional experimentation under state guidance.

Many interpretations of China's capitalist evolution have emphasised one aspect of the reform process over another. Yasheng Huang (2008) as well as Ian Bremmer (2010) and Minxin Pei (2006) hold that China primarily represents a state-centric system of capital accumulation. Huang in particular points out how, at the beginning of reforms, liberalisation allowed finance to flow to the development of rural Township and Village Enterprises (TVEs), thus creating a process of bottom-up equitable development. Reforms in the 1990s, however, recentralised powers in the state leading to economic de-liberalisation. This state-centric mode of development created an urban-focused and unequal form of development that is wasting scarce resources on state industrial, infrastructure and urbanisation projects.

A second interpretation sees China's political economy as primarily characterised by bottom-up network-driven dynamics. Authors such as Kellee Tsai (2007), as well as Victor Nee and Sonja Opper (2012), emphasise how constant informal institutional adaptations enabled the rapid growth of a private enterprise economy in China. Although Chinese private firms early on faced considerable discrimination from the Chinese government, entrepreneurs were able to create institutional innovations that enabled them to overcome the legacies of central planning to grow small, private manufacturing firms. Over time, new industrial clusters emerged that integrated various steps of production, as well as the provision of finance, labour, land and other crucial inputs. This clustering of private enterprises diffused rapidly throughout the coastal regions of China and eroded the market share of state-owned enterprises (SOEs). Once the fledgling private sector had become an engine of economic growth and job creation, the CCP sought to legitimise it as a way to sustain China's economic development. The success of Sino-capitalism in this view was due to a bottom-up process of networked entrepreneurship or *guanxi* capitalism.

A third interpretation stresses how China's development processes were propelled and conditioned by the outside-in forces of globalisation. You-tien Hsing (1998), David Zweig (2002) and, more recently, Ed Steinfeld (2010) stress how China absorbed various international forces to become a capitalist facilitator for global production and knowledge networks. In the 1990s, most international capital came from the diaspora networks of overseas Chinese entrepreneurs, which provided the bulk of foreign investment at the time. The gradual absorption of international best practices that resulted from these initial overseas Chinese investments allowed China later to incorporate crucial elements of the supply chains of global manufacturing networks. Outside-in forces also influenced many Chinese policy choices, such as openness to foreign direct investment, active use of both domestic and foreign equity markets, and the liberalisation of labour markets (Lee *et al.* 2002). The consequence has been the emergence of a form of 'state neoliberalism' (Chu and So 2010) or 'market-liberal state capitalism' (ten Brink 2011).

All of these accounts contain important analytical truths. Yet, they each only stress one aspect of Sino-capitalism's evolution. The crucial facet of Sino-capitalism is that it is based on counterbalancing institutional complementarities that are driven by top-down state-guided, bottom-up entrepreneurial, and outside-in globalised forces of capital accumulation. None of these analyses thus captures comprehensively the nature and logic of China's capitalist re-emergence. Rather, some, such as Huang's (2008) neoclassical economic perspective, risk falling into the dichotomy of state versus market or state versus private-sector forces. My analysis of Sino-capitalism, however, underscores that state forces and private-sector forces actually mutually conditioned and, ultimately, strengthened each other during the reform process.

The evolution of Sino-capitalism can only be understood by discarding the notion of a zero-sum game during which either state or private-sector forces are strengthened. Neither the statist nature of Sino-capitalism nor its bottom-up entrepreneurial character represents an exclusive aspect of China's development dynamic. In building on Kohli and Shue (1994), who proposed the concept of 'mutual empowerment' of state and society during developmental processes, I perceive of Sino-capitalism's evolution as primarily based on a process of mutual conditioning and strengthening of juxtaposed institutionalrealms, especially state and private-sector productive forces, as well as state and market. Put differently, China's capital accumulation has been driven by processes during which both state and private capitalist elements adapted to and empowered each other. This created cycles of induced reforms, where each small step at restructuring created pressures for further modifications (Jefferson and Rawski 1994; Naughton 1995; Solinger 1989).

To illustrate the nature of this evolutionary dynamic in Sino-capitalism's emergence, I briefly recap one crucial element in the history of China's reform process: the development of TVEs and their subsequent privatisation, laying the foundations for China's private sector. While this account only reflects one aspect of China's stunning economic take-off, it shows how state, market and private-sector forces mutually conditioned each other.

The surprising Township and Village Enterprises

The effects of China's reform and open door policy constitute undoubtedly an industrial 'success story'. China has experienced sustained economic growth, a marked increase in the manufacturing sector's share of total output, as well as a growing diversification of industrial production and a concomitant expansion of exports. These developments are especially noteworthy when China's original economic structure of a centrally planned economy is taken into account (Kornais 1992). What, ultimately, allowed China to transition rapidly from a centrally planned economy to a global export powerhouse?

In essence, a series of historical factors and policy changes enabled social groups within and outside of the Chinese party-state to form alliances in pursuit of break-neck economic growth. These 'growth alliances' overcame internal obstacles and established a dynamic and vibrant political economy outside of the centrally planned economy. In addition, these bottom-up entrepreneurial forces benefited from intensifying globalisation in the international political economy. Starting in the 1980s, overseas Chinese investment and the role of Hong Kong as economic mediator impinged on China. Within these new growth alliances, the role of the non-state sector of the Chinese economy, especially rural collectives or TVEs, is highly noteworthy.

Although following in broad strokes the Soviet model, already during the Maoist period the structure of China's centrally planned economy differed from its Soviet counterpart. China operated an industrial system that was relatively decentralised, multi-tiered and regionally oriented, with some responsibility for planning and coordination in the hands of local governments (Naughton 1995; Shirk 1993). This tendency became even more pronounced during the Cultural Revolution decade of 1966–76. Beginning in the early 1970s, a new wave of rural industrialisation was initiated. Under the heading of the 'five small' rural industries, the CCP leadership envisaged the building of cement, hydroelectric power, chemical fertiliser, farm implements, and iron and steel plants that would render small geographical units of the countryside autarchic. Ironically, these industries intended for autarchy would later form the backbone of China's light industrial export boom.

As the policy of 'reform and opening' began in the early 1980s, the CCP initiated a set of fundamental reforms in its governance of China. These included the dismantling of the commune system after 1979 and its replacement with two basic levels of local government: the *Xiang* (Township) and the *Cun* (Village). Second, the CCP's *nomenklatura* system – the system that is responsible for party personnel appointments – was instructed to evaluate local cadres not on their political correctness ('being red'), but on their ability to improve the economic performance of their jurisdictions (Huang 1996; Edin 2003). Third, reforms formally decentralised financial and material resources, as well as economic decision-making powers, to lower levels of government. The aim was to stimulate economic growth by fiscal and management decentralisation (Solinger 1991). The result: 'localities became independent fiscal entities that had responsibility for local expenditures and the unprecedented right to use the revenue that they retained' (Oi 1992: 103).

One of the biggest successes of the very early reform period was the rather spontaneous emergence of the rural household responsibility system in China's countryside (Kelliher 1992). The implementation of this system basically dismantled the communes, giving land back to farmers in long-term leases. This created strong incentives for individual farmers to raise their productivity and resulted in a meteoric jump in agricultural output up until 1984. Greater opportunities for farmers to sell their produce in open markets then substantially increased their disposable income and led to a rural consumer boom.

Rural collective firms originally based on the 'five small' industries benefited enormously from this boom. They also benefited from fiscal decentralisation and the new cadre incentive system. Local governments began to see the promotion of local industrial development as a means to harness new profit streams that could offset declining transfers from higher levels of government. New-found political autonomies further emboldened local cadres to undertake policy experimentation and sometimes outright circumvention of central rules. Quasi-market forces beyond the reach of the central state increased in strength, and, based on the original 'five small' industries, local governments expanded and funded productive ventures of their own: the TVEs.

TVEs under the management of local governments started to engage in all kinds of non-agricultural production that was not explicitly forbidden. Perhaps most importantly, the profit motive began to reign in TVEs. Many local governments, for instance, resorted to contracting out an enterprise to one manager, allowing this manager (either a private entrepreneur or a government official) to gain managerial autonomy as in a quasi-private enterprise. Managerial autonomy rendered smaller TVEs and other collectively run enterprises far more flexible than China's mostly larger SOEs. TVEs and other collectives were also not as burdened as larger SOEs with welfare obligations and could practise much more flexible labour practices, often hiring and firing workers at will in what was still predominantly a socialist political economy (Naughton 1995).

The rapid growth to prominence of TVEs was aided by one final and crucial factor. Although it practised fiscal decentralisation, the Chinese government did not replace the plan with a market economy in one fell swoop. Rather, the market sector was expanded gradually while maintaining parts of the plan. This macroeconomic policy meant that the high monopoly prices state industry could enjoy were at first left intact. This, however, created large empty niches for new entrants as market forces garnered strength. Whoever could enter an empty niche not filled by the state sector (often consumer goods that the state sector failed to supply adequately) and/or whoever could gain access to the monopoly markets enjoyed by state industry was able rapidly to reap large windfall profits. Especially in the early 1980s, TVEs' entrance into new niche and former monopoly markets led to very high profitability. In later years, as monopoly profits were eroded and new market niches became crowded, profitability declined (Naughton 1992, 1995).

Nevertheless, the lack of competition in markets not filled by traditional SOEs and monopoly profits in others enticed local governments throughout China to establish TVEs in large numbers. The rise of TVEs and other quasi-private enterprises allowed China to 'outgrow the plan' (Naughton 1995) and created conditions for a host of institutional innovations to take place (Tsai 2007). Different types of entrepreneurs, various branches of local government and in some cases overseas investors formed 'growth alliances' for profit. However, in many cases private entrepreneurs continued to suffer due to government discrimination and ideology. Under these circumstances, they enhanced their status by forming symbiotic relations with TVEs and other collectives affiliated with local government.

In Wenzhou, one of China's private-sector trailblazers, private entrepreneurs obtained legal status for their business transactions by borrowing for a fee an official identification from a collective or SOE. The private enterprise thus became legally a collective or state enterprise, though control remained in the hands of the individual entrepreneur. Many of the private operators in Wenzhou also formed 'partnership enterprises' with local cadres to ensure greater access to credit and other benefits that the local government controlled. Better connections or *guanxi*, on average, allowed these entrepreneurs to operate more profitably than their competitors. Every private entrepreneur thus tried to hook up with influential government cadres, and cadres became back-room supporters or even operators of many ventures (Liu 1992).

Over time, TVEs, some urban collectives and small SOEs began a process of quasi-privatisation, a process that primarily benefited former cadres who had been involved in enterprise management or well-connected private entrepreneurs. As this process unfolded, the institutional identification of collectives, small state firms and private enterprises began to blur. As Barry Naughton put it, 'Rural governments continued to register enterprises in the traditional categories, because this was ideologically more secure. In practice, though, the entire countryside was going through a massive process of privatisation' (Naughton 1995: 9).

With quasi-privatisation during the late 1980s and early 1990s, the organisational forms of many Chinese firms became very fuzzy, mainly moving in the direction of private management under the official 'hat' of state or collective ownership. This fuzziness also enabled overseas Chinese investors to enter China. Many TVEs in coastal regions entered into cooperative relations with these investors and traders, linking them with world markets and helping them to become internationally competitive. Finally, as the non-state sector continued to pick up steam, many SOEs subcontracted production processes to this more flexible and nimble sector. What emerged was a 'dual' economy with a relatively sluggish state sector and a rather dynamic collective, private and hybrid ownership sector. In fact, the 'state as entrepreneur' became a pervasive feature of China's drive to material wealth (Oi 1992: 118).

The surprising rise of TVEs created a massive expansion of industrial employment in China. The TVE workforce expanded from 24 million in 1980 to nearly 90 million in 1990, while employment in urban collective enterprises rose from 25.5 million to 35.5 million (White 1993: 172). Collective enterprises grew by 29.9 per cent per year, while the state sector grew by a respectable though much slower 8.49 per cent (World Bank 1992: 52). Already in 1990 the state sector produced only 55 per cent of total output, while urban collectives, TVEs, and individual and foreign enterprises provided 13 per cent, 22 per cent and 9 per cent, respectively (World Bank 1992: 56).

While the quasi-private sector suffered from the economic retrenchment and more restrictive ideological environment following the Tiananmen incident in 1989, it got a new shot of life after Deng Xiaoping's *Nanxun* (Southern Tour) in early 1992. This tour ushered in a renewed push towards market reforms, and enabled Deng Xiaoping to get his way during the 14th Party Congress of the CCP at the end of 1992. At this time, the CCP central committee proposed the establishment of a 'socialist market economy' in China, a move that opened the door to the establishment of more private enterprises and the restructuring of state and collective enterprises. The post-1992 period revitalised TVEs and other quasi-private enterprises. However, by the mid-1990s, markets had become extremely crowded and profit margins were rapidly eroding for TVEs. In 1997, as the Asian financial crisis began, the total number of TVEs and their overall employment declined for the first time (Li and Rozelle 2003).

In response to the declining performance of TVEs, which created an actual or potential drain on government resources, several local Chinese governments began experimenting with their formal privatisation around 1994. Wenzhou and Ningbo in Zhejiang Province, for instance, finished TVE privatisation by 1996 (Li and Rozelle 2003). These efforts benefited from an important legal move, the promulgation of the Chinese Company Law in 1994 enabling the establishment of limited liability corporations. Depending on their location and size, quasi-private firms could switch from corporate structures with murky ownership to limited liability corporations. In this process stakeholders converted their informal ownership into shareholding capital. As limited liability corporations, firms could acquire a stronger organisational identity with respect to their political and social environments. The implementation of this law also generated conditions in China for the governance structures of private and state firms to converge.

The strongest push for formal privatisation came around 1997 as the performance of TVEs and many small SOEs had declined markedly. In September 1997, the CCP held its 15th Party Congress during which Party Secretary Jiang Zemin announced that the legitimate rights and interests of all types of enterprises should be protected. The Party Congress also formalised the policies of *zhuada fangxiao* ('to grasp the large and let go of the small') and state enterprise *gaizhi* ('transformation'). The 'letting go of the small' element opened the door for relinquishing control over smaller state firms, including giving local governments authority to restructure, privatise or close down small SOEs and collectives, including TVEs. It also encouraged quasi-private firms to clarify and formalise their ownership structures as limited liability corporations.

The 'grasping the large' component indicated a focus on maintaining state control over the largest SOEs. Reforms encompassed wide-ranging efforts to transform large SOEs, including the shedding of labour and welfare burdens, setting up governance structures modelled on modern corporate systems (the

Modern Enterprise System), and various efforts at corporate restructuring, such as stock market listings, mergers and corporate streamlining (McNally and Lee 1998; McNally 2002).

As a result of these policies, most locales in China had begun the formal privatisation of TVEs by 1998, which then unfolded very rapidly. By 1999, almost 90 per cent of local government-owned firms had transferred their shares to private entrepreneurs partially or completely (Li and Rozelle 2003). Much of this happened via insider privatisation, whereby former managers bought out the business, perhaps representing one of the greatest episodes of privatisation in any transition economy.

Thereafter, the legal standing of the private sector was further strengthened by several constitutional amendments. In March 1999, the National People's Congress amended the Chinese constitution to redefine private enterprise as an 'important element' of the Chinese economy, while in March 2004 the Chinese constitution was amended once more to include the phrase 'private property obtained legally shall not be violated'. This put private property nominally on the same footing as state property, which is regarded as 'sacred and inviolable'. Finally, in March 2007, earlier constitutional changes triggered the promulgation of the much-awaited Property Law (*Wuquan Fa*). This law codifies earlier constitutional changes and affords equal protection to state and private property.

Mutual conditioning and strengthening of state and private capital accumulation

Chinese policies of recognising private enterprise represent the culmination of a long evolutionary process. This process saw a series of economic, legal and political initiatives resulting in quasi-private firms gradually clarifying their ownership structures and attaining a greater degree of organisational clarity vis-à-vis their social and political environments. As I will note later, this clarity is still circumscribed by the deliberate ambiguity of China's party-state governance regime. Nonetheless, the strides that the Chinese private sector has made are highly impressive. Chinese small to medium-size private enterprises have clustered into enormously competitive production networks, capturing global market share in sectors ranging from silk ties to lighters (Williamson and Zheng 2008). These vibrant and globally enmeshed networks of producers and traders have in fact allowed China to become a key component of the Western-led economic system, assimilating multinational production and knowledge networks into the Chinese economy (Steinfeld 2010).

In addition, the vast majority of Chinese firms in technologically fast-moving sectors are now privately managed, such as Huawei and ZTE in telecoms equipment, or Yingling and Suntech in solar voltaic panels. Many of these firms have hybrid ownership structures that include a degree of state ownership (Ernst and Naughton 2008). In the end, China's industrial success story could not have been possible without the emergence of competitive private and hybrid ownership firms, but this has not been a process divorced from state guidance and state reform. Quite the contrary, the dynamism of China's private sector, first in TVEs and other collectives, then gradually transitioning towards more formal private and mixed ownership structures, has only been possible due to the continuous adaptation of the CCP and the Chinese state (Dickson 2008; Shambaugh 2008; Nee and Opper 2012).

Private entrepreneurs have employed, as Kellee Tsai argues, a 'diverse range of informal coping strategies' (Tsai 2007: 207). These coping strategies have over time triggered responses from the Chinese party-state. The result: strategies that were often illegal or politically taboo at the outset were sanctioned post hoc, such as the recognition that quasi-private enterprises should be encouraged to formalise their ownership structures. In addition, the CCP has proven quite adaptive in integrating new elites, creating in the process a more inclusive and institutionalised polity that encourages large private enterprise owners to be engaged in formal political institutions. By the 2000s, the CCP had started to foster the needs and interests of private capital accumulation to a considerable extent (Dickson 2008).

Changes in state–private capital relations further triggered SOE reforms. As noted above, the rapid and surprising rise of TVEs in light industrial manu-facturing eroded the state sector's monopoly profits in these sectors. This put pressure on policy makers to undertake ever-more fundamental state-sector reforms. Already at the outset of reforms in the early 1980s the 'Expanding Powers and Yielding Profits' SOE reform tried to create a modicum of profit incentives for state firm managers. This was followed in the late 1980s by the 'Contract Responsibility System', which, following the lead of TVEs, attempted to yield operational autonomy to managers. The SOE reform process culminated in the implementation of the Modern Enterprise System and the policy of *zhuada fangxiao* from the mid-1990s onwards (McNally and Lee 1998; McNally 2002). This ambitious effort at SOE reform created a much more profitable state sector by shedding small uneconomical state firms and concentrating on large enterprises in key producer goods and basic network sectors. Moreover, remaining SOEs were corporatised under the Modern Enterprise System to enable the state to exercise its property rights more clearly, while opening the door to corporate restructuring and more profit-driven incentive structures.

In parallel to reforms in the governance of state firms, the Chinese state undertook several phases of reforms that streamlined and consolidated the government bureaucracy. In particular, all the line ministries in charge of SOEs in individual industrial sectors (e.g. the Ministries of Chemical Industry or Metallurgical Industry) were abolished, with only a few strategic planning functions retained. While adjusting to the demands of a developing and glo-balising market economy, the Chinese state bureaucracy thus kept an emphasis on indicative state planning. This is most clearly expressed by Chinese efforts to establish a supra-ministerial institution to implement industrial policy. Although fraught with bureaucratic rivalries for more than twenty years, these efforts came to fruition in 2003 when central bureaucratic reforms succeeded in establishing the National Development and Reform Commission as a hub to steer industrial development and upgrading.

At the same time, the State-owned Assets Supervision and Administration Commission (SASAC) was established to control the governance of large, central SOEs. This Commission exercises quasi-trustee control over state-owned assets. It oversees government holdings, appoints boards of directors in conjunction with the CCP's Central Organisation Department, and directs large mergers, combinations, acquisitions and divestments. SASAC's remit does not only suggest state control, but also contains elements of state corporate steering and transformation. As a result, the Chinese state sector is now populated by very large SOEs that in 2007 produced profits of about 6.2 per cent of GDP, an astounding number (Naughton 2008: 19). Under SASAC's management, most significant state firms have become profit oriented and their major operations are in units listed on stock markets. Large state firms also are mostly located in monopolistic or oligopolistic sectors while continuing to enjoy preferential access to loans, real estate and subsidies.

Thus, while state firms have retreated from the most competitive and least profitable sectors in the Chinese economy, they have kept a tight grip on a wide range of critical industries – the commanding heights. These include oil, gas and mining, the production of basic producer goods such as non-ferrous metals, steel and petrochemicals, essential network industries in telecommunications, transportation and utilities, and all major banking and financial institutions. This direct control over economic matters via state firms continues to enable central and local authorities to allocate financial resources and guide economic activities.

Clearly, the Chinese reform process does not represent a unilateral retreat of the state in favour of private entrepreneurial and market forces. However, neither does it represent the process of de-liberalisation and state-sector dominance that Huang (2008) conveys as having taken place since the mid-1990s. China's private sector has risen from non-existence to become the most dynamic element of the Chinese political economy. Surely, much of China's private sector is composed of small to medium-sized firms, often clustering in highly networked industries such as electronics, apparel and small household goods. Yet, China's private sector also has created giants like Huawei, Hai'er and real estate developers China Vanke and Soho. Conversely, while the state sector shrank markedly in relative terms during the reform era, it ultimately emerged strengthened and leaner. Some of the world's largest corporations are now Chinese state-controlled firms, including oil majors such as PetroChina and Sinopec, telecoms giants including China Telecom and China Mobile, and the four huge state banks: Industrial and Commercial Bank of China, China Construction Bank, Agricultural Bank of China and Bank of China.

The evolution of Sino-capitalism is therefore not purely the story of state-sector retreat in favour of liberalisation, privatisation and marketisation. Neither is it a story of initial liberalisation followed by a full reassertion of statist forces and a smothering of private entrepreneurship. The best way to understand

Sino-capitalism's evolution is to focus on how the development of private capital accumulation put pressure on the state to reform and adapt. State reforms in turn enabled further private-sector development while strengthening the ability of the state to govern and guide an increasingly sophisticated and internationally integrated capitalist political economy. This created the conditions for the unique institutional duality of Sino-capitalism to materialise.

3.3 The contemporary manifestations of Sino-capitalism

The conception of Sino-capitalism employed here attempts to provide a precise institutionally based definition of China's emergent capitalism. First and foremost, the emergence of Sino-capitalism has been generated by a process of medium- to long-term incremental evolution. Since the initiation of the reform and open door policy after 1979, China used an 'unusual combination of policy experimentation with long-term policy prioritisation' to undertake economic reforms (Heilmann 2010: 109). Full-scale liberalisation was consciously eschewed in favour of innovative experimentation and work-around solutions that attempted to keep state control intact. China therefore managed gradually to 'grow out of the plan' without experiencing the shocks generated by 'big bang' reforms in Eastern Europe and Russia (Naughton 1995). In a similar fashion, China's political economy 'grew out' of an economic system characterised by complete state ownership to incorporate large shares of private ownership and control (Oi and Walder 1999).

Throughout the Chinese reform process, market-oriented and rules-based, but also inter-personal networked, as well as more purely statist strategies have been creatively employed to develop innovative policy and institutional solutions. In fact, most Chinese policy initiatives have been cautious and experimental. Nonetheless, China has witnessed spurts of reform, showing how top-down state coordination and planning has been able to create important policy breakthroughs.

One advantage of this arrangement is that policy priorities only shift gradually in China, generating 'long-termism' as a feature of 'neo-etatist' planning (Heilmann 2010). In this system, the dominant role of the state is tempered by localised experimentation that includes pilot projects, special zones and trial regulations in such areas as attracting foreign investment, upgrading industrial structures and undertaking financial reforms. Such arrangements leave ample room for local ingenuity, learning and ad hoc tinkering. Successful local experiments often are then scaled to provincial and national levels with strong central state guidance and efforts at standardisation.

This combination of localised experimentation with top-down developmental planning and scaling has undoubtedly contributed to China's economic success. It allowed Chinese policy makers to employ a variety of strategies of economic organisation, technological innovation and industrial policy. Institutional hybridisation, layering and *bricolage* are thus characteristic of Sino-capitalism's institutional arrangements. Sino-capitalism is in the end a hybrid, drawing on

Western liberal, Asian developmental, socialist centrally planned, and Chinese traditional and modern elements.

Evidently, Sino-capitalism's institutional arrangements do not conform to ideal-typical notions of how capitalism is structured, especially liberal free-market capitalism. Under Sino-capitalism's unique compensating institutional arrangements, global integration, bottom-up networks of entrepreneurs and top-down state guidance all coexist and balance each other's strengths and weaknesses. The following will briefly describe each of these institutional realms and then focus on the nature and logic of Sino-capitalism's unique duality that juxtaposes top-down state coordination with bottom-up entrepreneurship and local initiative.

Outside-in: global integration

China's entry into the global capitalist system during an era of intense globalisation stands in contrast to what the economies of Japan, South Korea and Taiwan experienced. These late developers benefited from being front-line states in the Cold War, obtaining privileged access to US markets and technology (Stubbs 1999). China, on the other hand, belongs to a more contemporary wave of industrialisation in East Asia, a wave that roughly began in the 1980s as neoliberal globalisation accelerated.

The strengthening forces of globalisation offered both opportunities and challenges for China, and shaped institutional arrangements to a considerable extent. Compared to earlier developers in East Asia, China adopted more free-market principles. These principles include substantial access by foreign capital to China's manufacturing and retail sectors, the intensive use of Hong Kong's internationalised capital markets, and the fact that Chinese banks do not practise shared ownership in industrial firms (Lee *et al.* 2002; Chu and So 2010). In particular, China's opening to foreign direct investment is noteworthy. While overseas Chinese capital played a crucial role at the beginning, later more globalised players used China's coastal areas as critical manufacturing platforms (Hsing 1998).

The strong international pressures emanating from the neoliberal project of globalisation thus prodded the Chinese government towards developing one of the highest 'absorption capacities' for the forces of globalisation among developing economies. In other respects, however, China followed Japan, Taiwan and South Korea in their development strategies quite closely. For instance, China has used programmes of subsidised investment in 'strategic industries', pursued an export-led growth strategy and suppressed domestic consumption, while encouraging high savings and investment rates. Most prominently, China has followed its Asian predecessors by employing exchange rate controls to maintain an under-valued currency that fosters export performance. Despite some liberal impulses, therefore, Sino-capitalism features a substantial role for the state and emphasises the development of domestic industry and technology (Edmonds *et al.* 2008).

In sum, Sino-capitalism has aggressively embraced the global capitalist system and absorbed considerable industrial, technological and financial capacities from abroad. Sino-capitalism has in this manner welcomed networked globalised production, integrating itself with the contemporary industrial revolution that favours multi-firm, multinational networks in production and knowledge creation (Steinfeld 2010). In the process, a variety of liberal economic elements have been absorbed into China, not least of which are relatively liberalised labour markets. One institutional realm of Sino-capitalism is thus a form of market-liberal state capitalism (ten Brink 2011).

Put differently, to be successful China radically had to restructure its domestic economy to more market-like control systems and accept global integration. A host of liberal policy measures were adopted, culminating in China's entry into the World Trade Organization (WTO). Nonetheless, Sino-capitalism's global integration also relies on the proliferation of business networks based on interpersonal relationships that find their origin in Chinese culture.

Bottom-up: entrepreneurially driven network capitalism

Sino-capitalism is in part characterised by a form of network capitalism that drives capital accumulation bottom-up (Hamilton 1996; Nee and Opper 2012). Network capitalism in the Chinese context denotes how business organisations are built on distinct practices derived from strong tie networks of *guanxi* and thus differ qualitatively from Western capitalism (Hamilton 1998; Redding 1990). As noted, *guanxi* are conceived of as the cultivation of long-term personal reciprocal relationships that build enduring trust among members in a network. The concept expresses the centrality of personal networks in Chinese society throughout history (Gold *et al.* 2002). *Guanxi* as they are employed in capitalist business networks can facilitate collaborative ties among entrepreneurs, in the process generating a form of social capital among network members (Wank 1999).

Network capitalism in China further suggests that entrepreneurs, rather than relying on well-defined and enforced legal codes, make heavy use of interpersonal relationships and informal business networks. These business networks often encompass production clusters based on flexibly integrated small and medium-sized firms. China's network capitalism, however, comes in many forms and shapes. It is a variegated force, yet one that effectively integrates Sino-capitalism into global production, marketing and knowledge networks.

Politically, China's network capitalism enabled private entrepreneurs to gain political leverage as capital accumulation increasingly came to rely on them. As in many other late developers, private capital holders in China have become embedded in the Chinese party-state, creating an alliance of political and economic elites (Tsai 2007; Bellin 2000). *Guanxi* or network capitalism therefore has created deep structural changes in China's political economy. China now possesses a Leninist party structure that fosters the needs and interests of private capital accumulation to a considerable extent. At the same time, the Leninist nature of the system remains intact, and the CCP has carefully selected those entrepreneurs it deems trustworthy and reliable to enter the political system.

The institutional element of network or *guanxi* capitalism based on a Chinese form of clientelism/patrimonialism indicates that Sino-capitalism is not a purely state capitalist system. The bottom-up character of network capitalism imbues Sino-capitalism with a highly entrepreneurial private capitalist element. Ultimately, Chinese entrepreneurs have strategically adapted tradition to make network capitalism one of the most dynamic elements of Sino-capitalism. This, in turn, created a unique dualism of bottom-up entrepreneurially networked business activities juxtaposed with state-led development.

Top-down: state-coordinated development

As is common with late developers, the Chinese state has played a leading role in fostering and guiding capitalist accumulation in China (Gerschenkron 1962). Sino-capitalism encompasses a new application of state-led, state-coordinated or state-guided capitalism. Several state (and party)-guided elements are noteworthy.

First, the CCP's *nomenklatura* system is still instrumental in governing the basic Leninist incentives that shape the behaviour of local cadres. Since the 1980s, these incentives have focused primarily on retaining social stability and fostering economic growth (Huang 1996; Edin 2003). Second, the CCP party-state has retained control over the commanding heights of the economy via state firms. SOEs continue to loom large in Sino-capitalism and dominate a wide range of critical industries, giving the Chinese party-state considerable policy levers to guide economic development and upgrading. Finally, waves of bureaucratic reforms have created a state bureaucracy suited to the demands of a developing and globalising market economy, while retaining a wide range of regulatory tools amenable for indicative state planning (Zheng 2004; Yang 2004).

As a result of these three elements of state guidance, the Chinese party-state can utilise cadre incentives, control over the commanding heights of industry and finance, and the substantial regulatory purview of local and central state formations to guide the economy. Nonetheless, the very size of China means that central state guidance must rely on local initiatives and autonomies, a fact that tends to create a jumble of authority relations. Overlapping and incongruous features of the Chinese state apparatus have, in fact, created glaring local government interventions that run counter to central policies (Howell 2006).

In the final analysis, China must be seen as a late developer undertaking a form of state-led development. Like other late developers, China has used already developed economies as its model, often copying institutional arrangements and technologies. Evidently, this has triggered the absorption of both liberal market economy and Asian developmental institutions, creating hybrid institutional arrangements in the process. China thus has benefited from its 'advantage of backwardness', adopting international best practices rapidly throughout the economy (Gerschenkron 1962). Nevertheless, Sino-capitalism is rather unlike any other existent form of capitalism. It relies on an exceptional dichotomy whereby state capitalist features are balanced by vibrant entrepreneurial private capital accumulation and global integration.

Sino-capitalism's unique duality

While state intervention has undoubtedly played a key role in China's capitalist transition, Sino-capitalism might best be conceived of as a competitive state-coordinated economy, where multiple agencies and jurisdictional levels compete to create a relatively competitive market economy with state guidance. Top-down, therefore, China's capitalist development is driven by state guidance and SOEs, but bottom-up it is powered by myriad networked capitalist ventures, often involving global influences. Successful institutional hybridisation has allowed these two dissimilar types of capital accumulation to coexist and become co-dependent under Sino-capitalism (McNally 2008b, 2012).

The combination of vibrant private entrepreneurship and a dominant state bears a certain resemblance to the political economic structure of China's late imperial era (Faure 2006) from the Song to Qing dynasties: a dominant state-managed tributary system oversaw a system of commodity production by kin corporations (Gates 1996: 7). While history seldom repeats itself, China's political economy continues to display its historical roots. The state-dominant mode relies on oligopolistic competition with enormous support from state agencies, especially in terms of financing. Private entrepreneurial modes of capital accumulation, in contrast, depend on the savvy of individual entrepreneurs exposed to market pressures, often with little state aid. These two modes tend to meet at the lower levels of the state-administrative apparatus, where local cadres have played a crucial role in accommodating entrepreneurial capitalist practices (Dickson 2008; Tsai 2007).

The duality of Sino-capitalism is also evident in how China has harnessed the forces of globalisation. Strong incentives for local governments to attract foreign investment have generated policies that created industrial parks tailored to the needs of global capital. These parks are often segregated from the domestic economy at large and provide excellent hard and soft infrastructures. In the process, economic spaces that are divorced from China's domestic economy but highly integrated into global production and knowledge networks have emerged.

Deliberate ambiguity

The unique dualism of Sino-capitalism has had profound implications for state–capital relations in the political realm. The lack of autonomous institutions outside the party-state's control, such as an independent judiciary, and continued deep government involvement in economic affairs, gives local officials wide discretion. This is reinforced by a reliance on informal networks based on *guanxi* ties rather than transparent codes and rules. The discretion of local officials to intervene in society and economy, in turn, generates deliberate ambiguity – ambiguity over how economic rules and laws will be enforced, even in sectors, such as technology development, where the government is highly supportive, and institutional ambiguity tends to be lower (McNally 2011).

Most fundamentally, any private entrepreneur of considerable commercial success is likely to have committed some illegal act during his/her career. The party-state can in this manner always find a business person guilty of a transgression, providing it with an effective deterrent to political challenges from economic elites. Deliberate ambiguity is therefore the lubricant that binds private capital to the state in a particularistic fashion while assuring state control. It is upheld by the state for this purpose, as well as to introduce flexibility in economic governance (Ho 2001).

Therefore, despite a trend towards greater recognition and institutionalisation of private property rights in China, private entrepreneurs do not yet enjoy fully secure property rights. Certainly, formal legal mechanisms have been proliferating in China, but overall the institutional logic of *guanxi* continues to hold sway in mediating relations between China's dynamic private sector and the CCP party-state (Michelson 2007). Most private entrepreneurs continue to employ *guanxi* networks to compensate for institutional uncertainty and to create profit-making opportunities (Wank 1999). According to Western standards, China does not fully enjoy the rule of law.

Sino-capitalism's unique duality clearly encompasses simultaneously deep tensions and symbiotic dynamics. Despite the increasing use of contracts, formal institutional arrangements and modern corporate forms in China's private sector, ambiguity in rules and institutions persists. Institutional ambiguity navigated by *guanxi* relations has actually been crucial in enabling private entrepreneurs to translate wealth into political influence (Dickson 2008). Deliberate ambiguity further aids the state in retaining a measure of control over society and economy by fostering a deliberate lack of transparency about laws and rules (Cartledge 2007). Rather than establishing autonomous institutions outside the party-state's purview, party-state officials continue to possess wide discretion. As Andrew Nathan notes, 'The regime is willing to change in any way that helps it to stay in power, but is unwilling to relax the ban on autonomous political forces' (Nathan 2009: 39).

Consequently, deliberate ambiguity has been essential to the CCP's quest of retaining power in the face of rapid economic change. Sino-capitalism's *guanxi* capitalist element forms a link between the logics of Leninist control and entrepreneurial capital accumulation. While the CCP has fostered rapid capitalaccumulation by private interests, it also has captured part of the newly generated wealth for its own statist purposes, such as the expansion of military power and governmental infrastructure. Sino-capitalism's unique dualism calibrates state–private capital ties by retaining an opaque and uncertain business climate for pri firms while yielding particularistic benefits to individual entrepreneurs loyal to the political elite. The result: a state–capital symbiosis in which large private businesses have gained in political influence and been co-opted into party-state bodies. Deliberate ambiguity has allowed the Chinese party-state to maximise its ability to retain political power while fostering dynamic private capital accumulation.

Capital–labour relations

At the outset of reforms, farmers were tied to the land, while urban workers held the 'iron rice bowl' – a cradle-to-grave system that allocated jobs, housing, welfare benefits and more generally regulated the lives of urban workers in their *danwei* (unit). This socialist legacy has more or less disappeared during the reform period. State-sector reforms in the late 1990s led to mass lay-offs in SOEs. All newly hired workers lost the assurance of life-time tenure that the 'iron rice bowl' brought. Even workers in media organisations like the *People's Daily*, in cultural organisations like symphony orchestras, and in universities have lost tenure unless they were hired before the 1990s. All new hires are contract workers with fixed renewable terms.

China therefore has utilised highly liberal as well as repressive elements to increase labour market flexibility, including a constitutional change in 1982 that abolished the right to strike. By now, the hiring and dismissal of employees has become extremely flexible, even in the state sector. As Mary Gallagher (2005) argues, the timing and sequencing of foreign direct investment in SOE joint ventures weakened labour's role. This enabled state-sector reforms to unfold in the late 1990s that allowed SOEs to shed 28.7 million workers between 1997 and 2000, about 40 per cent of the state sector's workforce in 1997 (State Statistical Bureau 1997: 136; State Statistical Bureau 2001: 116). These reforms also further weakened the political status of SOE workers and allowed SOEs to shed their welfare burdens, including much of the last remnants of the 'iron rice bowl'.

Although there are substantial regional and sectoral differences, capital–labour relations in China are by now characterised by strong management control over basic working conditions. This is not much different from other examples of labour regimes in late-developing East Asian economies. However, China distinguishes itself by the lack of any trade union organisation that could act independently from state and capital (Luethje *et al.* 2011). Although the All-China Federation of Trade Unions (ACFTU) with its around 200 million members is the largest trade union in the world, it is not regarded as an independent union. Its upper echelons are controlled by the CCP party-state and cannot freely advocate the interests of workers. Moreover, the ACFTU is the only trade union organisation that is formally allowed to represent workers in China, yet its leaders are usually paid and beholden to the management of the companies in which they operate. The ACFTU is thus co-opted by management and used as a tool of worker control (Chan 2008).

The regulation of capital–labour relations in China is also concentrated at the level of individual companies. This localisation of industrial relations fragments the representation of worker interests. The result is a considerable differentiation of production regimes, with substantial regional and, particularly, sectoral variation. General characteristics of China's capital–labour regimes, though, include extremely high employment flexibility, a lack of job-security provisions, low base wages with high amounts of variable pay, long working hours, strong wage hierarchies and substantial status discrimination among migrant workers, women and temporary workers (Luethje 2012).

Two characteristics are especially noteworthy. First, basic wages are often only 50 per cent of total wages, indicating that the payment of overtime and bonuses to supplement wages is extremely common. This flexibility in employment relations has created huge opportunities for private entrepreneurship, yet heightened social cleavages and economic inequalities. Although after 2009 productivity and wage growth have become more synchronous, throughout the mid-2000s, productivity growth in China's manufacturing sector has been considerably higher than wage growth. The result has been low hourly compensation costs throughout China's manufacturing industries in international comparison (Bannister and Cook 2011).

Second, a deep urban–rural divide continues to shape industrial labour markets and production regimes in China. Back in the 1980s, TVEs began to take advantage of the large rural surplus labour pool, transforming peasants into peasant workers (*nongmin gong*). In the 1990s, SOEs, like the Shanghai Textile Corporation, began to subcontract much of their manufacturing to TVEs in adjacent semi-urban areas. Rapidly increasing foreign investment, especially by the Chinese diaspora, also took advantage of flexible labour relations in hiring peasant workers migrating to cities along China's eastern seaboard. Migrant workers subsequently emerged as a very large force in China's labour relations, numbering by 2011 around 252 million, a bit less than a fifth of China's overall population (Mozur and Orlik 2013).

Migrant workers remain second-tier workers since their permanent migration to cities is restricted by the *hukou* system. Under this system, rural residents are tied to their villages and cannot enjoy permanent residency in cities and the ensuing urban welfare benefits. Rural migrant labour has in this manner emerged as a highly flexible buffer for China's export industries. In a downturn, these workers can easily be laid off, as they return to their home villages where there is some (though minimal) economic support. China's two-tiered labour market thus diminishes the impact of large lay-offs on urban social stability.

China's formal urban workers often enjoy better conditions than migrant workers. For example, the core workforce of automotive makers in China enjoys extensive welfare benefits and some limited participation in industrial relations (Luethje 2012). Nonetheless, automotive manufacturers make use of arrays of subcontractors that practise a low-wage regime with mostly migrant workers. China's capital–labour relations thus reveal a final duality in Sino-capitalism: there is considerable segmentation and polarisation of the workforce along a line dividing better-paid urban workers in core assembly plants from migrant workers with poor pay at the lower tiers of the supply chain.

This two-tier system of industrial relations has shown increasing strain. The number of labour conflicts, including demonstrations, riots and strikes, has risen in recent years. In the auto industry, a massive strike wave in Guangdong during May/June 2012 at auto parts suppliers showed how the systematic discrimination of migrant workers in supplier pyramids creates deep social tensions. Similarly, in the information technology (IT) industry, the sad suicides of migrant workers at the massive contract manufacturer Foxconn during 2010 brought the company's autocratic regime of flexible mass production to the public eye.

The CCP party-state has taken a variety of initiatives to address the threats to social stability that result from China's profit-driven accumulation regime. These include setting up a universal social security system and state-driven legal efforts to create better labour conditions. The Labour Contract Law introduced in 2008, for instance, aims to limit some of the worst consequences of employment flexibility on workers. Nevertheless, its impact has been limited. Contractual safeguards are often circumvented by management and there is no serious form of negotiated involvement by labour. Indeed, often local governments tacitly support local enterprises to violate national labour laws in their drive to attract investors and accelerate economic development.

Addressing the polarisation that China's two-tier system of industrial relations creates is also of utmost importance in rebalancing China's economy away from low value-added exports and state-driven investment towards domestic consumption-driven demand. The *hukou* system slows the transition of migrant workers into a more stable, productive workforce that forms the core of urbanisation and domestic consumption. Although in recent years the lot of migrant workers has been improving – manufacturing wages grew at close to 20 per cent in 2010 and 2011 – reform of the *hukou* system is needed to stop the exclusion of even longer-term migrants from urban opportunities.

In sum, there are no effective institutions to balance the interests of labour vis-à-vis those of private and state capital in China. Some reforms, as those in Guangdong Province, have attempted to create a controlled autonomy for trade unions at the firm level, while supporting large minimum-wage increases to create a better distribution between profits and wages. These efforts, however, remain state based and state driven. While they could open up new opportunities for reform in China's capital–labour relations, the CCP is unlikely to yield substantial autonomy to the ACFTU or, even more improbable, to allow independent unions to register. Similar to capital–state relations, the CCP's quest is to assure its ability to retain political power while fostering dynamic private capital accumulation and gradual state-driven efforts to redistribute wealth.

3.4 Conclusion

Sino-capitalism stands at the forefront of a major global shift of financial and economic power away from the USA, Japan and Western Europe. Emerging market economies are beginning to generate the bulk of global economic growth, becoming new dynamic centres of global economic activity. However, the prominent role of the state in these political economies and their hybrid forms of capitalism place them largely outside the varieties of capitalism that the rules-based international economic order has so far accommodated in the post-Second World War era (Kahler 2010). In this context, I address three major analytical implications that the study of Sino-capitalism generates: first, with regards to the study of comparative capitalisms in general; second, with regards to the study of emerging market economies, especially the BRICs; and third, with regards to the impact that Sino-capitalism and other emerging political economies could have on the international system.

Theoretically, employing the conceptual lens of comparative capitalisms to explore China's emergent political economy opens up novel dimensions. The key contribution of the comparative capitalisms literature is that it highlights how modern capitalism represents a heterogeneous force. Capitalism is not a monolithic, impermeable block that is ideologically coherent, but rather a complex socio-economic system that adjusts to the various ways of different nations, cultures and times. Sino-capitalism is no exception. As a conceptual perspective, it provides an integrative and encompassing framework for understanding China's political economy. Yet, it also points to how the rigid binary framework of the Varieties of Capitalism approach is inadequately open to be applicable to the case of China.

Specifically, the Varieties of Capitalism approach emphasises how institutional complementarity shapes economic competitiveness. Complementarity, in this context, is perceived of as different institutions aligning to reinforce each other's incentives, thus creating institutional coherence or isomorphism with few contradictory incentives. This emphasis on institutional fit or coherence becomes especially problematic when applied to Sino-capitalism. Sino-capitalism is first and foremost a complex hybrid. It is structured by a duality where institutional complementarity is based on a basic compensatory mechanism that allows bottom-up entrepreneurial forces to temper state-coordinated development. Under Sino-capitalism, institutional arrangements compensate for each other's weak points rather than pushing incentives in the same direction. This can result in a balancing of institutional realms, but also in contradictory incentives and friction.

The importance of compensatory institutional complementarity has been highlighted in several analyses stressing that institutions can balance certain one-sided incentives, such as extreme self-interested behaviour, and make up for each other's deficiencies (Kenworthy 2006; Campbell 2011; Crouch 2005c). Compensatory institutions are therefore perhaps just as important as, if not more so, than coherent reinforcing sets of institutions. We must therefore accept that there are more than two ideal-typical forms of capitalism, and that the nature of capitalism does not necessarily prioritise reinforcing sets of complementary institutions. Counterbalancing, hybrid and even contradictory realms of institutions can coexist with reinforcing institutions. There is no perfect way of organising capitalism.

The logic and nature of Sino-capitalism therefore directly contradicts one of the major findings of the Varieties of Capitalism analytical framework by proposing that hybrid compensatory institutional arrangements can work just as well as coherent reinforcing sets of institutions. In Sino-capitalism, the state-guided realm and the entrepreneurial private (including globalised) realm compensate for each other's weaknesses and meld, especially at the local level. The study of Sino-capitalism points to how we must adopt broader and more open conceptualisations than the precise, yet static models put forward in the Varieties of Capitalism framework to understand emerging forms of capitalism.

The unique duality of Sino-capitalism further elucidates that the degree of stateness of a given political economy must form an important defining characteristic of its variety of capitalism (cf. Schmitter 2012). In fact, the degree and nature of state involvement in the economy is a prominent characteristic of emerging market economies, especially the BRICs. As noted in the introduction by Uwe Becker, the BRICs are united by being large and discontent to a certain extent with the current world order. They also are institutionally connected by efforts to employ state measures to accelerate the process of industrial catch-up. All of the BRICs and most other emerging market economies are practising refurbished state capitalism (McNally n.d., forthcoming).

In recent years, several authors have noted how novel forms of state capitalism have begun to challenge the established Anglo-American order based on free market capitalism (Choate 2009; Bremmer 2010). In their view, the rapid rise of powerful forms of state capitalism in China, Russia, India and Brazil could undermine the established global economic consensus.

Although state capitalist systems have often been identified with Stalinist central economic planning, they are actually associated with a range of political economic frameworks, ranging from communism and socialism to neo-corporatism, mercantilism and fascism. A precise definition of state capitalism highlights the higher degree of stateness in a capitalist system. It denotes a political economy in which the state directs and controls key productive forces, yet follows capitalist principles.

Twenty-first-century refurbished state capitalisms thus have little to do with Stalinism and socialist central planning. They encompass a rather diverse range of capitalist systems in which the state continues to perform key economic functions. Undoubtedly, there are considerable differences in the role of the state, the reach of SOEs, and degrees of openness to foreign investment and capital flows among the BRICs and other emerging market economies. Refurbished state capitalism is a variegated force. Moreover, the BRICs are all continental or at least sub-continental sized and thus contain distinct sub-national economic units.

Nonetheless, there are several institutional and ideational patterns that characterise refurbished state capitalisms (McNally n.d., forthcoming). First, after 1990, no economy that desired rapid industrialisation could afford to shut itself out from globalisation's accelerating trade, knowledge and capital flows. As a result, practitioners of refurbished state capitalisms absorbed many neoliberal precepts, from liberalising labour markets to opening up capital markets. Even in the management of SOEs and other state entities, governments have introduced capitalist practices such as performance incentives for top managers, mergers and acquisitions, advisory services by international fund managers, international accounting standards, stock market listings, and other efforts at restructuring and improving corporate governance.

The leading practitioners of refurbished state capitalism today are deeply enmeshed in the international trading system and practise different degrees of open trading and investment relations. They host multinational corporations and attempt to take advantage of global production and knowledge networks.

Second, refurbished state capitalisms like Sino-capitalism are hybrids. They espouse mixed economies with often substantial domestic private sectors. Yet, they all have more state involvement in the economy than is envisaged by the liberal conception of free-market capitalism. Specifically, there is a considerable distrust of full-out economic liberalisation. This does not mean that markets are unimportant. To the contrary, practitioners of refurbished state capitalism are fully aware that experiments with socialist central planning failed. Markets are needed to set prices, direct supplies of scarce resources and create competitive pressures. However, this is a pragmatic use of markets. As in China, all refurbished forms of state capitalism share a strong belief in the potential benefits of state power, a belief that undergirds their economic management philosophies.

Institutionally, all refurbished forms of state capitalism make wide use of industrial policy tools, foster national champions and employ sovereign wealth funds to manage state investments in a variety of domestic and global financial markets. Sino-capitalism in particular has harnessed China's domestic financial systems to support industrial policy goals and the building of national champions. This is similar institutionally to earlier efforts by Japan and South Korea to build globally competitive conglomerates, such as the Keiretsu and Chaebol. However, these conglomerates were privately owned, while most Chinese national champions are either state owned or of a hybrid ownership structure.

Sino-capitalism in this sense exemplifies a new breed of refurbished state capitalisms in the early 21st century. Indeed, China is widely seen as the world's leading practitioner of state capitalism. As in most other emerging political economies, Chinese policy makers view markets with more scepticism than in the advanced industrial economies of North America, Europe and Japan. Sino-capitalism, ultimately, differs in its ideas, interests and institutions from the ideal-typical neoliberal conception of capitalism as it is based on a hybrid system that combines state-led development top-down with entrepreneurial private capital accumulation bottom-up.

In terms of Sino-capitalism's impact on the global political economic order, its influence has so far been limited. Historically, late developers have had very little sway over how the international political economy functioned and thus had to adjust to its rules, institutions and power relations. The USA's influence over the international political economy began long after its economy became the largest globally in around 1870. For instance, only after 1913 did the US dollar start being an internationally accepted currency (Eichengreen 2011). Nonetheless, China's sheer size and rapid development mean that Sino-capitalism is likely to have a greater and earlier impact on the global political economy. What will these impacts be? Will China try to undermine the global political economic order based on neoliberal precepts? Or will China gradually adjust and become a 'responsible stakeholder'? Indeed, can the neoliberal order adjust to Sino-capitalism's emergence and incorporate other refurbished forms of state capitalism in Brazil, Russia and India?

The conceptual tool of Sino-capitalism shows the need to move beyond dichotomous debates on the possible future influences of the BRICs, and

China in particular. Sino-capitalism's rise is unlikely to be one-dimensional, but rather riddled with complexities and contradictions. The distinct duality of state-guided capitalist accumulation coexisting with bottom-up entrepreneurial forces and considerable global influences means that Sino-capitalism posits a statist challenge to the neoliberal order while at the same time developing into a key component of it (Steinfeld 2010). To be successful, China had to restructure its domestic economy radically to more market-like control systems. At the same time, though, policy makers consistently endeavoured to keep state control over key economic aspects intact.

The study of Sino-capitalism hence encourages us to take more expansive and open perspectives concerning the likely consequences of the rise of China and other emerging market economies on the global order. Sino-capitalism, ultimately, represents a new emergent system of global capitalism centred on China that is producing a dynamic mix of mutual dependence, symbiosis, competition and friction with the still dominant neoliberal free market model of capitalism. As Sino-capitalism gains in global importance, its precepts are certain increasingly to challenge the neoliberal model, altering the global capitalist status quo in its wake. Already the international policy consensus has started to move away from the pure neoliberal Anglo-American stance of the 1990s Washington Consensus to embrace more state-managed solutions (Kahler 2010).

To illustrate, the International Monetary Fund (IMF) took a substantial ideological shift in December 2012 by accepting the use of direct capital controls to calm volatile cross-border money flows. This represents a sharp change from the IMF's enthusiasm for liberalising capital accounts during the 1990s under the precepts of the Washington Consensus (Beattie 2012). The IMF's shift has vindicated measures employed in recent years by emerging market economies, including Brazil, Thailand, South Korea and China. Nonetheless, the Brazilian representative at the IMF noted that the fund was still too cautious and regarded capital controls as a last resort rather than a standard policy choice. Clearly, pressure on the global policy consensus to legitimise more state-managed solutions will continue from the BRICs and other emerging market economies.

The BRICs thus are testing the existing global institutional architecture much more directly than before the 2008 financial crisis. Major economic powers, both new and old, must acknowledge that, while they are growing ever-more closely intertwined economically, they champion different forms of capitalism. However, this does not imply an all-out struggle for global supremacy of one form of capitalism over another. The more likely outcome is a gradual shift in the global policy consensus as more state-coordinated forms of capitalism like Sino-capitalism gain in prominence (McNally 2012). The next twenty years are likely to see a new and messier reality of global capitalist heterogeneity and resulting policy diversity.

4 Continuity and change in Indian capitalism

Surajit Mazumdar

The year 1991 certainly marks a discontinuity in the history of Indian capitalism – probably the most significant one since the country's independence from colonial rule in 1947. There was no fundamental political change comparable to that earlier event, but in 1991 Indian economic policy made a decisive break from the earlier strategy of 'planned economic development', a euphemism for a state-led process of capitalist industrialisation and development. Instead of its relative autonomy maintained by the earlier strategy, Indian capitalism after 1991 has been pushed towards a greater degree of integration into the global economy. The attempts at state direction of the course of the economy have been abandoned in favour of relying on spontaneous market forces. This has meant a shift in emphasis from the public sector to private capital as the driver of growth and a dismantling of the whole regime of controls that had been erected to partition economic activity between the public and private sectors and to bring the latter within the framework of planning.

India's shift towards economic liberalisation has of course reflected a global trend. That it has been a significant enough development to be the basis for demarcating a very distinctive phase of the post-independence history of Indian capitalism would not be disputed by anybody. The only debate relates to the dating of the beginning of this phase, given that the more dramatic 'economic reforms' after 1991 were preceded by a limited liberalisation in the 1980s. The transition to a distinctly new phase in the life history of a particular capitalism does not, however, mean that it undergoes a complete change in its type. This holds true for Indian capitalism's transition to its liberal phase too. If attention is focused merely on the purely formal aspects of state economic policy and its rationalising ideology, the Indian transformation would indeed appear to be dramatic – from a highly statist or coordinated market economy to a liberal one. However, if one goes beyond the surface, a significant element of continuity can also be discovered between the past and the present of Indian capitalism. No understanding of the origins, the nature and the consequences of Indian liberalisation can be complete without acknowledgement of these continuities. When these are taken into account, Indian capitalism does not appear to be on a trajectory in which it is converging towards a universal model of liberal capitalism in the age of globalisation. At the same time, its experience of standstill and movement also poses challenges in the path of developing a general analytical framework for understanding capitalist diversity.

4.1 The prehistory of Indian liberalisation: the making and development of an agriculture constrained Third World capitalism

Capitalism in India emerged almost by default in the second half of the 19th century when India was under colonial rule and Britain's most important colonial asset. This peculiar origin of Indian capitalism had two significant long-term implications. On the one hand, it created a strong tendency for this capitalism to be caught on the wrong side of the international division of labour. Reinforcing this was the second implication, that of an incomplete emergence of capitalism – unaccompanied by any significant agrarian transformation. Throughout its history, the limited development of agriculture itself acted as a barrier to capitalist industrialisation and development that would comprehensively move the major part of the economy into non-agricultural activities.

Colonialism and the incomplete emergence of capitalism

In the second half of the 19th century, India's designated role in the British imperial order required it to be kept forcibly open to serve as the most important market for industrialised Britain's export-oriented industry. At the same time, India was also a large exporter of a variety of primary commodities, mainly produced by its agrarian sector, the destinations of which were increasingly the industrialising economies of North America and Europe. India's large trade surplus was siphoned off through the colonial tribute transfer mechanism and played an important role in enabling Britain to meet its international payment obligations by offsetting its deficit.

A small capitalist industrial sector emerged in such a background, stimulated by the railway development that the colonial rulers promoted for their own reasons. The dominant impact of the railways on Indian manufacturing, however, was the carrying forward of the process of de-industrialisation, the destruction of India's traditional artisanal manufacturing industry, which had begun in the early part of the 19th century as British-manufactured goods began penetrating the Indian market (Ray 1994). In other words, capitalist industry was established in India when it was actually rapidly receding from its position as one of the great manufacturing regions of the world of the pre-Industrial Revolution era.[1]

The capitalist class emerged mainly through segments of the mercantile community using their trading activities as the springboard for entry into industry (Ray 1994). In the period before the First World War, the emerging modern industrial sector was dominated by European merchants. The balance started shifting towards the indigenous Indian capitalists after the War as the profitable opportunities for capitalist enterprise moved away from the sphere of international trade and towards the domestic market. This growth of native capitalists and the rising tide of nationalism served mutually to reinforce each other.

The capitalist industrial sector in the colonial period remained a small enclave of the economy. At India's independence, it was still dominated by the relatively technologically unsophisticated light manufacturing industries, accounting for only 8 per cent of the economy's aggregate output and less than 2 per cent of employment. Even the surviving traditional manufacturing sector was larger in size. Agriculture continued to be the main sector of the economy, accounting for over half of output and three-quarters of employment. While it had not remained unchanged through the history of colonialism, Indian agriculture was still a primarily peasant agriculture in which no radical transformation had happened in the way production was organised or the techniques that were used (Patnaik 1999). Agricultural productivity was low and, while agriculture supported an extremely wealthy class of landowners, much of the agrarian population, which included not just a differentiated peasantry but also a class of agricultural wage workers, remained in extreme poverty.

Capitalism's original emergence in India was thus neither a product of any widespread reorganisation of Indian society, nor did it result in one. The capitalist sector in the colonial period had served as the cradle for the emergence of new social classes and of conflicts amongst them.[2] The numerical proportions of these classes had, however, remained limited and each in their own way was underdeveloped. Much of the working class continued to have strong links with the countryside. The fractured development of the industrial capitalist class reinforced its underdeveloped nature so that its native component still strongly reflected its mercantile roots. It was not their mastery over production or technological innovativeness but instead accumulations through trade and commerce and their connections and skills in that sphere that had formed the basis for the emergence of India's industrial capitalist class (Ray 1994). This combined with the colonial background to shape an attitude towards technology of long-term significance. Technology was not something to be developed but simply something to be acquired in the market and from foreign sources. India's industrial capitalist class never fully shed this attitude acquired as a result of its specific origin.

The making of the corporate structure

Capitalist enterprise in India also acquired certain durable institutional characteristics in the colonial period. An early emergence of a *corporate* sector was one of these, enabled by the enactment of a general incorporation law in the middle of the 19th century soon after a similar legislation in Britain. Both Indian and European enterprises made extensive use of joint-stock companies for undertaking industrial ventures in the colonial period with share capital issues as the major means for financing fixed investment (Rungta 1970;

Lokanathan 1935). Capital was, however, typically raised from a relatively small circle of people and the class of shareholders in India remained relatively small. Independent of this, however, proprietary control over companies was ensured by the extensive use of the *managing agency* system.[3] While instances of managing agency firms managing a single company were quite common, some European-controlled firms pioneered the system of centralising control of a number of companies in a single managing agency firm – the *managing agency house* (Ray 1985). Indian-controlled businesses also subsequently assumed a multi-company form and thus emerged the business group as the typical unit of decision making in the Indian corporate sector.

However, the managing agency system was only an instrument through which promoters of 'public' companies could gain virtually impregnable control over them individually and thereby centralise control over many. It did not reflect the emergence of any kind of 'managerial capitalism'. Indian business groups instead were typically family-controlled firms. While they at first imitated the European houses, they did not necessarily confine themselves to using a single managing agency firm for controlling a number of companies. After-independence, they developed the mechanism of inter-corporate investments to play the same role and replace the managing agency system, which was eventually abolished by law (Hazari 1966; Sengupta 1983). The legacy of the corporate structure created under colonial conditions is visible to this day.

Independence and the new context: opportunities and constraints

India's independence did not change the basic economic structure that had taken shape under colonialism but did transfer power to the locally dominant classes. The national movement had, however, also politicised to a degree other social classes too. One of its consequences was the coming into being after independence of a formal political structure of representative democracy based on universal adult suffrage. This also influenced the way in which the social conflicts inherent in the economic and social structure expressed themselves, developed over time, and were responded to.

Independence on the one hand set the stage for the active and instrumental use of the state to promote capitalist industrialisation. The presence of powerful landed interests, however, severely constrained the ability of the state to bring about the agrarian reform necessary to remove what was called the 'built-in depressor' in India's agrarian structure (Thorner 1956). Even though it was constructed around a simplified picture of the division of agrarian society into three main classes – *maliks* (landlords), *kisans* (peasants) and *mazdoors* (agricultural labourers) – the concept of the depressor served to highlight three important inter-related features of the agrarian structure. First, that a parasitic class of landed interests who were a small minority of the agrarian population monopolised a major part of land ownership and extracted a significant part of the produce from tenant farmers in the form of rent and usurious interest. Second, that such a structure was inimical to investments in agricultural productivity and gave rise to a prevalence of small-scale agriculture. Third, that it gave rise to a highly concentrated distribution of agricultural income, meaning that the vast majority of the rural population had barely subsistence levels of income.[4]

For India's industrialisation, the issue of agrarian reform had become more important by the time of independence. India's long-standing export surplus built on its agricultural exports had disappeared by then. Land, once the most important source, no longer contributed anything significant to government revenues. The population was larger and increasing and this was happening in the wake of the trend of declining per capita food production that characterised the last half century of British rule (Blyn 1966). Moreover, there was very little surplus land left to which cultivation could be extended. To add to all of this were the adverse effects of the partition that accompanied India's independence.[5] In such circumstances, let alone the limited ability of agriculture to be a foreign exchange earner as it was earlier, food imports and imports of producer goods for industry (including agricultural raw materials) became potential competitors for scarce foreign exchange. Similarly, food and cash crop production had also become potential competitors for scarce land. Unlike earlier when agriculture contributed majorly to state revenue, it became a potential claimant on the scarce resources of the state.

India after independence also confronted challenges from its international context, as did every Third World country attempting late industrialisation. Independence did offer India an opportunity to reorder its international economic relations in the direction of promoting its industrialisation. The country could therefore take advantage of the new geo-political realities that emerged in the second half of the 20th century and made conditions more conducive for the diffusion of industrialisation to the Third World. Yet industrialisation was not possible by completely disengaging from the international structure of capitalism, in which India, like many others at first, necessarily occupied a subordinate position.

While India was a Third World capitalism, it would not be appropriate to call it a *dependent* capitalism if that expression implies a capitalism only capable of a responsive expansion to the expansion through 'self-impulsion' of the advanced economies (dos Santos 1978). However, the autonomy of its dynamic and development were *relative*. One important reason for this had to do with technology, one sphere where the expression 'dependence' had a meaningful application. In technological terms, in fact, Indian factory industry by independence had fallen further behind than it had been at the start of its development 90 years earlier. Like all late industrialisations, a combination of partial dependence on imports of capital goods and substantive dependence on transfer of know-how in general was therefore a necessity for India's industrialisation.

Indian dirigisme and the agrarian constraint

The strategy of import substitution industrialisation and 'planned' economic development adopted after independence in India in principle meant the state taking on the role of guiding and directing economic activity. Restrictions on inflows of products, capital and technology were one part of the strategy, though a window was always kept open for all of these. Indian dirigisme also partitioned non-agricultural economic activity between the private and public sectors. The public sector was supposed to dominate key industries and sectors such that it could occupy the 'commanding heights' of the economy. The private sector was allowed to dominate manufacturing activity with public-sector financial institutions being, however, the main source of industrial financing. State direction of private investment in accordance with planned priorities was also part of the scheme. An elaborate system of controls on private capital was created for this purpose, the centrepiece of which was a system of industrial licensing.

Notwithstanding the rhetoric of the 'socialistic pattern of society', the post-independence strategy was one of accelerating capitalist industrialisation. Indian big business actually offered no significant resistance as the strategy was put into practice in the 1950s. In fact, they had played an active part in the process of developing the basic blueprint of that strategy and the consensus around it in the closing years of British rule (Ray 1985). The interaction between businessmen and the future political leadership of the country that had taken place in that process carried forward the process of development of networks of relations between the worlds of business and politics. This carried within itself the potential for working at cross purposes to and even undermining the very planning process to which it contributed in giving birth. That is precisely what did eventually happen.

Private big business was not quite crushed under the heavy arm of the state under what came to be pejoratively called the 'license-permit raj'. Instead, the Indian state failed to impose any meaningful discipline on private capital, distinguishing the Indian case from others like Korea (Chibber 2004). Big business firms, with the assistance of the discretionary decision makers in the state apparatus, routinely abused, manipulated and circumvented the system of controls to their advantage. Clientelism, cronyism and corruption thus came extensively to characterise the actual working of the control regime. It is widely acknowledged that this became more pronounced in the second half of the control regime, after circa 1970 (Goyal 1979; Kochanek 1987; Virmani 2004). To add to this were severe fiscal difficulties, partly a result of private capital successfully thwarting any significant revenue mobilisation effort, and recurrent crises. After the mid-1960s, these promoted short-termism in economic policy and a slippage of public investment growth.

Clientelism and cronyism did not mean, however, that a fixed and exclusive set of favoured business firms remained the beneficiaries of state patronage throughout or that there were no other imperatives to which the state responded. In fact, the overarching setting of an interventionist economic policy regime also provided a context for significant autonomous state action. For instance, the period of the most intense economic difficulties, from the mid-1960s to the late 1970s, also saw the high tide of nationalisation. Major sectors like banking, general insurance, mining and oil came within its ambit. In addition, there was a spate of permanent government takeovers of many stricken private-sector companies.

Overall, however, the ultimate consequence of Indian dirigisme remained very far from giving rise to a highly coordinated or organised capitalism. It was far less statist than appears at first sight. The public-sector share did increase over time but only to about a quarter of national output by 1991, two fifths of which was accounted for by general government. However, this contrasted with the relatively steady share of the formal private sector, which remained at around 15 per cent. Tax mobilisation and public expenditure levels also remained extremely low, at less than a fifth and 30 per cent of gross domestic product (GDP), respectively.[6]

Agriculture, which was overwhelmingly private, was one of the key sources of the difficulties that capitalist industrialisation faced in India. Like Indian planning, the agrarian reform programme also fell well short of its stated objectives – the redistribution of land ownership and provision of security of tenures. However, there were other ways in which the state did get involved in the agrarian economy and there were also incremental changes in the agrarian structure over time. The key areas of the state's intervention in agriculture were public investment in agriculture and rural development in general; promotion of technological change involving a shift to high-yielding varieties of seeds and increased use of inputs and some element of mechanisation, including through subsidisation of inputs and the facilitating of increased flow of subsidised credit to the rural sector; promotion of credit and marketing co-operatives and intervention in trade in agricultural products, and particularly food, encompassing imports, government purchases as part of a price-support mechanism, a limited public-distribution system and maintenance of stocks. The agrarian structure changed as a result of the cumulative effects of the impetus provided by this state intervention, the spontaneous influences arising from within the agrarian structure and its interaction with the development of the non-agricultural sector, agrarian movements and the operation of demographic factors.

The changes that took place in agriculture contributed to a modest easing but by no means elimination of the agrarian constraint on industrialisation. The slow agricultural growth with declining per capita production was replaced by a fluctuating growth of a slightly higher order barely above population growth and marked by a greater degree of regional unevenness (Rao 1994; Patnaik 1994). Over time, the dependence on food imports did come down, but only with per capita food consumption levels remaining relatively flat.

Apart from being unable to provide resources for financing capital formation in industry, a slow-growing agriculture constrained industrial growth and generated instability in many other ways (Nayyar 1994). It gave rise to supply and demand constraints, which were reinforced by the resultant inflationary barrier to industrial growth supporting public investment. Limited industrial growth inhibited the growth of non-agricultural employment and an increasing pressure on land constrained slow-growing agriculture and the low-productivity non-agricultural informal sector as the population expanded. For a large part of the workforce, whether self-employed or in wage employment, this made any escape from a low-income situation next to impossible. This in turn made for a tendency towards the Lewisian unlimited supply of labour situation becoming a permanent feature of Indian capitalism. This labour-market situation also inhibited the growth of wages in the formal private sector, where some kind of collective bargaining and protection through labour regulation were present.

The record of Indian dirigisme

Overall, the achievements of India's import substitution industrialisation between independence and 1991 were limited by its inherent historical constraints. The pace of industrial growth was greater than in the colonial era (Sivasubramonian 2000) and the industrial base became wider in terms of industrial diversification. Per capita levels of industrial production, however, remained low as did the industrial sector's share in aggregate output.[7] The major part of the workforce remained in agriculture and formal employment remained confined to barely 10 per cent of the workforce. India ceased to be a mainly primary product exporter but did not become a significant exporter of manufactured products and these exports were also dominated by low-tech, labour-intensive products.

Formal employment expanded more in the public than in the private sector, and formed the core basis for an expansion of the middle class. State intervention in agriculture also benefited a stratum within the agricultural population, including the upper segments of the peasantry. These two processes along with some expansion of informal sector small businesses founded on a low-wage context enabled some degree of market widening.

Iniquitous development under Indian dirigisme did give rise to significant social and political conflict. Authoritarian tendencies also emerged in response but parliamentary democracy survived and checked these tendencies.[8] The political structure, however, served more as a pressure valve than as an effective antidote to the iniquities inherent in the economic and social structure.

Import substitution industrialisation did enable a significant, albeit also limited, development of Indian big business (Mazumdar 2008a). Indian big business firms grew in the sheltered environment provided by protectionism. They built businesses that were mainly 'national', producing, selling in and raising finances from the domestic economy. Their scales of operation were considerably smaller than international scales and technological gaps still existed. The most important weakness, though, was their continued dependence on foreign technologies (Alam 1985; Tyabji 2000). Yet the private large business sector expanded in tandem with the rest of the economy, whose chief beneficiaries were new and old Indian business groups. Sectors originally dominated by foreign multinational firms were also increasingly penetrated by Indian firms (Encarnation 1989). These Indian groups also reflected most the significant changes in the industrial spread of corporate capital that accompanied industrial diversification. They moved away from being confined to a few traditional industries such as textiles into others such as steel and steel products, chemicals, cement, automobiles and automobile products, industrial and other machinery, and consumer electronics. This expansion in newer and more 'modern' industries increased the level of technological sophistication with which Indian big business dealt. They learned to find, absorb, adapt and use technologies and technological advances across the industrial spectrum even if they themselves did not develop them.

Industrialisation did not produce, thus, in India the kind of overall transformative impact that it had in many other Third World countries. By 1991, India was also not amongst the likes of South Korea, which had built internationally competitive firms and industrial structures. Despite these, the shift to liberalisation happened. While it was initially triggered by a foreign exchange crisis, Indian big business support to it imparted durability to the shift. The basis for this support lay in the fact that both the strengths Indian big business had acquired through import substitution industrialisation and its surviving weakness on the technological front worked in the same direction (Mazumdar 2008a). Opening up was necessary for Indian business to get the kind of access to technology that its new stage of development required. Thus, the state–business consensus on liberalisation has been as great as if not more so than, it was on dirigisme.

4.2 From dirigisme to liberalisation: a regime change?

India entered into the process of increased integration with the global economy with its background of failed institutional reform in the agrarian sector and a limited level of industrialisation. The swing towards liberalisation to begin with was thrust down from above – a foreign exchange crisis necessitating recourse to an International Monetary Fund (IMF) loan with its associated conditionalities. Neither changes in the balance between political formations or the emergence of new ones nor a new social compromise evolving through the democratic processes of India's polity were the source of the shift. However, once set in motion, the process proved immune to political ups and downs and the numerous changes in governments that India has witnessed in the last two decades.[9]

The initial set of 'economic reforms' with which the new era of Indian capitalism announced its arrival certainly had a dramatic character. Industrial licensing was virtually abolished as were various restrictions on expansion of large private business firms that were integral elements of India's anti-trust legislation, the Monopolies and Restrictive Trade Practices (MRTP) Act. The list of sectors reserved for the public sector was also pruned and many were opened up for private-sector involvement. Imports were liberalised through a significant reduction in import controls and tariffs. Foreign direct investment and foreign technology agreements up to a limit and in a number of industries were brought under the ambit of automatic approval. Foreign institutional investors were also permitted to invest in the Indian stock market. The administered exchange rate was done away with and the rupee was put on the road to convertibility. Banking sector reforms were initiated, which undermined the directed credit programme and changed the regulatory framework in a way designed to shift the orientation of the public-sector-dominated system from a social to a commercial one. India's industrial development banks were also put on track virtually to disappear over the next few years. The commitment to fiscal conservatism – maintaining low tax rates and low deficits – was also declared in letter and in form.

Despite this flush of measures in the early stages of the process, and despite there being no ambiguity regarding its direction, it still remains true that liberalisation in India has been a comparatively slow and gradual process. Instead of a one-shot adoption of free trade, protection levels were brought down in stages and still are higher than in many other parts of the world. Capital controls in general, and specifically the policy towards foreign investment, have also been liberalised progressively rather than in one go. Caps on foreign investment, some still existing and others gradually raised, have also been used in many sectors. In addition, some foreign exchange earning obligations were imposed in the earlier stages of liberalisation. The retreat from state monopoly in many sectors has also not taken the form of a swift wholesale privatisation. Instead, it has been undertaken in a phased and somewhat controlled manner. While creation of new public enterprises has virtually completely ceased and some old ones have been privatised, a significant public sector still survives in India today in many key sectors like oil and banking.

Agriculture, the labour market and inequality

Completing the institutional reforms in agriculture was of course never part of the liberalisation programme. Instead, fiscal compression and other measures associated with liberal economic policies contributed to the emergence of the deep-rooted agrarian crisis in India since the 1990s (Patnaik 2003, 2007; Reddy and Mishra 2008). Over 200,000 suicides by farmers since then is one symptom. More generally, the agrarian crisis had adverse consequences for those still dependent on the sector for its livelihood, whose proportion still is around 53 per cent of the total workforce. The only exit from the sector that has happened has been distress driven into the informal sector, even as a backward agriculture has contributed to holding down the reservation wage in non-agricultural activities.

Formal employment has virtually stagnated since liberalisation (Table 4.1). One major reason has been the shrinking of employment in the public sector as economic policy has moved towards a greater emphasis on the private sector playing the leading role. The public sector share in aggregate GDP as well as that of the organised (formal) sector has declined from its levels in the early 1990s – from a quarter to a fifth and from 64 to 45 per cent, respectively. Faster growth of the private formal sector has not, on the other hand, generated

Table 4.1 Reported organised (formal) sector employment in India (million persons)

Sector	1991	1997	2004	2008	2010
Total organised	26.74	28.25	26.44	27.51	28.65
Public sector	19.06	19.56	18.20	17.67	17.86
Private sector	7.68	8.69	8.25	9.84	10.79

Note: Employment in the private sector relates to non-agriculture establishments employing 10 or more persons. Employment in the public sector relates to all establishments irrespective of size.
Sources: (GOI 2010; 2012)

sufficient additional employment to compensate for the decline in public-sector employment. Moreover, this additional employment even in the formal sector has been entirely of an 'informal' kind – irregular and casual, and lacking the work benefits typically associated with formal employment (Government of India 2007). While India's workforce still has a large proportion of self-employed workers (many in agriculture), the decline here is being increasingly absorbed by the casual workforce (Table 4.2).

The distinctive labour market conditions associated with India's agriculture-constrained capitalism have therefore been reinforced by liberalisation. India's workforce is not becoming less but more concentrated in the informal sector. Not only are the vast majority of those workers employed in agriculture, but also more than 70 per cent of workers in industry and services are employed in the informal components of these sectors. In addition, the always fragile and limited leverage that the small segment of organised labour had enjoyed under dirigisme has been severely eroded. Working in tandem with the presence of large quantities of surplus labour, the pressures emanating from globalisation and the attitudinal changes that liberalisation has brought to the working of public agencies and the judiciary has made the context more hostile even for those formally employed (Bhattacharya 2007; Papola and Sharma 2004; RoyChowdhury 2005). A movement towards increasingly flexible labour markets, erosion of collective bargaining and the greater role of capital in setting the terms of work has resulted, even though the legal framework of labour regulation has remained relatively unchanged.

Table 4.2 Distribution of India's workforce by employment status (% shares)

Employment status	2004–05	2009–10
Self-employed	56.5	51.0
Regular workers	15.2	15.6
Casual workers	28.3	33.5
Total	100	100

Source: (NSSO 2006, 2011)

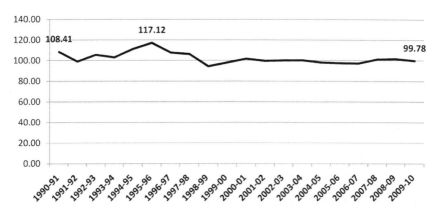

Figure 4.1 Index of real wage per worker in India's organised industrial sector, 2002–03 = 100

Source: (CSO 2012; GOI 2010, 2012)

One implication of this has been the holding down of wage levels even in the formal sector (Figure 4.1). This has accompanied significant increases in productivity so that the share of wages in industrial value added has been brought down greatly. In the 1980s, this share had been reduced from over 30 per cent to around 20 per cent. Now it has been reduced to a mere 10 per cent.

In India's circumstances, these organised sector wage trends can be considered indicative of what has happened to a large category of incomes. Indeed, the grim agrarian situation has underlain the extremely low levels of income of a large part of the Indian population and their exclusion from the growth process under liberalisation (Sengupta *et al.* 2008; Vakulabharanam 2010). Even food consumption levels have fallen for large segments of the population from the already low levels of the pre-liberalisation days. Indicating this is the fact that per capita expenditure on the items making up the bulk of food consumption in India has generally been lower than at the beginning of the 1990s (Figure 4.2).

The one segment of employees who have escaped income depression and stagnation associated with globalisation have been the growing but relatively small number of white-collar workers in the formal private sector, including those who have become part of a geographically mobile global workforce. Salaries in this segment have increased considerably and this in turn has exerted upward pressure on government salaries. These have enriched a segment of India's middle class, many of whom have also consequently become vocal supporters of globalisation and liberalisation. However, the widening of the middle class that had been happening earlier has ceased. Indeed, the relatively small increase in such high-salaried employees is indicated by the fact that the distribution of income within the private formal sector has shifted decisively in favour of surplus incomes.

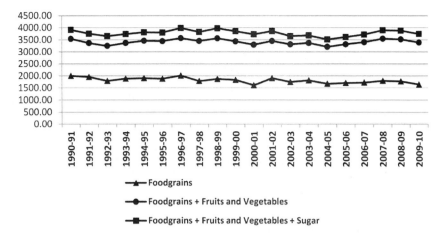

Figure 4.2 Per capita expenditure on major food items in India at 2004/05 prices, 1990/91 to 2009/10 (Rupees)
Source: (CSO 2011a, 2011b)

As Table 4.3 shows, the share of the private organised sector within the Indian economy's aggregate output has increased very sharply since liberalisation. This has reflected the exceptionally rapid growth that the private corporate sector has experienced. Corporate growth has been significantly faster than that of the rest of the economy – and more than twice in the period of the highest growth between 2003–04 and 2007–08. The rise in the share of the private

Table 4.3 Shares of the private organised sector output and its components in India's aggregate net domestic product (NDP) (%)

Component	1999–2000 base year series					
	1990–91	1996–97	2002–03	2003–04	2004–05	2007–08
Compensation of employees	7.72	6.01	6.61	6.69	6.46	6.82
Operating surplus	6.35	11.44	11.96	12.56	14.08	16.62
Total private organised NDP	14.07	17.45	18.56	19.26	20.54	23.44
	2004–05 base year series					
	2004–05	2005–06	2006–07	2007–08	2008–09	2009–10
Compensation of employees	6.35	6.48	5.93	5.80	5.70	5.55
Operating surplus	13.21	15.55	17.24	17.85	17.27	16.78
Total private organised NDP	19.55	22.04	23.16	23.65	22.97	22.32

Source: (CSO 2008a, 2008b, 2009, 2011b)

corporate sector in aggregate income, however, has not been reflected by the part of it going towards compensation of employees. In other words, surplus incomes have cornered the entire increase.

In recent times, India has drawn attention for being one of the largest economies in the world and amongst the fastest growing. Yet its per capita income is still below the levels crossed in Western Europe and North America over a century ago, and a good distance behind even China, the other exceptionally large developing economy. Some 80 per cent of the Indian population lives on less than US$2 a day. By any indicator, therefore, India is still economically an extremely poor country, which makes the trend of income stagnation and depression over large segments of its population a particularly striking phenomenon.

Market constraint and industrialisation

Liberalisation in India has not only aggravated income inequalities but also sharply reinforced the narrowness of the domestic market. A high degree of concentration of income increases at the upper end of the distribution spectrum has meant that the aggregate consumption demand pattern has been shifting in favour of services and the share of consumption of manufactured commodities in it has been consistently declining. At the same time, its status as a low-wage economy has not enabled Indian manufacturing to find too many niches in the internationalised system of production characteristic of the globalisation era in which it is competitive. India's manufactured exports have grown and in the current century also have experienced some change in composition. However, the levels of these exports have not been very high and imports of manufactures have tended to grow even faster. India's greatest export success since liberalisation, in fact, has been in services and that, too, in a very specific category of information technology (IT) and IT-enabled services.[10] A significant surplus in its invisible trade (made up of a surplus in services trade and large inflows of remittances) has also kept India's current account deficit within manageable limits in the face of a ballooning trade deficit. India's emerging position in the international division of labour therefore appears to be quite different from many of its Third World counterparts.

In the absence of significant domestic and external market growth, industrial growth in India has become excessively dependent on demand generated by investment, in particular private corporate investment. Given that this investment has a strong tendency to be also concentrated in manufacturing, instability in both investment and industrial growth has resulted (Mazumdar 2008b). This has completely stalled India's industrialisation process – while industrial production has been increasing, the share of industry and manufacturing in aggregate GDP stopped growing entirely in the mid-1990s (Mazumdar 2010). At that time, this share was under 30 per cent, well short of peak levels attained not only in the advanced industrialised countries but even in the late-industrialising East Asian economies or countries in Latin America.

Growth sans *industrialisation and Indian big business*

With liberalisation, the Indian economy did not experience severe contraction of the kind that Latin America and Africa had in the 'lost decade' of the 1980s. After initially maintaining the levels attained in the 1980s, when India started growing faster than the world economy, a further growth acceleration was achieved from 2003/04 onwards. Post-liberalisation growth in India has been even more services-dominated than earlier (Mazumdar 2010), however. Services have not faced similar demand constraints as industry, with income distribution trends, India's competitiveness in some fast-growing tradable services and the non-tradable nature of many others all contributing to this. The corporate sector's unprecedented growth under liberalisation has also been heavily reliant on business firms finding profitable opportunities in the fast-growing services and of late also in construction. In the process, these have decisively displaced manufacturing as the principal spheres of private corporate activity (Mazumdar 2008a).

Indian business groups have clearly been the principal beneficiaries of rapid corporate growth. A major part of capital imports into India has been through portfolio investment and even a significant component of direct investment has had a similar 'financial' nature (Chalapati Rao and Dhar 2011). Directly and indirectly, the financing of Indian firms has benefited from such inflows. However, while the presence of foreign multinational firms has also certainly become more pronounced since liberalisation, and they dominate a few sectors, no foreign takeover of the Indian corporate sector has happened. Multinational interest in India has been mainly of the market-seeking variety and remained limited in terms of its spread. At the same time, Indian firms have taken important steps in the direction of greater internationalisation, mainly through acquisitions abroad (Nayyar 2008; Athukorala 2009).

Indian big business thus has been able to find ample space for its own growth and development in the process of India's integration into the global economy. Partly this reflects the strengths it had acquired in the earlier stage of industrialisation, but not the elimination of the old weakness in the technological sphere. Indeed, the evidence suggests that, barring the pharmaceutical industry, there is no indication of any significant increase in the innovative capacity of the Indian private sector (Mani 2009). Even in pharmaceuticals, Indian firms lack drug development capabilities (Chaudhuri 2008; Jha 2007). The pharmaceutical sector has also seen of late some prominent Indian firms getting taken over by international drug majors. In the other highly internationalised sector, software, innovative activity in India has been mainly by foreign research and development (R&D) units (Mani 2009), and Indian firms have found their niche in a relatively subordinate position to the internationally dominant firms in the sector (d'Costa 2004). In other sectors, Indian firms have circumvented their limited technology development capability in a variety of ways like sourcing technology in part or as a whole from specialised technology suppliers, outsourcing to foreign firms, and wherever possible through the older traditional routes of technological collaboration and joint ventures with multinational firms. The pattern of growth has also helped because, in a number of services and construction activities, the role of self-development of technology in any case tends to be limited. Even the foreign acquisitions by Indian firms, enabled mainly by their financial strength, have been perhaps attempts to acquire missing competitive strengths like innovative capacity (Nayyar 2008).

The state–capital relationship under liberalisation

Liberalisation has hardly meant either the 'retreat of the state' or the development of arm's-length relationships between the state and private capital. Instead, it has served as the background for an even closer relationship between the state and private capital, which has been important for the success of Indian capital in global competition and also reinforced its domination domestically.

The gradual and calibrated, and in some respects restricted, nature of Indian liberalisation contributed to checking foreign acquisition of Indian assets, facilitated the adaptation and adjustment of Indian big business to the new competitive context, and helped them set themselves up in many of the new sectors opened up for private capital in which they had no previous experience.

Where liberalisation measures resulted in significant threat to Indian business from foreign capital, the state also showed a willingness to take countervailing measures. One prominent example of this is the virtual killing of the 'market for corporate control' that was sought to be established in the initial flush of liberalisation. Indian big business argued that it was unfair that, while foreign firms were being allowed to hold large blocks of shares in companies, they were still subject to restrictions on inter-corporate investments. This made their companies apparently vulnerable to takeovers by big foreign firms. The state responded to big business lobbying and eased these restrictions, and introduced other measures that would enable them to increase their stakes (Chalapati Rao and Guha 2006). As a result, incumbent managements of most large companies in India, domestic or foreign controlled, became virtually immune to hostile takeover.

If Indian dirigisme provided a setting and a smokescreen for clientelism, cronyism and corruption to be associated with the state–capital relationship in Indian capitalism, liberalisation has done so to an even greater measure. One of its ideological justifications had been that liberalisation would make market competition rather than cosy relationships with politicians and bureaucrats the ultimate arbiter of the fortunes of business firms. However, experience has shown this notion to have been a myth (Mazumdar 2008c).

The state can under certain circumstances confer tremendous benefits on favoured business firms by refusing to intervene in the functioning of markets. The context of deregulation provides a handy rationalisation for such inaction. Privatisation of public-sector firms and of different sectors, integral parts of the liberalisation programme, also carried within them a similar potential. In almost all the major sectors that have been de-reserved and/or opened up for increased participation of the private sector – telecommunications, power, mining, petroleum and gas, banking, insurance, airlines, etc. – the state has had to set up the rules of entry and mechanisms for regulating them since these are not sectors where competitive markets can function. The withdrawal of the state in one form therefore necessitated its reappearance in another. There are also other markets like financial markets where regulation is a permanent necessity. Public–private partnerships in infrastructure development including special economic zones (SEZs) have further institutionalised state engagement with private capital in what was originally primarily the state's domain.

Right through the liberalisation period, the influence of extraneous considerations and favouritism over big-ticket decisions of the state have been discussed. A permissive attitude towards capitalist lawlessness has also been a perceptible feature of this period. Recent exposures of a massive scam in the allocation of spectrum to private telecommunication companies, of the active intervention and influence of big business houses in politics, of illegal mining, etc., have brought the existence of these phenomena to prominence. The real structural consequence of Indian liberalisation has therefore not been the elimination of the state as an important factor in the economy, but instead the increased leverage of private capital with the state by virtue of the fiscal and other restrictions imposed by liberalisation and opening up on the latter.

Constrained in its ability to drive the economy's growth process through public investment, the state has to induce the private sector to play that role. Policy has therefore had to be oriented towards encouraging private investment and that, too, in a context of global competition. This placing of the private sector in a privileged position has also made the adoption of a friendly attitude towards it a part of the general culture of state functioning in India. In a federal set-up like India's, the leverage of private capital over the state has been enhanced by the competition for investment between states into which liberalisation has forced them. At the same time, large business firms that have established themselves in key sectors have increased their clout and thus influence on regulatory policy in them. Liberalisation has also fostered a culture that greatly celebrates money making with the all-pervasive erosion of values being its joint product. This has increased the proneness to corruption of public officials, while the greater permissiveness towards international transactions has added a new dimension to the possibilities of graft. Moreover, in a globalised context, private business enterprises have also become the standard bearers of 'nationalism', 'national interest' and 'national achievement' so that national success tends to be seen as something that coincides with their success. In this background, granting 'concessions' and providing 'incentives' to private capital, and maintaining through these the 'state of confidence', has become normal fare. The implications of these measures for state revenues have further reinforced the dependence on private capital. The state in India has also been actively involved in the process of private capital acquiring land on a vast scale for industrial projects, special economic zones and real estate projects.

The status enjoyed by corporate capital in India and its voice and influence over policy-making process have perhaps never been greater than has been the case under liberalisation. Using this, Indian big business enterprises have been able to secure significant individual and collective benefits and dictate policy priorities. Their stranglehold over the state has meant it effectively tilting against the interests of other claimants to the state's attention – industrial labour, the urban and the rural poor, the agricultural and unorganised sectors. The narrow social base of development under liberalisation has meant the absence of any broad social consensus on liberalisation. Electoral verdicts have consistently revealed this, as have the overt conflicts erupting from time to time. Yet the march of Indian liberalisation, actively backed by big business, has continued uninterrupted. For a brief period since 2004, with exceptionally high growth (particularly of corporate profits) swelling the government's coffers, India's poor did receive some attention compared to the complete neglect of the previous decade and a half. Measures like the National Rural Employment Guarantee Scheme (NREGA) were introduced during this period. Even such modest efforts at redressing the worst effects of India's growth trajectory, however, have run into difficulties as the fiscal situation has deteriorated since the global financial crisis.

The inability of India's political structure to ensure the responsiveness of the state to the aspirations of large sections of Indian society, or more precisely a significant increase in the degree of this non-responsiveness, has been a perceptible change evoking comments like the following:

> It is, then, plausible to suggest that this latest phase of independent India is characterized by an intensification of conflict in the economy, in the polity, and in the interaction between economy and polity. There can be no doubt that the need for conflict resolution is much greater than ever before. But the task has become more difficult. And the effort is much less.
>
> (Nayyar 1998: 3129)

4.3 Continuity and change in Indian capitalism: summing up

From the colonial period to the current phase of liberalisation, Indian capital has experienced a development or motion that has been more than mere quantitative expansion. It initially emerged in the shadow of colonialism and the dominance of foreign capital and then became the more dynamic segment of capital as the balance started shifting after the First World War. It gained further strength through a relatively autonomous development within a domestic space after independence and then moved further on and stepped onto the world stage in the age of globalisation. To that extent, Indian capitalism can be called an 'emerging' capitalism, whereby its location within the international structure of capitalism has been changing.

Through this development, however, associated with Indian capitalism have been some fundamental features that have proven durable and unyielding to change. These have played their part more in shaping the trajectory of Indian capitalist development. One of these is the existence of an agrarian constraint resulting from the initial incomplete development of capitalism. Albeit in somewhat different ways in the different stages of its development, the agrarian constraint has constrained capitalist development sufficiently enough to prevent its own elimination. One specific expression of this has been Indian capitalism's inability to achieve full-fledged industrialisation. This in turn has reinforced the technological dependence of Indian capital, a feature that initially reflected both its larger context as well as the mercantile roots of Indian capital. A related consequence of the enduring agrarian constraint has been the creation of a permanent labour surplus situation and high levels of informalisation. The consequence of these has been that Indian capitalism has been characterised by an inherent tendency for uneven development – an imbalance between the advance of its capitalist sector and its larger transformative impact on Indian society.

Neither of the above features of Indian capitalism or their expressions is disappearing under the impact of liberalisation. If anything, they are being reinforced and therefore are important qualifications to the notion of the 'emergence' of Indian capitalism, and more so perhaps than may be the case with many other important Third World capitalisms. Correspondingly, Indian capitalism's escape from a subordinate position in the international structure of capitalism remains significantly incomplete. Moreover, the evidence hardly permits an unequivocal conclusion that it is only a matter of time before it decisively moves into the core of global capitalism.

An integral feature of capitalism in India has also been the substantial reliance of capital, not only collectively but also individually, on state support of its development. The nature of the former kind of support has changed over time because of capitalist development, and that underlies the shift in economic policy from a dirigiste to a liberal one – from promoting a relatively autonomous development to enabling them to succeed in the face of global competition at home and abroad. In each stage, the state has obviously not been unconstrained in its ability to support capital, but it has remained an important factor in the economy throughout. Active manoeuvring by business groups to make advantageous use of this, something that originally may have come to them instinctively in view of their origins, has become an entrenched feature of business behaviour in India. This is also because, as the state has historically evolved in India, it has also exhibited a persistent tendency to be so manoeuvred. Consequently, the spontaneity of Indian capitalism has not proven particularly amenable to taming by the state, allowing it to exert a decisive influence on its trajectory. Even if its composition has not remained static, Indian capitalism has always been characterised by the domination of the corporate sector by a relatively small number of business groups controlled by well-connected and powerful business families and individuals. Liberalisation has not changed either of these but instead has taken the business–state nexus to a different level where the stakes involved have become larger and the state's ability to act autonomously has become more restricted. Big business has always been a powerful social force in India. It has become even more so as capitalist priorities have pressed down harder on a state constrained in many new ways as a consequence of the opening up of India's economy.

4.4 Indian capitalism and the Varieties of Capitalism perspective: some reflections in lieu of a conclusion

Indian capitalism has certainly displayed a set of temporally stable characteristics, or continuities, and a related trajectory of movement over time that cannot be generalised to all capitalisms. Moreover, it is clearly not converging towards any universal model of liberal capitalism even as it is changing under an impetus created by changes in its economic policy regime and the country's consequent increased integration into the global economy. To that extent, the case of Indian capitalism reinforces the founding basis of the Varieties of Capitalism (VoC) perspective. Yet, the Indian case also serves to highlight that it is not so simple to find places for such capitalisms in the existing typological schemes. The most essential features of Indian capitalism that shape its working and outcomes, for instance, include the presence of a significant agrarian sector and an agrarian constraint. These are, however, hardly the features that are emphasised as sources of distinctiveness in the standard classification schemes.

As argued by Uwe Becker in the Introduction to this volume, the standard classifications are also ill equipped to deal with change, given their static nature. The importance of this observation is also brought home by the case of Indian capitalism, the deep-rooted continuities of which have been combined with very important changes, say in the transition from dirigisme to liberalisation. Becker's methodological approach to dealing with the combination of heterogeneity and movement, one that involves identifying a limited number of ideal types and then distinguishing between ideal types and actual cases, should be in principle capable of accommodating the Indian case. What needs to be noted, however, is that the case of Indian capitalism brings to the fore the importance of taking into account variations in space and time along two axes – the distance from what might be called a full-fledged capitalist industrial economy and the relative position in the international structure of capitalism.

Indian capitalism, given the significance and character of its agrarian economy, is clearly not a classic capitalist industrial economy. Its historical origins have also firmly placed it in an unequal position in the international structure of capitalism. These two factors are essential elements in its temporally stable configuration and are critically important factors explaining the very distinctive set of outcomes Indian capitalism has produced in the longer run as well as in its more immediate liberalisation phase. To a lesser or greater extent, these were also distinguishing features of many of today's 'emerging' capitalisms half a century ago. Since then, they have all moved from their initial situations but in greatly varying degrees and even perhaps directions. Most, however, are still clearly distinguishable from the advanced capitalisms of the core, and Indian capitalism very sharply so. The VoC perspective has been criticised for reifying the national economy, ignoring the fact that no such economy is entirely autonomous (Watson 2003). In the process, it has also not given importance to the hierarchical element in the mutual interaction of economies.

In the end, one might highlight an additional complication that Indian capitalism – and its distinctive combination of standstill and movement and uneven development – brings out. Since a single quantifiable variable does not decide the degree to which a particular capitalism approximates an ideal type, actual variations between them or their changes over time may not also be along an 'ideal' path. Any exercise of constructing a typology of capitalisms needs to address this problem too.

Notes

1 Even if these are considered only very broadly indicative of what really happened, Paul Bairoch's estimates (cited in Simmons 1985) bring out India's industrial regression during the 19th century. According to these estimates, India's share in world manufacturing production fell from just under 20 per cent at the beginning of the century (it was nearly 25 per cent in 1750) to under 2 per cent by the end. During this period, India's per capita industrialisation level fell to one sixth of its original level.

2 Intermittent strikes by industrial workers began in the 19th century, and a modern organised trade union movement came into being in the period after the First World War. The growth of Indian nationalism and the Russian Revolution of 1917 inevitably also contributed to the working class and its movement going beyond mere economic struggles and acquiring an increased political orientation (Sen 1997). It became a significant enough political force in Indian society for the ideas of 'socialism' to penetrate even into the mainstream national movement, and for Indian capitalists to become self-conscious of the need politically to meet this challenge side by side with their battle against European dominance (Ray 1985).

3 This system involved the contractual vesting of the responsibility for managing the affairs of a company to a managing agency firm in return for a remuneration or commission. However, notwithstanding their formal position, managing agents were not really providers of services for a fee. Instead, they were in fact the active agents in promotion of companies they managed.

4 The figures given in Bettelheim (1977: 25–26) illustrate this: the average annual income per person in 1950–51 was Rs 3,200 for *maliks*, who constituted 17 per cent of rural households, Rs 130 for *kisans*, whose share in households was 45 per cent, and Rs 104 for the 38 per cent of *mazdoors*. At the same time, the per capita national income was Rs 265.2, which, as Bettelheim noted, was in any case amongst the lowest in the world.

5 This took outside the ambit of the Indian Union some of the most irrigated tracts of the sub-continent, a food surplus region, and major areas of production of the two most important industrial raw materials produced by the agrarian sector, namely cotton and jute.

6 For central and state governments together.

7 Particularly since 1980, it was a growth of services more than that of industry that contributed towards faster GDP growth and the increasing share of the non-agricultural sector in total output (Mazumdar 2010).

8 The Emergency, which lasted from 1975 to 1977, was the biggest test.

9 Virtually every political party in India, national and regional, has been part of one or more of three different alliances that have formed national governments since 1991. Most have also been at one point or another ruling parties at the regional (state) level.

10 While salary levels in the concerned sector are exceptionally high by Indian standards, India's low-wage economy still underlies this export success. The additional factor has been the longstanding existence of an English language-based tertiary education sector, a legacy of both the country's colonial and dirigiste past.

5 Continuity and change in Russian capitalism

Alexandra Vasileva

5.1 Introduction

The development of the Russian political economy presents observers with an intriguing combination: on the one hand, in the wake of the collapse of the Soviet Union, Russia has introduced basic institutions of a market economy. At the same time, the Russian political economy has maintained many features of the old system, in particular clientelism, patrimonialism and a pronounced role of the government and the bureaucracy. The Russian politico-economic system is often referred to as 'Kremlin capitalism' (Blasi *et al.* 1997), 'patrimonial capitalism' (King 2007: 314), 'state capitalism' (Zudin 2006) or 'bureaucratic capitalism' (Petrov 2011: 61).

The objective of this chapter is to analyse change and continuity in the Russian political economy since 1992, focusing on state–economy relations but leaving some space for capital–labour relations. I grant special attention to the elements of continuity in the process of change – an aspect that has not yet received the consideration that it deserves. The main finding is that, after the initial liberalisation in the 1990s and the early 2000s, change in Russian capitalism manifests itself in etatisation, expressed foremost in the increased role of the state in the political economy since approximately 2003. Continuity manifests itself in the persistence of patrimonialism, expressed in the enduring corruption, in the partial fusion of the state and the economy, and in the spread of the informal state–business and capital–labour relations. In the last part of the chapter, I take a look at the endurance of patrimonialism and its influence on the changes in the Russian political economy through the lens of the mechanism of 'power-ownership'. This mechanism describes how Russian bureaucrats use their positions in the state apparatus in order to control the cash flow from property (e.g. local business) as if it belonged to them.

I follow the critical mainstream of both Russian and international scholars of Russian capitalism (for example, Aslund, Gudkov and Zaslavsky, Kapelushnikov, Kryshtanovskaya, Pappe and Galukhina, Rutland, and Shevtsova, to name a few), but also develop my own distinct argument. Unlike the mainstream, I do not divide the timeframe into the 'Yeltsin period' and 'Putin period', but rather distinguish the periods of 'liberalisation' and 'etatisation', which only partly coincide with the respective presidencies; neither do I treat President Medvedev as a liberaliser but argue that he was an integral part of Putin's team and continued Putin's etatist policies. Furthermore, I argue that the often cited interpretation, according to which Russian capitalism underwent a change from 'state capture' in the 1990s to 'business capture' in the 2000s (Hellman *et al.* 2000; Fries *et al.* 2003; Yakovlev 2006), falls short of providing a comprehensive account of the processes that were underway in Russian capitalism in the past two decades. Instead, I emphasise that behind the superficial change from 'state capture' to 'business capture' lies the continuity of a partial fusion of the state and the economy.

My argument draws on the theory of comparative capitalism, where the state of the art is largely defined by the mainstream and the critical accounts of the Varieties of Capitalism (VoC) approach (Hall and Soskice 2001; Streeck and Thelen 2005; Crouch 2005a; Becker 2009). This framework is best suited for the analysis of the macro level and provides useful analytical tools for capturing change in political economies. Adopting the typology of capitalist varieties by Becker (see Chapter 2 in this volume), I deploy three ideal types of capitalism – the liberal, the statist and the patrimonial type – and emphasise the strict distinction between the ideal types and empirical cases. In this context, my case – Russian capitalism – is understood as a certain mixture of elements of the ideal types of capitalism at any given point in time. The identification of the shift in the proportion of the statist, liberal and patrimonial elements in Russian capitalism in the last two decades is the central endeavour of my account.

The method of analysis is explorative, meaning that it explores an open question – how did the Russian political economy evolve over time? – rather than testing theoretically derived hypotheses. Focusing on one case, the analysis adopts a holistic perspective that seeks to understand the phenomenon as a whole by tackling its complexity, rather than reducing the analysis to a few discrete variables (Vromen 2010: 257). I start the analysis of the Russian capitalist development in 1992, when the first round of privatisation was initiated, and track it to the present day or at least as late as data are available. The analysis draws on both quantitative and qualitative data – their combination helps to 'unpack' the complex Russian political economy, in which formal rules are often at odds with actual practice.

Compared to other BRICs countries, Russia is somewhat an outlier: its heavy dependence on hydrocarbons and minerals, the underdeveloped manufacturing as well as some signs of economic decline are not typical of most emerging economies. In this context, a brief note on Russia's general economic situation seems relevant. The continuous oil boom helped to sustain spectacular gross domestic product (GDP) growth between 1999 and 2008 and secured windfall export revenues. The downside of the reliance on petrodollars has been the lack of diversification of the economy and the neglect of manufacturing. Apart from some promising companies in the defence, aircraft, automobile and metallurgy sectors, many industries remain uncompetitive and desperately need investment. The perils of oil dependency have become particularly clear since the 2008 financial crisis: the Russian economy shrank by almost 8 per cent in 2009, plunging into a much deeper recession and recovering slower than other emerging economies. The natural resource bonanza has also served as a source of corruption and cronyism (see the Introduction to this volume).

These imbalances, exacerbated by the heavy and often predatory interference of the state in the economy, have produced an unsound business climate. It leads to a short planning horizon, underinvestment and capital flight and may have a negative impact on Russia's economic development. Some signs of the economic decline are already visible and include an increased occurrence of technical catastrophes and the deterioration of the notoriously old industrial equipment and infrastructure, including oil and gas pipelines on which Russia relies for its exports. Additionally, mismanagement and endemic corruption have led to a degradation of public services such as policing, education and science. The shrinking and ageing population, coupled with the brain drain to Western countries, contribute to a fairly grim economic prospect (*The Economist*, 14 July 2012; Petrov 2011: 61).

In the following sections, I will turn to the major changes in Russian state–business relations, distinguishing the stages of liberalisation (1992–2002) and etatisation (since 2003). The next sections will address the continuities in Russian state–business relations and then review the development of capital–labour relations. A conclusion and several open questions close the chapter.

For the sake of systematisation I will analyse the state–business relations along three dimensions. The political dimension comprises state capacity (the state's capability to design and implement policies) and the composition of the dominant political elites; the legal dimension deals with the rule of law and the security of property rights; the economic dimension comprises the economic policy of the state towards business. It has to be noted that the choice of the year 2003 as a dividing line between the 'liberal' and the 'etatist' periods concerns primarily the change in the state policy towards business and thus should not be viewed as a sharp dividing line that denotes changes in every aspect of state–business relations.

5.2 Change in Russian state–business relations (1992–2002): liberalisation

The political dimension

Along with the general collapse of statehood in the course of the break-up of the Soviet Union, the Russian state was weak in every aspect of state capacity. The 'strategic' state capacity can be characterised as feeble throughout the 1990s since many institutions were dysfunctional or had to be built from scratch, the state apparatus was notoriously underfinanced and a new legal framework had to be developed. Yeltsin, who was elected president in 1991, faced a constant blockade from the communist-dominated Supreme Soviet (parliament) so that regular policy formulation was hardly possible. The new constitution, adopted in 1993, endowed the president with much power and helped to overcome the stalemate, allowing Yeltsin to rule by decree and to push through the liberal reforms against the conservative, pro-communist mindset of the deputies in the parliament. As a consequence, many key government decisions, including much of the privatisation programme, were introduced by presidential decrees (Zaznaev 2008: 33).

The 'administrative' state capacity was also low in the 1990s as the federal state was losing control over the increasingly autonomous regions. The 89 provincial executives were making use of President Yeltsin's initial proposal 'to take as much sovereignty as they could swallow' and increasingly resisted Moscow's policy, refusing to pay taxes to the federal government and issuing their own laws and even currencies. The fact that the policy-making authority quickly devolved from the centre to the regions arguably brought Russia to the brink of disintegration and led in the case of the Republic of Chechnya to a civil war. Furthermore, the Russian state could not effectively collect taxes due to rampant corruption, the spread of barter and the sprawling shadow economy (Stoner-Weiss 2006: 109).

The 'coercive' state capacity decreased as the Russian government attempted to dispose of the compromised secret service, the KGB – the embodiment of Soviet coercive practices – in an effort to build a democracy. Having restructured the KGB and dismissed more than 300,000 of its employees, Yeltsin curbed the power of this formidable agency. At the same time, the state was unable to cope with the surging crime rate (not least because the police force was underfinanced and corrupt) and was hardly capable of enforcing the rule of law and guaranteeing the protection of the nascent private property (Kryshtanovskaya 2005: 125f).

The Russian political elites in the 1990s were fragmented but generally comprised two groups of people. 'The liberals' were young, progressive economists and reformers around President Yeltsin, many of whom were newcomers to politics. 'The conservatives' had their background in the communist party *nomenklatura*: these genuinely Soviet elite groups were not confronted by a rising counter-elite in the course of transition and thus managed to retain their positions (Gelman and Tarusina 2000: 320). The conservatives included the so-called *siloviki*, or 'power-agents' – individuals and networks with a background in the armed forces, law enforcement bodies or intelligence agencies. Having been the backbone of the Soviet regime, the *siloviki* continued to constitute a shadow political elite in post-Soviet Russia, not acting on the political surface yet being very influential (Shevtsova 2007: 97).

The balance of power between the liberals and the conservatives changed in the course of Yeltsin's presidency. In the first half of the 1990s, the young liberal elites headed by Prime Minister Gaidar were dominating (Higley *et al.* 1998: 22f). By the second half of the 1990s, Yeltsin's team began losing popularity due to the painful effects of the radical reforms such as the dramatically declined living standard and the loss of personal savings. The unpopular war in Chechnya and the 1998 financial crisis exacerbated the situation (Gudkov and Zaslavsky 2011: 67, 73). Confronted with the waning support, Yeltsin was looking for a stable power base and a trustworthy successor who would guarantee the security of Yeltsin's clan. Having ultimately chosen the former KGB officer Vladimir Putin, Yeltsin shifted the power base from the liberal elites to the *siloviki* (Aslund 2007: 189). Eager to compensate for the missed opportunities during the privatisation, the *siloviki* gradually expanded their influence in politics and the economy in the course of the 2000s, as will be shown later.

The legal dimension

Although Yeltsin's liberal government gave high political priority to the establishment of a stable legal environment, the rule of law remained weak throughout the 1990s, which was a manifestation of the low state capacity. The adoption of laws crucial for the establishment of a new politico-economic order was delayed by the confrontation between the parliament and President Yeltsin in the early 1990s and complicated by the resistance of the first Russian businessmen who understood how to take advantage of the opaque legal situation. Negotiation of exemptions from rules between the bureaucrats and their crony businessmen often required more time than the drafting of the general rules of the game. Once adopted, laws could not always be enforced in a proper way since the largely dysfunctional state could hardly claim a monopoly over the use of force (Schröder 2008: 5ff; Pappe and Galukhina 2009: 76).

In the early 1990s, more than 14,000 criminal groups with about 57,000 members took advantage of the legal vacuum, which led to a surge of crime and violence. Business relied on these gangs and various private 'violence-managing agencies', responsible for racketeering, contract murders, protection and contract enforcement functions. The physical survival of Russian business in the early 1990s often depended on such criminal groups providing protection services – the so-called 'roof'. Criminal 'roofing' virtually substituted the missing rule of law in the 1990s (Volkov 2002; Myant and Drahokoupil 2010: 152f).

Ownership rights were opaque throughout the 1990s and could not be guaranteed by the state. Ownership did not imply automatic control over business, let alone the entitlement to profit. Moreover, stock owners were supposed to be 'useful' for the company, ensuring good relations with the bureaucracy, negotiating exemptions from rules or the like. 'Idle' owners could be forced to sell their shares or would be edged out. By the same token, the rights of 'not useful' minority shareholders were virtually ignored (Pappe and Galukhina 2009: 69ff).

The economic dimension

In the wake of the break-up of the Soviet Union, Russia faced a deep economic recession, coupled with hyperinflation and the spread of the shadow economy. In this environment, the team of young reformers around President Yeltsin endorsed a radical liberal economic policy (the so-called 'shock therapy') that aimed at a rapid transition to a market economy. By mid-1994, the first stage of the liberal reforms had been finished and a market economy had been formally introduced. The reforms included a macroeconomic stabilisation, the liberalisation of most domestic prices and foreign trade, and large-scale privatisation. The first informal round of privatisation, the so-called 'spontaneous privatisation', occured already in the last years of the Soviet Union under Gorbachev (1989–91) and served as a source of early fortunes (Aslund 2007: 57ff). Yeltsin's team continued with the voucher privatisation programme in 1992.

Every Russian citizen received a voucher that represented a share in the whole national economy and could trade it or use it at voucher auctions to bid for shares in former state enterprises. As a result, approximately half of the formerly state-owned firms had been transferred to private hands. However, the voucher privatisation did not lead, as expected, to the dispersion of ownership throughout society, but to its concentration, as vouchers accumulated in the few hands of people who had benefited from Gorbachev's reforms – foremost the former enterprise managers – and had enough start-up capital at their disposal and bought up the vouchers (McCarthy *et al.* 2000: 260f).

Thereafter, between 1995 and 1997, the major trend of the state's policy towards business was further liberalisation and privatisation. In order to understand the mode and the result of the reform, we need to be aware of the new business actors who had a profound and lasting impact on the Russian political economy – the so-called oligarchs. These billionaires, whose resources typically combined banking, sections of industry and the mass media, had both economic power and a considerable political influence.[1]

The future oligarchs typically originated in the Soviet *nomenklatura* (notably the cadres of the youth communist organisation Komsomol) and started accumulating their wealth in the course of Gorbachev's Perestroika of the late 1980s, profiting from insider information and access to the financial resources of the communist party, coupled with waning state control and partial trade liberalisation. Banking was a particularly lucrative source of early fortunes since it allowed the accumulation of profits from currency speculation and export arbitrage.[2] Furthermore, in the absence of a strong treasury system, banks owned by the oligarchs ensured enormous profits by becoming 'authorised' to manage state funds for a wide variety of government agencies (Aslund 2007: 57f; Hoffman 2007: 345).

In the absence of strong institutions and a firm legal environment, political ties allowed the oligarchs to shape the reform process and the distribution of wealth in the nascent Russian market economy. The channels of influence included participating in agencies such as the Government Committee for Questions of Economic Reform, buying votes of the members of parliament and, most importantly, directly approaching the decision makers and especially Yeltsin's inner circle (Schröder 1999: 972–78). Some of the oligarchs formed an integral part of this circle and exercised informal yet decisive influence on policy making, appearing to have 'captured' the state (Hellman *et al.* 2000).

However, this was rather a relationship of mutual dependence – the dubious loans-for-shares privatisation and Yeltsin's subsequent re-election in 1996 are the most striking examples.

The 1995–97 loans-for-shares privatisation was pivotal for the rise of the oligarchs. It allowed them to obtain the country's most valuable assets at favourable conditions set up by themselves. According to the scheme, devised by the oligarch Potanin, the cash-strapped Russian state auctioned off valuable shares of 29 major oil and mineral producers and received loans from the winners in return. The winners would be entitled to keep or to sell the shares if the state failed to repay the loans after one year. Given their political connections, the oligarchs organised and controlled the auctions and, by using shell companies, made sure that banks owned by themselves could win. As the government failed to pay back the loans, the oligarchs were able to keep the shares. As a result, a favoured group of insiders acquired the shares of the country's leading enterprises – such as Norilsk Nickel, Yukos and Sibneft – at a fraction of their potential market value.

Yeltsin, who was gradually losing support, turned a blind eye to this manipulation since he preferred to foster powerful allies among business instead of achieving the highest price possible. Indeed, the oligarchs provided massive financial and media support to Yeltsin's election campaign and ensured his re-election in 1996 (Hoffman 2007: 353–57). In the same year, Yeltsin launched the second wave of the loans-for-shares privatisation, widely perceived as a payback for the election support. Apart from that, dozens of businessmen were appointed to positions in the state apparatus, thus demonstrating the interpenetration of business and government that defines an oligarchy (Aslund 2007: 161–64).

The result of the privatisation programme was an extreme concentration of ownership: by 2001, the country's 23 largest firms, controlled by a mere 37 individuals, were estimated to account for 30 per cent of Russia's GDP, while large parts of the population did not profit from the privatisation (Rutland 2008a: 1055). The ownership and management relations in the business empires of the 1990s were often non-transparent, mostly involving offshore affiliates, which gave numerous opportunities for asset stripping and tax evasion (Pappe and Galukhina 2009: 71ff).

Although the bulk of the state-owned firms (70 per cent) was transferred into private ownership in the course of the privatisation, many of them were essentially operating in the same way as they did in Soviet times, remaining inefficient, overstaffed and heavily reliant on government subsidies – particularly in the energy and defence industries. Some economic sectors were preserved as 'natural monopolies', such as the Russian Railways or the gas giant Gazprom. The small and medium-sized enterprises (SMEs) developed sluggishly given the weak legal environment and the excessive tax burden. The number of SMEs registered each year declined from 1994 on, so that in 1997 SMEs accounted for barely 12 per cent of GDP, while in the advanced market economies the number is close to 50 per cent (Gustafson 1999: 110). The state budget was in trouble due to massive tax evasion and the ramifications of the 1998 financial meltdown.

The financial crisis of August 1998, caused by heavy government borrowing and the slump of world oil prices that eroded Russia's account surplus, was a significant blow to the oligarchs. They had been profiteering from high-interest treasury bonds that helped trigger the crisis, but lost much of their fortunes when the state defaulted on its debts and the rouble lost 75 per cent of its value (Aslund 2007: 173–80). In this way, the pervasive influence of the oligarchs on policy making decreased, symbolically marked by the denial of admission into the government building. On the whole, in the wake of the crisis the government of Prime Minister Primakov (1998–99) pursued a liberal, market-oriented policy and thus the state did not increase its presence in the economy, contrary to some assessments (Pappe and Galukhina 2009: 92).

President Putin's assumption of power in 2000 coincided with an improvement of the economic situation. Backed by the surging world oil prices and a rouble depreciation that boosted exports, the economy had averaged 7 per cent growth from 1999 until 2008, resulting in an increase of wages and real disposable incomes, the reduction of unemployment and the emergence of a nascent middle class. Given this favourable economic situation, Putin enjoyed great popularity and was able to continue the market reforms. He endorsed a liberal economic programme, which put the primary emphasis on deregulation and the improvement of the business climate (Gudkov and Zaslavsky 2011: 77).

The programme included a tax reform, which alleviated the overall tax burden and was supposed to boost tax revenues,[3] a new Land Code that legalised the private ownership of land and liberal reforms targeted primarily at the SMEs. Instead of having to be approved by several government agencies in a lengthy process that could easily take weeks, a business could be registered with one agency within only five days. Furthermore, new laws cut the number of mandatory inspections for business and reduced the number of business activities that required licensing (Rutland 2008a: 1053ff).

From the beginning of his presidency, Putin attempted to strengthen the state's authority over business and to formalise relations. He urged business to join associations such as the Russian Union of Industrialists and Entrepreneurs, which were supposed to channel the consolidated information from business to the government. However, business associations contributed to the institutionalisation of state–business relations only marginally and gradually lost their significance in the course of the 2000s. Most business lobbying in the 2000s, as in the 1990s, took the form of direct approaches to government officials by particular businessmen or business groups. Many 'deals' seemed to be concluded in a shadowy way (Pappe and Galukhina 2009: 160).

Contrary to Yeltsin's relations with the oligarchs, Putin created a centralised hierarchical system of relations in which the government assumed the dominant position. This re-alignment was fostered by the weakening of the 'first generation' oligarchs in the wake of the 1998 financial crisis and by the advancement of new, more cautious business players. At the same time, following the unwritten 'deal of equidistance', the state appeared to guarantee the inviolability of the oligarchs' businesses and immunity from prosecution over privatisation as long as they stayed loyal to the Kremlin and did not interfere with politics (Sandschneider 2001: 23). Those magnates who respected the new unwritten rules multiplied their fortunes – by 2008, there were more than 80 oligarchs with combined assets worth US$455 billion.[4] Oligarchs who did not comply were forced into exile, like the media tycoons Gusinsky and Berezovsky, or were prosecuted, like Khodorkovsky, the owner of the oil giant Yukos (Rutland 2008a: 1057).

In this context, in the 2000s, big business appeared to be 'captured' by the resurgent state (Yakovlev 2006: 1033f). However, the renegotiation of the government's relations with business did not imply a dissolution of the partial fusion between the state and business typical of the 1990s. Many of the loyal businessmen were co-opted into politics (Kryshtanovskaya and White 2005: 303ff), while others continued to rely on clientelist networks and informal modes of interaction with the authorities. At the same time, some politicians became full-blown 'state oligarchs' on boards of state corporations, managing whole swaths of the economy at their discretion and extracting rents (see below).

5.3 Change in Russian state–business relations since 2003: etatisation

The political dimension

President Putin saw the strengthening of the state as his political priority. Putin's attempt to improve the capacity of the Russian state was focused on the consolidation of the political power of the president. The creation of the so-called 'vertical of power' implied a centralisation and the co-optation of the regional leaders (Stoner-Weiss 2006: 109f), but also included the control of the independent sources of power such as the mass media and non-governmental organisations (NGOs) as well as the subordination of the parliament and the establishment of the pro-Kremlin 'party of power' United Russia (Shevtsova 2007: 174). Although formally committed to democratic principles, the government gradually compromised on them under the pretext of national security and the danger of terrorism – the war in Chechnya providing an ideal breeding ground for this discourse (Gudkov and Zaslavsky 2011: 182). The 'rise of the state' was bolstered by the surge in world oil prices and was backed by the Russian public, who associated the economic hardships of the 'wild 1990s' with the failures of the democratic reforms and perceived the new regime as successful in attaining economic growth and restoring order.

Despite the partial strengthening, the Russian state remained weakly institutionalised, with clans and informal networks of patronage being the basic unit of the state apparatus, just as they were in Soviet times. The state also maintained its poor strategic capacity: it was not successful at promoting a comprehensive modernisation strategy or at diversifying the economy, and tax collection remained difficult. The implementation of ambitious national projects and programmes for socio-economic development suffered from administrative weakness, bureaucratic inertia and corruption (Bertelsmann Foundation 2010: 18). Furthermore, excessive centralisation has made the state inert, inflexible and less responsive to crisis situations. Instead of routinely addressing arising problems, the state has often resorted to 'manual steering', which requires the involvement of the top political authority (Petrov 2011: 55). All in all, the paradox combination of the increased authority of the central state and of its coercive capacity on the one hand and the persisting weakness of the state's strategic capacity on the other hand can be called 'consolidation of the weak state' (Gudkov and Zaslavsky 2011: 95).

The constellation of the dominant political elites changed dramatically in the course of the 2000s. From the beginning of his presidency, Putin faced a rivalry between different factions and was eager to establish his own reliable team consisting of people who were personally devoted to him. Putin recruited both the liberals and the conservatives, most notably people from the former KGB, who shared with Putin the professional background. The remaining members of Yeltsin's elite left the government in the wake of the Yukos affair in 2003–04, marking a shift in the balance between the elite groups in Putin's administration. By Putin's second term the *siloviki*, in particular their ex-KGB wing, had clearly become Russia's dominant political elite, occupying influential positions in virtually all political spheres (Sandschneider 2001: 12; Kryshtanovskaya 2005: 150–55). Once in power, the *siloviki* made an effort to catch up on property redistribution and significantly shaped state–business relations, as will be addressed in more detail later.

The election of President Medvedev, who can be viewed as an integral part of Putin's team, allowed the incumbent elite to stay in power, Putin's return to the president's office in May 2012 being a testimony. Despite his liberal rhetoric, President Medvedev contributed to the consolidation of the political regime that emerged under Putin. For example, Medvedev extended the duration of the presidential term by two years and considerably expanded the power of the KGB's successor FSB to control the population (Kynev 2012: 35). In a similar vein, much of the liberal rhetoric regarding human rights and fundamental freedoms was not put in place (Rogoza 2011: 15).

The legal dimension

Putin's announcement to establish the 'dictatorship of the law' indeed entailed some legal improvements. Major amendments to the Civil Code and the Criminal Code were adopted, jury trials were introduced in all Russian regions and the resources allocated to courts and judicial bodies were greatly increased (including judges' salaries), reducing the dependence of judges on regional authorities in terms of basic needs and premises (Frye 2011: 121f; Hendley 2010). The activity of the 'violent entrepreneurs' and criminal 'roofing' were pushed back. The attitude of business to the establishment of the rule of law changed, too: while in the 'wild 1990s' many businessmen became rich overnight and were not interested in transparent laws, after 2000 they had a vested interest in a functioning judiciary in order to legalise and protect their wealth (Gudkov and Zaslavsky 2011: 95).

However, despite formal legal improvements, law enforcement remained weak throughout the 2000s. The judicial practice was highly selective and often depended on the political loyalty of business, on the personal interest of policy makers and on the compliance of the courts with the political will (Myant and Drahokoupil 2010: 151, 158). The confiscation of the oil company Yukos in 2003 and the legal prosecution of its owner Khodorkovsky, widely perceived as politically motivated, is a case in point. The Yukos affair demonstrated that business could count on legal security only in return for political loyalty and gave rise to the term 'telephone justice', referring to the political interference into the judicial process and the dependence of the courts (Ledeneva 2011). As a consequence, business preferred to rely on informal personal networks rather than on the regulative institutional pillar, which perpetuated the vicious circle of the weakness of the rule of law.

The Yukos affair paved the way for the interference of the authorities with business and put the violations of property rights, raids and expropriations back on the agenda.[5] However, the hostile illegal takeovers of the 2000s were carried out not by criminals like in the 1990s but by corrupt state agents who deployed intelligence networks, state prosecutors and armed forces to intimidate business or to persecute business rivals (Golovshinskii *et al.* 2004: 27f). In this sense, the practice of 'roofing' de facto remained intact.

Legal uncertainty was exacerbated by corruption: litigant parties could influence the judge's decision by competing to pay a bigger bribe, or business could bribe the law-enforcement authorities to prosecute the undesirable competitor (Satarov *et al.* 1998: 32). Even the lowest, municipal level of law enforcement was corruption-prone due to legal 'loopholes': blanket provisions (legal provisions that have a general character), subject to the discretionary power of local authorities, provided numerous opportunities for extortion (Golovshinskii *et al.* 2004: 16).

Overall, judicial rules and legal procedures became formally more institutionalised in the 2000s compared to the 1990s. However, even though thousands of mundane cases had been resolved without political interference, the rule of law remained fragile, selective and susceptible to manipulation by the authorities. Law enforcement remained weak, too. In this context, unwritten rules, informal arrangements and illicit actions continued to shape the Russian state–business relations and often appeared more important than the legislation.

The economic dimension

While Putin's economic record during his first term can be characterised as largely liberal, the dominant stance of Putin's policy towards business during his second term was etatisation. In particular, the state increased its stake in strategic economic sectors via nationalisation and created vertically integrated state corporations.

The partial re-nationalisation occurred primarily in the lucrative hydrocarbon sector. The government re-asserted its control by acquiring the assets of companies that had been privatised under Yeltsin, by limiting foreign investment and by putting pressure on private companies to sell the majority stake to the state-owned companies.[6] As a result, by 2007, the state controlled over 50 per cent of the oil sector, compared to less than 20 per cent in 2004, and brought the controlling stake in the gas monopoly Gazprom under its control (Cooper 2009: 13).

Between 2004 and 2006, the government took control of several private companies in other strategic sectors such as aviation, power generation and machine building. At the same time, the state increased its stake in firms where it already had shares: the percentage of firms in which the federal government held a majority stake increased from 25 per cent in 2005 to 61 per cent in 2008 (OECD 2011d: 80). The overall percentage of state ownership in the economy increased from 30 per cent (1994–2004) to 35 per cent (EBRD n.d.).[7]

Another measure concerned the creation of vertically integrated state conglomerates called *goskorporacii*. Governed by separate laws and exempt from most auditing and reporting obligations, *goskorporacii* included many state-owned companies in strategic economic sectors such as nuclear energy, nano-technology and defence, but also absorbed some private firms. The directors, appointed by the president, had considerable leeway to manage the assets of the corporations (Luzan 2009: 280). Putin ensured that the leading state corporations were headed by the people loyal to him, placing the incumbent members of the executive branch – foremost the *siloviki* – on corporate boards (Treisman 2007: 143ff). In this way, whole swaths of the economy were entrusted to the 'state oligarchs'. Even though most of them had to leave their positions on corporate boards following an order by President Medvedev, their aides filled their positions, securing the control of the incumbent clan (Rogoza 2011: 17).

I suggest considering the emergence of the state corporations and the 'state oligarchs' from the perspective of 'power-ownership', a concept by Runov and Tambovtsev (2009) largely unknown to Western scholars. *Vlast-sobstvennost*, literally power-ownership, is essentially a factual property right tied to the position in the state bureaucracy. Thus, power-ownership refers to the power of the bureaucrats to control property (business) as if they owned it. Such de facto property rights apply only as long as the incumbent is in office and concern primarily the cash flow from property, but not the debts, liabilities and risks associated with legal ownership. Most importantly, factual property rights, which obviously lack a legal status, appear to be better protected than the legal rights since the latter can be successfully contested by the state in a dependent court. At the same time, state agencies are able to prevent or manipulate a lawsuit brought against corrupt bureaucrats or raiders. As part of a vicious circle, the factual property right – power-ownership – becomes strengthened in the long run at the expense of the legal ownership (Runov 2009: 69ff).

Viewed from the perspective of power-ownership, the policy of the 2000s seems to be not a nationalisation but rather a redistribution of property to the benefit of the incumbent clan. The *siloviki*, having been weak as an elite group up until the late 1990s, for the most part failed to take part in the distribution of property in the course of the privatisation of the 1990s. Once in power, they were eager to compensate for the lost opportunities. Having acquired key positions in the state bureaucracy under President Putin, the *siloviki* profited from the nationalisation of lucrative economic assets and their concentration in state corporations. Viewed from the perspective of power-ownership, in this way the *siloviki* obtained factual property rights, or access to the cash flow from property under their control. In other words, the state's economic policy in the late 2000s appears not as a genuine *nationalisation* in the sense of a return of strategic economic assets into state ownership as part of a particular development strategy, but rather as a *re-privatisation* in favour of the *siloviki* (Tucker 2010: 172ff). Thus, the concept of power-ownership offers an interpretation of the changes in the Russian political economy in the 2000s, revealing the underlying continuity of the partial fusion of the state and business.

The state policy towards business since late 2008 can be seen as a continuation of Putin's statist policy, despite President Medvedev's verbal commitment to the reduction of the state's role in the economy. The economic record comprised the anti-crisis programme and the pursuit of large-scale national projects, such as the Sochi Winter Olympic Games, Skolkovo innovation centre or Asia-Pacific Economic Cooperation Leaders' Summit in Vladivostok (Rogoza 2011: 29).

The 2008–09 financial crisis hit Russia particularly hard as oil prices plummeted and the foreign credits upon which Russian banks and firms relied dried up. The crisis invariably entailed an increase in the state's interference in the economy. Tapping the vast reserves accumulated during the boom years, the government launched rescue and stimulus packages for troubled banks and companies and later reduced the corporate tax rate to stimulate investment (Cooper 2009: 19). As a result, the share of budgetary subsidies and transfers reached 7.1 per cent of GDP in 2009, compared to 3.7 per cent in 2004 (EBRD n.d.).

State support was given primarily not to the SMEs but to large 'system relevant' firms such as Gazprom or Russian Railways in order to prevent large-scale job losses, especially in single-industry towns (see section 5.4 below). The military and defence sector alone accounted for one quarter of governmental support (Gudkov and Zaslavsky 2011: 163). More recently, an upsurge of inflation driven by food and energy prices has resulted in a number of ad hoc interventions by the authorities, such as the prevention of real increases in electricity prices, a ban on the export of grain and the imposition of a prohibitive tax on petrol (OECD 2011d: 80).

The new wave of privatisation announced in 2010 did not reduce the overall share of state ownership since the privatisation concerned only minority shareholdings in state-owned companies (OECD 2011d). Other liberalisation attempts by Medvedev, including the attempt to liquidate state corporations, were de facto not implemented. The SMEs continued to develop slowly – Russia has seven SMEs per 1,000 inhabitants, while the European Union has about 45.

Also the share of the GDP generated by the Russian SMEs – 12 per cent – remains low (OECD 2011d: 69). Most of the 'natural monopolies' as well as the subsidisation of parts of the economy have endured, too. For example, domestic energy prices are kept artificially low, allowing the cross-subsidisation of domestic manufactures (Rutland 2010: 168).

5.4 Continuity in Russian state–business relations

The legacy of patrimonialism

Entrenched patrimonialism has been traditionally characteristic of the Russian political environment. In a patrimonial system, the state does not pursue the public good but operates in the interest of clans and informal networks that 'privatise' the state institutions for personal enrichment. This implies a system of government administration in which state officials are responsible to the top political leadership but at the same time are given wide leeway and treat their jobs as income-generating property (Brinkerhoff and Goldsmith 2002: 40).

In Russia, a system of personalised exchange relationships and clientelist politics has flourished since tsarism, blurring the distinction between politics and the economy. The Soviet patrimonial system was marked by hierarchical chains of personal dependence between party leaders and their underlings, who extracted economic rents from the state property under their control (Jensen 2001: 34). Since the old Soviet elite largely remained in control of the state apparatus after the collapse of communism, Russia has inherited the patrimonial character of the Soviet public administration.

At the heart of Russian patrimonialism lies the tradition of entrenched paternalism, rooted in social passivity, the legacy of forced labour and the ingrained respect of authority. For instance, the Russian workers prefer to rely on informal, paternalistic relations with the enterprise managers rather than join collective action to defend their interests (see the next section). By the same token, having 'made friends' with the authorities or having agreed on a kickback scheme, businessmen are eager to retain informal contacts with the bureaucrats instead of following the official rules. In a similar vein, the Russian public, accustomed to being patronised by the 'father state' and at the same time disbelieving that anything could be changed 'up there', seldom attempts to contest the official rules of the game but rather seeks unofficial ways to circumvent them. This has resulted in particularism and the pursuit of private gain as the guiding social principles in Russia, as opposed to universalism and the pursuit of the common good.

The dominance of particularism has led to the society-wide spread of informal relations, unwritten rules and ad hoc arrangements that count more than laws and written contracts. *Dogovoritsa* – a Russian verb that refers to all kinds of 'private solutions' negotiated between the bureaucrats, businessmen and workers – affects virtually every aspect of the Russian political economy and, most importantly, is regarded as 'normal' by large parts of the Russian public.

According to a recent poll, virtually nobody in Russia believes that all court decisions are made in accordance with the law (OECD 2011d: 78). All in all, the persistence of paternalistic attitudes and the dominance of informal ways of interaction sustain and reproduce Russian patrimonialism. One of its most salient manifestations is the enduring corruption.

Corruption

Corruption, or abuse of public power for private gain, goes back to tsarism and to the informal activities (*'blat'*) and the shadow economy under state socialism (Pleines 2001: 283; Ledeneva 1998). Given the weak legal environment and payment arrears in the state bureaucracy in the aftermath of the collapse of the Soviet Union, corruption flourished and basically served as a substitute for the universal rules of the game (Satarov *et al.* 1998: 24f). Rampant but somewhat 'randomised' corruption of the 1990s gave way to systemic and 'institutionalised' corruption of the 2000s. While in 2002 14.7 per cent of firms identified corruption as a major constraint to doing business, in 2009 the figure reached 50 per cent (BEEPS 2009). According to one estimate, the monetary value of corruption flows equals up to one quarter of Russian GDP (Nemtsov and Milov 2010).

Despite the formal ease of the administrative burden under President Putin, bribery and extortion persisted and even increased in the 2000s. When interacting with the Russian authorities, businessmen occasionally give 'gifts' for obtaining licences, for receiving preferential treatment or for letting the bureaucrat turn a blind eye to illegal conduct. Thereby it is estimated that the amount of an average 'gift' in 2001 equalled the cost of a 30 sq.m flat, whereas four years later an average bribe already 'bought' a 200 sq.m flat (INDEM 2005: 14).

The authorities in their turn treat business as a 'cash cow', resorting to corrupt methods such as unofficial charges or arbitrary fines. Most infamous are the state agencies authorised to register and inspect firms, such as the fire-fighting service and the sanitary-epidemiological agency. Controlling authorities often impose arbitrary fines, drop in for an unofficial check-up on the eve of a holiday and expect 'gifts', demand expensive 'training' for the employees as a condition for obtaining business permits or impose more expensive and less efficient solutions, for instance forcing the purchase of security equipment from specific suppliers. The same applies to the police force, which is authorised to undertake practically any kind of business check-up (Golovshinskii *et al.* 2004: 24–28).

In the environment of corruption, administrative decisions turn into goods that are traded on a shadow market. Creating an artificial shortage of rights (such as the right to open a business), bureaucrats generate a source of rents. In this way, any Russian firm becomes a forced joint venture with the local bureaucracy. Beyond bribes or extortion, the state officials are eager to institutionalise this profitable 'partnership' by imposing ongoing obligations on business, such as the renovation of the bureaucrat's office or organisation of a banquet. The existence and survival of firms often depend on the fulfilment of these obligations.

In this context, firms treat the expenses associated with the maintenance of 'good relations' with the authorities as a reasonable investment (Kliamkin and Timofeev 2000: 94–97).

The Russian energy sector represents a particularly lucrative source of rents that happen to end up in the pockets of the state officials and their crony businessmen. Hydrocarbon trading is one of the most conspicuous examples of the enduring corrupt practices. Both private and state-owned exporting energy companies have been using shell companies, shadowy subcontractors and off-shore banking for selling oil and gas at low prices and then re-selling it via subsidiaries at higher prices, embezzling huge profits. This corrupt practice extends back to the 1990s but became even more entrenched in the 2000s. Today about 30 per cent of Russian oil exports are channelled through a Swiss-based intermediary Gunvor, which is owned by Putin's close associate Timchenko (Rutland 2008a: 1058).

A form of corruption that became prominent in Russia in the 2000s is the so-called *raspil*, literally 'sawing-through', or a system of institutionalised kickbacks in public procurement. The mechanism behind *raspil* is that public contracts are awarded not according to the best price or quality, but as a result of collusion between state officials and their crony businessmen. For instance, firms owned by persons with close ties to Putin or to the ministers get awarded lucrative procurement contracts for constructing large infrastructural facilities.[8] Thereby the cost of the service exceeds the market price while the government allows itself to be overcharged. The resulting price difference is the kickback. The scope of kickbacks in Russian public procurement is estimated at 30 to 60 per cent of the contract volume, leading to the embezzlement of billions of dollars annually (Rogoza 2011: 18; Makarov 2011).

5.5 The transformation of capital–labour relations

In the Soviet centrally planned economy, labour relations were regulated primarily by the state, which guaranteed full and stable employment in exchange for labour peace. The Soviet labour model represented an 'organised consensus' and included secure jobs, largely egalitarian incomes and a ban on strikes. The trade unions never fulfilled the function of institutionalised channels for the workers' interest articulation but rather formed part of the Soviet authoritarian enforcement and control machine in charge of labour discipline and mobilisation of workers for fulfilling the plan. In this context, Soviet workers had to rely on informal relations with the enterprise managers to address their needs and problems. Thus, paternalism was at the heart of the Soviet labour model and represents perhaps the most enduring continuity in Russian industrial relations (Sobolev 2010: 22f; Gudkov and Zaslavsky 2011: 31, 39f).

The Russian labour model that emerged in the 1990s and consolidated in the 2000s differs from the Soviet model given the social, political and economic changes that accompanied the transition from the planned economy. Yet at the same time Russian labour relations were shaped by Soviet legacies and enduring continuities, and arguably underwent an 'adaptation without restructuring' (Kapelushnikov 1999: 91). The core elements of the Russian labour model, which will be discussed in detail below, are:

- stable employment loosely correlated with GDP fluctuation;
- a small role for trade unions and low strike activity;
- the spread of informal capital–labour relations instead of reliance on institutionalised channels; and
- a gap between the rigidity of formal regulations and the flexibility of their application.

Partial liberalisation in the 1990s

The economic breakdown and the 'shock therapy' of the early 1990s made high unemployment (at least 25 per cent) seem inevitable. Mass layoffs were bound to happen given that the Soviet enterprises were notoriously inefficient and overstaffed, experts warned. However, things turned out differently. Unlike the transition economies of Central and Eastern Europe, Russia experienced a much deeper recession but at the same time a disproportionately low and slow rise of unemployment. Bankruptcies were rare and official unemployment reached its peak of just 13 per cent in 1998 and has decreased ever since. There is no doubt that the factual unemployment figure was considerably higher than the formal one, let alone the proportion of people who registered as unemployed, since many troubled enterprises continued to employ excess workers only nominally, pushing them into the informal economy. However, on the whole, the nascent Russian labour model proved to be successful at amortising shocks and crises, as will be discussed below. Yet at the same time the Russian labour model has hampered the transformation of labour relations in the long run, encouraging informal relations between the managers and the workers at the expense of the institutionalisation of labour relations (Kapelushnikov 1999: 71ff, 92).

President Yeltsin sought to free the workers from state control and to democratise relations between the tariff partners. In the course of the 1990s, a new labour legislation was issued. It included a right to strike and to form independent trade unions; a process through which firms could legally dismiss workers; a minimum wage; basic unemployment benefits; rules for tariff negotiations; and a tripartite system of social partnership (Sil 2005: 7; Gudkov and Zaslavsky 2011: 26, 40).

However, the institutionalisation of labour relations remained largely nominal. Just as many other legal provisions in the 1990s, formal regulations governing labour relations were often at odds with the actual practice – given the weakness of the legal system and the low enforcement capacity of the Russian state. In this context, the 'Russian labour miracle' can be explained rather by the informal adaptation strategy adopted by the troubled enterprises and their workers under adverse economic conditions of the 1990s. The adaptation strategy, which decisively shaped Russian labour relations, comprised two fundamental elements: first, the prevention of mass unemployment via flexibilisation of working time and wages; and second, the spread of informal labour relations (Kapelushnikov 1999: 91ff).

The first component of the adaptation strategy implied the retention of excess workforce at the cost of economic efficiency. Russian enterprises were reluctant to initiate mass layoffs and continued to keep redundant workers on the payroll, reducing labour costs by cutting both the working time and the wages. The wage-reduction strategy included real wage cuts, exacerbated by galloping inflation (real wages fell by 60 per cent between 1991 and 2000), mounting payment arrears (at their peak in 1998 wage arrears encompassed three quarters of Russian workers), the cancellation of bonus payments, which used to constitute up to 20 per cent of the wage, the spread of in-kind payments and cuts in social benefits. The average yearly working time decreased between 1991 and 1996 by one month, or 12 per cent (15 per cent in industry). Many workers were routinely sent on unpaid leave (Kapelushnikov 2009: 12–16).

Concerned over labour unrest, the Russian government supported the adaptation strategy of the enterprises for the sake of social stability. This decision – possibly rather spontaneous than considered – was not in line with the liberal reforms, especially with the minimum wage provisions and the regulations authorising dismissals. However, the government used carrots and sticks to make factories retain personnel, continued to subsidise many enterprises and avoided mass layoffs in the public sector by drastically cutting wages. As a result, the continuity of over-employment endured: in 1997 of 75 million people of working age, 8 million were unemployed and an additional 12–13 million constituted excess personnel (Gudkov and Zaslavsky 2011: 19, 24–27). In this context, wages decreased, often falling below the subsistence minimum in the public sector, thus providing a fertile breeding ground for corruption and at the same time serving as an excuse for low wages in private companies (Sobolev 2010: 26).

The second equally important aspect of the adaptation strategy was the spread of informal labour relations. As real wages were decreasing and payment arrears skyrocketing, the dramatically deteriorating living standard of the workers left them at the mercy of enterprise managers, who granted workers access to shadow salaries constituting up to 40 per cent of official wages, non-wage supplements and informal mechanisms that allowed the workers to earn additional income. The tangible benefits from covert earning schemes promoted a personal dependence by workers on the enterprise managers and thus strengthened the paternalistic ties that used to be at the heart of the Soviet labour model (Sobolev 2010: 22f; Birdsall 2000). As a result, the workers, who often had no alternative to their current employment, notably in single-industry towns, did not rely on the trade unions as defenders of their rights and were reluctant to join a strike despite their deteriorating economic situation (Gudkov and Zaslavsky 2011: 41ff; Sil 2005: 10).

The fact that the workers preferred to turn to enterprise managers rather than to the trade unions to address their problems and pressing needs, coupled with a low level of trust in the unions, certainly hampered the transformation of the trade unions into viable workers' organisations in the course of the 1990s. Unions that belonged to the newly established Federation of Independent Trade Unions of Russia, which was carved out of the Soviet trade union apparatus, were afraid to lose members and continued the old practice of distribution of social benefits, although they lacked the resources. New, genuinely autonomous trade unions struggled for members and often faced difficulties and even harassment since both the state and business continued to view the trade unions as nuisances (Sil 2005: 11). As a result, the traditional paternalistic alliance between the enterprise managers and the workers has endured at the expense of the institutionalisation of Russian labour relations and has decisively shaped their further development.

Adaptation without restructuring in the 2000s

The 2000s witnessed an improvement in the economic situation of the workers along with the general recovery of the economy. Unemployment was steadily decreasing and fell to 6.3 per cent in 2008. The average working hours increased, having grown by 16 per cent in the industry by 2008. Real wages increased threefold between 1999 and 2008, and wage arrears almost disappeared, affecting merely 1 per cent of workers (Kapelushnikov 2009: 13–18). However, wages were lower than the cost of the reproduction of labour and were in decline as a proportion of production costs, a study by Sobolev (2010: 34–37) shows. At the same time, Russia's senior managers were much better paid than their counterparts both in the West and in the other BRICs, indicating a huge gap between the workers' and the managers' salaries (*The Economist*, 11 September 2008).[9]

Just as in the 1990s, in the 2000s, enterprises attempted to keep labour costs as low as possible, reducing the share of fixed payments and increasing the 'black' part of the so-called 'black-and-white salaries' that were widespread both in private companies and in the public sector, where the black cash originated in kickbacks or from *raspil* in public procurement. Not fixed in any contract, the 'envelope payments' could be cut at any time, keeping labour costs flexible and at the same time enhancing the personal dependence of the workers on the employer. In this context, it is not surprising that strike activity remained low in the 2000s (with the exception of the traditionally well-organised mining industry). Similar to the 1990s, workers preferred to rely on personal informal relations with the management instead of collective bargaining (Sobolev 2010: 37; Kapelushnikov 2009: 63).

In terms of legislation, the Putin government pursued the institutionalisation and formalisation of labour relations. A new Labour Code adopted in 2001 can be considered rigid as compared to international standards, granting the state a great role in the control of capital–labour relations (Ashwin and Clarke 2002:

111–14). For instance, under the new Labour Code, enterprises had less leeway to cut wages and working hours, and layoffs became a particularly costly and sophisticated undertaking. Also the enforcement of the labour legislation improved in the 2000s compared to the 1990s in line with the general increase in state capacity. A successful fight over wage arrears and the improved observance of collective agreements are the most telling examples (Kapelushnikov 2009: 20f, 55).

These improvements were put in perspective by the 2008–09 economic crisis. The preference of the state for employment stability, the informal adaptation strategies of enterprises and the low strike activity of the workers revealed the continuity of the labour model that emerged in the 1990s.

In the wake of the crisis, the Russian labour market showed its resiliency yet again. While GDP dropped dramatically, unemployment increased inconsiderably, reaching 8.7 per cent in 2009 and already decreasing again the following year.[10] The state was again concerned over social unrest and interfered heavily in the economy to prevent mass layoffs. The case of the Russian single-industry town Pikalevo became emblematic of the Russian crisis response. In 2009, three concrete plants owned by the oligarch Deripaska were to be closed down, leaving 4,500 people (almost the whole working-age population) without jobs. Demands by the trade unions were ignored by the local authorities. Thereupon, the workers started massive protests and blocked one of the main federal roads. In a demonstrative rescue operation, Putin arrived in the troubled town by helicopter and forced Deripaska to resume the work of the factories and to guarantee employment to the citizens of Pikalevo in front of running cameras. The very same day the state compensated wage arrears equivalent to $1.3 million from the federal budget (*Vremia Novostey*, 5 June 2009; *Izvestiya*, 30 December 2009).

Just as in the 1990s, firms reacted to crisis with flexible working hours and wages, although the room for manoeuvre was clearly limited under the new rigid legislation. However, it was perhaps the very rigidity of formal regulations that encouraged firms to seek new, often illegal ways to circumvent the regulations and to cut labour costs. This pushed labour relations further into the shadows in line with the popular Russian wisdom that reads 'the imperfection of our laws is compensated by their non-observance' (Ledeneva 2001: 2). For instance, employers cut wages by cancelling bonuses and shadow payments. Another popular method was the proliferation of unpaid 'voluntary' leave and 'voluntary' layoffs, which did not require financial compensation. Under informal agreements, the employees continued to work and received their salaries 'in envelopes'. This de-formalisation of labour relations has strengthened the paternalistic interdependence of the workers and managers (Kapelushnikov 2009: 61ff).

To conclude, the Russian labour model was formed in the 1990s and, having undergone an 'adaptation without restructuring', consolidated in the 2000s. Russian labour relations are marked by stable employment achieved through flexible wages and working hours; by feeble development of the trade unions and a low level of industrial conflict; and finally, by the spread of informal, paternalistic relations between the workers and managers, at odds with the rigid labour legislation.

Similar to the development of state–business relations, the main direction of the adaptive change of Russian capital–labour relations was etatisation, expressed in the somewhat enhanced enforcement of labour legislation, coupled with the increased involvement of the state in labour relations. The pronounced role of the state became conspicuous during the 2008–09 crisis when policies directed at employment stability were pursued. The main continuity of Russian labour relations is – similar to state–business relations – entrenched patrimonialism, expressed foremost in the de-formalisation and individualisation of capital–labour relations. Instead of stable institutions and independent organisations of entrepreneurship and interest representation, Russian labour relations are based on a web of paternalistic and semi-legal relations of personal dependence.

The paradox of the Russian labour model lies in the contradiction between the rigid formal regulations and the largely informal, paternalistic relations between the managers and the workers that allow a flexible adaptation to crises. The gap between the formal rules and the actual practice indicates yet again the weakness of the rule of law, the low level of enforcement of the general rules of the game and the dominance of particularistic, patrimonial practices. This tendency echoes the theory–praxis gap in state–business relations and thus appears to be typical of Russian capitalism as a whole.

5.6 Conclusion

The development of the Russian political economy is a complex interplay between continuity and change. 'Capitalism Russian style', which emerged in the wake of the collapse of the Soviet centrally planned economy, has undergone a transformation in the course of the last two decades but has maintained some Soviet-era characteristics that continue to shape the Russian political economy.

Viewed against the backdrop of the statist, liberal and patrimonial ideal types of capitalism, the main direction of change in the Russian political economy is expressed in the shift in the proportion of liberal and statist elements. While between 1992 and 2002 Russian capitalism can be characterised as largely liberal, after 2003 the trend towards increased statism became pronounced. The etatisation of Russian capitalism was expressed in the partial increase in state capacity, in the shift from the liberal to conservative political elites, and in the partial nationalisation of strategic economic assets, coupled with an overall increase in the state's involvement in the economy and labour relations.

The major continuity of Russian capitalist development was found in the persistence of patrimonial elements. The continuity of patrimonialism is expressed in the pervasive weakness of the rule of law, in the endurance and perhaps even increase in corruption, in the partial fusion of the state and business, and in the spread of informal state–business and capital–labour relations, which are at odds with the formal regulations governing these relations.

My analysis has pointed out that the continuity of Russian patrimonialism underlies the change towards increased statism: behind the etatisation of Russian state–business relations in the second half of the 2000s was arguably a redistribution of property to the benefit of the incumbent clan of the *siloviki*. This process was facilitated by the feeble rule of law, by the insecurity of property rights, by the dominance of particularism and corruption and, finally, by the political environment in which clans and networks of patronage and informal exchange supplanted formal state institutions.

In order to understand the mechanisms behind Russian patrimonialism, we need to address factors, contexts and circumstances that serve the bureaucrats as power resources and enable them to extract administrative rents from property under their control. We also need to research the scope of Russian patrimonialism and the eventual differences between the 1990s and the 2000s. All in all, considering change in the context of continuity may contribute to a better understanding of the changing capitalism in Russia and possibly in other emerging countries.

The final remarks regard Russia's possible trajectory in the future. Recent developments provide a mixed picture. On the one hand, given World Trade Organization (WTO) accession, Russia may be exposed to the pressure to liberalise its economy. Additionally, the diminishing Russian hydrocarbon reserves and the lack of diversification may soon reveal the limits of the resource-driven rentier development and ultimately push for change; at the same time, the discovery of shale oil and gas in the USA may reduce the importance of Russia as a gas supplier for Europe and bring the gas price down, which would be a serious challenge for Russia's budget (see also Chapter 9 in this volume).

On the other hand, Putin's return to the president's office in May 2012 and the continued political dominance of the *siloviki* point to the likely perpetuation of the trajectory that Russia has taken since the second half of the 2000s. However, public approval of Putin, though still comparatively high, was at an historic low of 62 per cent in January 2013, down from over 70 per cent throughout Putin's first two presidencies (Levada Centre n.d.). The public protests since the December 2011 Duma elections and the timid awakening of civil society also point to the limits of Putin's consensus based on loyalty to the incumbent regime in return for oil-driven economic growth. In this context, it is unclear whether there is a prospect for change or whether Russia will rather face the consolidation of the statist-patrimonial regime.

Notes

1 Among the most influential oligarchs of the 1990s were Alekperov (Lukoil, oil), Potanin and Prokhorov (Interros-Oneksim, nonferrous metals), Khodorkovsky (Yukos-Menatep-Rosprom, banking/oil), Vinogradov (Inkombank group, banking), Berezovsky and Abramovich (SBS-Agro-Sibneft-LogoVaz, banking/oil/automobile), Fridman (Alfa group), Ivanishvili (Bank Rossijskij Kredit group, banking), Gusinsky (Most media group, TV) and Yevtushenkov (AFK Systema, telecommunications) (Pappe and Galukhina 2009: 53f).

2 The partial trade liberalisation in the late 1980s allowed the '*nomenklatura* capitalists' to make use of the highly varied exchange rates as well as to purchase commodities at

government-controlled prices and to re-sell them at great profit on foreign markets. Export arbitrage in metals, oil and gas accounted by 1992 for approximately 30 per cent of Russia's GDP (Aslund 2007: 58; Rutland 2010: 163).

3 The number of taxes that residents and businesses faced was reduced from about 200 to 16; a progressive income tax that peaked at 30 per cent was replaced by a flat tax of 13 per cent in 2001; the payroll tax was cut to an average rate of 26 per cent and the corporate profit tax was cut from 35 to 24 per cent; four social taxes were compressed into one; finally, tax collection was centralised into one agency (Cooper 2009: 10).

4 Among the influential oligarchs of the 2000s were Deripaska (Base Element-Rusal, aluminium), Abramovich (Sibneft, oil), Alekperov (Lukoil, oil), Potanin and Prokhorov (Interros-Norilsk Nickel, nonferrous metals), Abramov (Evrazholding, steel) and others. While the 1998 crisis weakened the position of the Moscow-based oligarchs, many of whom were engaged in banking and finance, it paved the way for the rise of the provincial oligarchs who headed new industrial groups, for example Mordashov (Severstal, steel) and Lisin (Novolipetsk metallurgical combine, metallurgy) (Guriev and Rachinsky 2005: 133; Kryshtanovskaya and White 2005: 302ff).

5 For instance, Putin's public harassment of the private metallurgic giant Mechel (2008), accused of dumping, cost the company 30 per cent of its value on the Russian stock exchange (*Vesti* broadcasting station, 28 July 2008; www.vesti.ru). Prominent cases of hostile illegal takeovers include the expropriation of three subsidiaries of the international investment fund Hermitage Capital in 2008 as well as the corporate raid on Yevgeny Chichvarkin's mobile communication company Evroset, carried out by several police officers (Frye 2011: 123; OECD 2011d: 78).

6 For instance, the Russian government forced Royal Dutch Shell (2006) and British Petroleum (2008) to cede controlling stakes in major gas fields to the state-owned Gazprom by claiming environmental violations or revoking licences (Rutland 2008a: 1059).

7 It has to be noted that this figure includes only formal state ownership. According to other estimates that include informal state control, by 2008 state ownership had reached 40–45 per cent (Kudrov 2009: 44), or even 60 per cent (Gudkov and Zaslavsky 2011: 161).

8 For example, in 2011, the company Stroygazmontazh, controlled by Putin's aide Rotenberg, became the general contractor for the construction of the Nord Stream pipeline; Rotenberg's Mostotrest received contracts for building the Olympic facilities in Sochi and other sports facilities worth $100 million (Rogoza 2011: 18). Similarly, between 2008 and 2010, a construction company that belonged to a friend of the transportation minister won 30 tenders with a cumulative volume of more than $3.6 billion (Makarov 2011).

9 A survey conducted by Hay Group, a consultancy, calculated the disposable incomes of top chief executive officers (CEOs) in 51 countries, having adjusted the salaries for taxes and living expenses. Russian CEOs are ranked ninth in the survey, while managers from Japan and the USA rank 39th and 41st, respectively. China is ranked 17th in this survey, Brazil 23rd, South Africa 36th and India 38th (*The Economist*, 11 September 2008).

10 Apart from the adaptation strategies to crisis chosen by the Russian state and enterprises, other factors prevented the explosive rise of unemployment in the wake of the 2008–09 crisis. Among them is the smaller share of excess workforce as compared to the 1990s, the structural change of the Russian economy towards services and the expansion of the non-corporate and informal sectors (Kapelushnikov 2009: 60f).

6 Politics and trajectory in Brazilian capitalist development

Renato Raul Boschi

6.1 Introduction

This contribution discusses some of the issues that are part of the research agenda proposed by Becker (2009) in an earlier work and taken up in Chapter 2 of this volume in a more systematic way. The analysis seeks to shed light on particular aspects of the Brazilian case, as part of a group of middle-income countries known as the BRICs, which share some common characteristics, yet differ in substantial ways. In the same vein as the one proposed by this author, this chapter reiterates the difficulty in framing empirical cases to ideal types, something that depends on the prism that is used in defining the contours of different productive regimes. It also reiterates the need to explain institutional change emphasising both endogenous and exogenous factors leading to transformation – in particular, the cumulative long-term effect of changes based on short-term uncertainty on the part of strategic decision makers and economic actors. Fundamentally, this contribution underlines the need to consider systematically the effect of the trajectory of historical development in the configuration of a given variety of capitalism, thus escaping the trap of static views based on fixed complementarities and stable equilibria. One can say that, although the comparative statics of fundamental dimensions of the institutional environments in which enterprises and businesses operate constitute the basis for efforts to refine the characterisation of varieties of capitalism beyond the categories of liberal market economy (LME) and coordinated market economy (CME), empirical cases should be treated as uncompleted and changeable realities. As a consequence, the chapter also points out the need to distinguish a path-dependent from an open-systems perspective on processes of change as a result of the elite's contested frames of reference.

I try to carry the analysis beyond the idea that the state matters in the configuration of varieties of capitalism. As is well known, state interventionism was typical of the process of capitalist development among latecomers in general and peripheral countries in particular. It is important to stress that, while complementarities are central in determining the varieties of capitalism at stake, the crucial aspect of the role of the state lies precisely in the ways the state acts in terms of making up for absence of complementarities at the level of firms.

Furthermore, I try to go beyond the recognition that political institutions are fundamental in determining the characteristics of capitalist varieties. In this analysis, I stress which political institutions mattered in shaping the characteristics of a given productive system: those having to do with the institutionalisation of capital–labour relations in a first moment, and those related to the role labour played in institutionalising democratic competition in a more recent phase. In this long process over time we also stress how state institutions were affected by the introduction of market reforms, that is whether effectiveness of the former was preserved and somehow complemented by the latter. Hence the importance of considering trajectory effects in the characterisation of varieties of capitalism.

In the case of the productive regimes in Latin America, which share a similar location in the (semi-)periphery of the capitalist system and constitute societies marked by accentuated structural inequalities, it is possible to identify a wide-ranging diversity of cases, despite the importance of the state's strategic role in each one of them. These variations can be explained precisely as a function of the very specific trajectories of capitalist development and the differentiated role of political institutions in the definition of national models, which in turn affect each economy's perspective of competitive insertion in the current scenario of globalised capitalism (Boschi and Gaitán 2008a, 2008b, 2009b). A crucial point in this regard is the articulation of interests connected to labour with institutions of representative democracy.

The Brazilian case, marked as it is by structural inequality and heterogeneity, presents variations not only when its trajectory is considered, but also when examined at a single point in time. It definitely moved from a strictly statist model of coordination in the early phase of industrialisation in the 1930s to something closer to a liberal variety of capitalism. Import substitution industrialisation (ISI) came to an end amidst the serious debt crisis in the 1980s and neoliberal reforms were implemented in the 1990s, and eventually acquired a somewhat social democratic facet with policies of social inclusion after Lula's administrations since 2003. If this analysis were to be carried out in a single time frame but based on a micro perspective from the viewpoint of enterprises, it would still reveal, in addition, enormous differences according to regional and sector criteria. Yet, from a macro perspective, the Brazilian case could be best described as a more state-oriented variety of capitalism[1] or, still, as a considerably corporatist variety of capitalism, according to the typology advanced by Becker, if emphasis is given to forms of industrial relations based on strong state intermediation.

Industrial relations in Brazil have been strongly marked by a labour legislation protecting formal employment. On the other hand, the corporatist legislation that favoured such forms of protection of labour did not provide for the political incorporation of the working class on equal footing with the type of incorporation of business. The latter had formal access to decision-making and policy-making arenas of the state apparatus, in addition to permission to organise and form associations outside of the official structures of interest representation.

For labour, more flexible patterns of organisation only materialised with the emergence of a new trade union movement in the late 1970s, which pushed for the creation of multiple industry associations. Still, the principle of monopoly of representation at the local level was maintained, the creation of more than one trade union by branch of activity being forbidden up to the present day. Yet, the new trade union movement lies behind the creation of the Workers Party as the political organisation that would stimulate both the transition to democracy in the 1980s and new forms of political incorporation for the working class in the wake of successive electoral campaigns at all levels of the Brazilian political system.

The attainment of the presidency with Lula's election in 2002 also meant new possibilities for labour from the point of view of participation in policy-making arenas, in addition to the extension of social protection to segments hitherto excluded. I argue that such a possibility drastically changed the configuration of Brazilian capitalism, both because it opened up the perspective for an inward process of development in the highly competitive and unstable scenario of contemporary globalisation, and because new forms of social policies increasingly became an integral part of the political agenda, favouring the reduction of persistent structural inequalities.

Route corrections did occur in the Brazilian trajectory of the ISI-model development in the course of time and, more crucially, at the crossroads of the 1990s double transition towards liberal reforms in the economic realm and democratisation in the political realm. In the economic realm, liberal reform was successful in terms of guaranteeing currency stability, promoting fiscal adjustments and privatisation, while it was not able to dismantle the pockets of bureaucracies constructed during the ISI development period. However, significant reform of the financial system was carried out during this period, furthering and deepening the modernisation that had begun in the 1970s (Kasahara 2011). Market reforms also introduced new forms of regulation based on the operation of autonomous agencies in different segments of economic activity.

Meanwhile, in the political realm, the gradual institutionalisation of a workers' party and its ascension to power through the ballot introduced the issue of inequality onto the agenda. In addition to bringing union and labour interests to the core of the political system, it led to the implementation of social inclusion and income distribution policies. Furthermore, another important consequence of this process of adaptation of labour to the rules of electoral competition was the inception of a type of societal corporatism that corrected the bi-partite (business + state only) model of the first-phase capitalist development.

In addition to endogenous processes, external variables must also be taken into account insofar as they substantially affect domestic trajectories. In particular, the impact of systemic crises may be responsible for major realignments, changes in the content and nature of economic policies and, therefore, in internal arrangements in the productive regimes.[2] Although not in a systematic way in terms of characterising Brazilian capitalism, my analysis focuses on some of the trajectory dimensions that played a part in facing the crisis of 2008. Some of the responses of the Brazilian economy to the financial crisis will be examined in order to underline how the pattern of economic growth based on social inclusion and the domestic market opened up the possibility of an inward-based strategy of growth based on the consumption of newly emerged middle classes.

I want to start by focusing on the establishment of a strong state-corporatist tradition in the early stages of Brazilian industrialisation in the 1930s and its role in shaping capital–labour relations. The analysis will address the continuity of state institutions in the context of liberal reforms at the end of the developmentalist cycle in the 1990s showing which market mechanisms were created and how and why some state capacities were preserved. Finally, I will focus on the more recent phase of institutionalisation of electoral democracy and the emergence of a labour-based party, and some of the policies and strategies adopted to face external crises and open up new perspectives for a model of capitalist development based on social inclusion and inward growth.

6.2 Trajectory and continuity: the pervasiveness of corporatism and state interventionism in the early phase

As emphasised, the role played by the capital–labour axis is definitely a central aspect of Brazilian capitalist development, both from the point of view of political incorporation of the entrepreneurial class and of the working class, and in terms of the forms of social protection geared towards the formal segment of labour that were implemented at the time of the first critical juncture in the 1930s. This period corresponds to the national revolution which redefined the basis of the Brazilian economy from an agro-export model to an urban industrial one, characterised by increasing state intervention and deepening the process of import substitution industrialisation.

In the framework of a closed economy, the central role of the executive branch as an inducer of modernisation starts to gain prominence, thus pushing ahead a relatively late, though efficient process of state making. In fact, if it is possible to identify one line of continuity in the role and activities of the Brazilian state, this would be the preponderance of the executive branch. It lasted for several phases of development from the 1930s onwards, from the crisis of the state-led model to the period of neoliberal ('state-shrinking') reforms up to the current phase marked by the re-strengthening of state intervention against the market coupled with insertion in global circuits.[3] State capacities were developed through the creation and subsequent Weberian-style modernisation of bureaucracies basically by means of public recruitment along universalist procedures.

Corporatism as an institutional arrangement dominant throughout the developmentalist period can be seen as a form of public–private organisation based on the interaction between the practices of organised groups, particularly of capital and labour, and state action. Rather than a deliberate move of the state with the intent of submitting society to corporatism in order to ensure long-term economic development, this arrangement provided the institutional basis for the expansion of industrial capitalism in Brazil. The corporatist legacy of the developmentalist period provided a framework in which new relationships were engendered, this being precisely the case of the structure of interest representation of the entrepreneurial class and the working class in the post-reform scenario (Diniz and Boschi 2004, 2007).

The corporatist structure of interest representation, set up during the first *Estado Novo* administration of President Getúlio Vargas after 1934, constitutes, along with the labour legislation, one of the most expressive continuities of the institutional trajectory of Brazilian capitalism. Indeed, here we can talk of path dependence in the sense that this structure provided early incentives for the organisation of labour and the entrepreneurial class through the maintenance of the so-called trade union tax (*imposto sindical*), which finances the activities of both entrepreneurs' and workers' unions. One of the most noticeable characteristics of this type of corporatism was the asymmetry of business vis-à-vis the labour organisations. The latter were not allowed to create parallel entities nor move beyond the strict limits of monopoly of representation. For this reason, this corporatist institutional architecture was very controversial and received substantial criticism when it was first implemented. In the beginning, corporatism was also criticised for its role in the Brazilian political system. This was due to its potential for co-optation, the control of labour and the perpetuation of a weak business class. More recent evaluations sustain that current new corporatist arrangements are reminiscent of the authoritarian principles of the *Estado Novo* and create obstacles for the flexibilisation of the labour market. However, on a positive note, it is possible to show that thanks to corporatism the foundations for organised collective action of the business sector as well as for conflict regulation between capital and labour were established, and reasonably effective channels of public/private interlocution were set in place.

Specifically in the case of the organisation of business interests, the structure has changed and adapted to modern times. This is indicative of its flexibility and propensity to change and also due to its survival as the main mechanism of articulation between the business sector and the state. Despite the diverse and fragmented formats of business collective action (cf. Diniz and Boschi 2004, 2007), and despite a performance that is possibly inferior to other mediation structures (Pedersen 2008; Schneider 2004), the centrality of corporatism in the organisation of the productive Brazilian regime is undeniable.

In its broader contours and as an asymmetric arrangement between classes, corporatism was shaped by resources such as the capacity for collective action of some social actors. Related to the control exerted by the state through its monopoly over representation and the labour unions, tax corporatism expanded and its class base became increasingly fragmented and differentiated. Regarding labour, control and the impossibility of organisation outside the official structure prevailed. When the control over the centralised labour entities was diminished in the late 1970s, this led to the multiplication of unions with local bases and the fragmentation of leadership. Regarding the entrepreneurial class, fragmentation became expressed in the creation of parallel associations at the edges of the official structure. This process started in the 1930s, became intensified in the 1950s and particularly in the 1970s and 1980s. At the top of the structure, this was translated into the absence of a hegemonic entity capable of representing capital as a whole. With respect to access to the state apparatus fragmentation also implied multiple interventions of multiple agents in different spheres of this apparatus at different stages of the decision-making process. This originally authoritarian and generally hierarchical form of corporatism with a minor role of labour was called bi-partite or state-oriented and contrasted with the inclusive and centralised neo-corporatism that emerged in Europe, especially in social democratic Scandinavia.

The market reforms of the 1990s implied a new effort to adapt business and working-class associations to the requirements of competitiveness in the open, globalised economy. In spite of the fragmentation of capital and the exclusion of labour, the changing corporatist structure proved to be relatively effective for continued interaction of business groups with the state. Overall, this transition was characterised by some centralisation of corporatist coordination and the adjustment to the liberalisation component of the reforms. The very fast reaction of the entrepreneurs to these institutional changes was remarkable. They demonstrated pragmatism and a high capacity to adapt to increased market competition.

As liberalisation went together with re-democratisation in the 1990s, Congress (the Brazilian parliament) passed legislation that restricted business rights and therefore became a target of collective action and intensified lobbying by the business sector. Business organisations, anchored in a dual structure with compulsory and voluntary forms of collective action, had been transformed in successive moments since the beginning of the state-led industrialisation in the 1930s. In the liberalisation and democratisation context of the 1990s, they had evolved towards a complex combination of segmentation and centralisation. In a quick adaptive effort, with this structure the business organisations showed themselves suited to playing a central role in the coordination of the new productive regime by moving towards associations articulating productive chains (Diniz and Boschi 2004).

The National Confederation of Industry (CNI), the peak-level entity of capital in Brazil, went through a process of significant modernisation and created a coordination office for legislative affairs – COAL – which follows up demands made by the industry to Congress (Mancuso 2004, 2007). Through studies on productivity and innovation, the CNI also engaged in creating analytical capacities for deeper involvement in policy making. A series of sector associations and productive chains have, however, proven very effective in the defence of their interests against centralisation, although this also occurred by coordinating their interests. In sum, we observe a process of adaptation to modern times in the associative sphere of the private sector, especially regarding the articulation of firms (Diniz and Boschi 2004).

During the authoritarian regimes and in the democratic interludes, labour's relative autonomy was not as expressive as that of business. More recently, the incorporation of labour-related organisations in the bureaucracy created new patterns of state–society relations that resulted in a significant democratisation of these formats of interaction. Ultimately, these changes were responsible for the development of a more articulate interaction between the private sector and the state and, moreover, they gave a voice to labour interests.

In sum, the corporatist model implemented in the 1930s can be interpreted as an institutional synthesis, drawing a line between the public and private spaces, yet still covering up the appropriation of the private by the public within the grey area of personal contacts, clientele connections and the establishment of networks. Corporatism also led to the mobilisation and organisation of social classes through the representation of their interests, however. Be it from the viewpoint of state intervention in the political arena, or from the viewpoint of social policy formulation through the regulation of labour relations and the definition of social rights, the state executive strengthened itself through its capacity to intervene. In each of these two areas, the 'expansive' aspect of the state's presence can be noticed. On one side, it occurred by defining through the growing intervention the enhancement of economic growth as well as the creation of an environment for public and private economic actors. On the other side, this aspect became visible to the political generation on the conditions for the mobilisation of popular forces and their entry into politics. In the deconstruction of the Vargas legacy that coincided with an expansion of political and social rights in the 1988 constitution and, simultaneously, a crisis of statism, the corporatist structure became perhaps the most durable and stable of all republican institutions, due to its capacity for flexible adaptation.

6.3 Market reforms of the 1990s and the maintenance of patterns of state interventionism

In the mid-1980s when, due to the economic crisis, the deepening of import substitution industrialisation could no longer be sustained, a process of deconstruction of developmental structures was set in motion, thereby endangering the accumulated state capacities. The imperative of macroeconomic stabilisation internally, plus the need for competitiveness and the integration of Brazil into the globalised circuit established the logic of restrictive state intervention. The deconstruction process of the previous order started with the reform of the state itself, as the state's expansion, especially in the productive sphere, was identified as a component of the crisis. The conjunction of the three axes that prevailed in the early phases of state-led development – economic growth, expansive social policy and restricted political participation – turned out to result in the reverse: severe restrictions on potential economic growth, the decline of social policy, the impossibility to enforce the social rights as granted by the 1988 constitution (as well as those acquired previously), and, finally, an ascending trend of political participation.

The executive branch was at the centre of the reorganisation that took place in the institutional environment of liberalisation. It led to the redefinition of the state's strategic role vis-à-vis organised actors and the relations amongst them. This reconfiguration of the relative role of the state and social actors was characterised by the redefinition of intervention forms. The rule of the market became the foundation for the interaction between state and society. The main objectives were the opening-up of markets, privatisation and economic stabilisation. The opening of markets, together with the dynamics of selective competitiveness, led to a reconfiguration of domestic capitalism. This was true in the industrial sphere, with its influx of foreign capital, displacement of activities and restructuring of property in various sectors through an extremely intense process of fusion and acquisition. Privatisation also operated as a vector for the appropriation of public property by globalised capital circuits, notably in segments that demanded strong investment and technological innovation. Liberalisation and privatisation provided the input for the stabilisation policy carried out by the executive branch, and in turn highlighted its strategic mediation role ultimately materialised by the new regulatory framework that was set in place.

Liberalisation introduced new actors and new forms of regulation, created agencies governed by the principle of autonomy, but was not able to erase the legacy of the interventionist state and the strong executive branch. On the contrary, the new institutions imposed themselves upon previous ones and now operate in an environment with more regulation. Examples are new agencies in the sphere of economic policy and other areas of public policy.

Together these processes moved Brazilian capitalism in the direction of liberal variety. The role of capital markets as a mechanism of financing increased and huge enterprises emerged. In addition to integration in financial circuits, new forms of market coordination were created, especially with a regulatory matrix based on the operation of autonomous agencies, as already mentioned. None of this would have been possible without the stabilisation plan that created a new currency – the Real – following a very well-established strategy of control of the banking system. Fiscal responsibility also became a fixed rule to be followed by governments at all levels of the federation. Fear of a return of inflation became a central aspect in the dynamics of the economy, and would remain so in the period to follow, when new state-centred mechanisms were set up after the ascension of the Workers Party to power.

Elements of this liberal orientation, especially those related to the principle of monetary stabilisation (autonomy of the central bank, fiscal restraint, high interest rates and fluctuating exchange rates), became established and framed the economic policies of the post-reform governments. However, the late timing of the reforms occurred at a conjuncture when the deepening of the state-centred developmental model engendered resistance to contested frames of reference. Even the elites – entrepreneurial, political and bureaucratic – took quite a long time to embrace the neoliberal credo. Trade unions, free to organise in the context of a newly installed democratic regime, opposed privatisation. While the state was reduced in size by the reforms, it nonetheless preserved intervention capacities through the maintenance of several strategic bureaucracies and the control of some public enterprises in areas such as oil exploitation.

Another dimension that reveals continuities in terms of early choices of the developmentalist tradition concerns the nuclei of efficient state bureaucracies. The state reform implemented during the Fernando Henrique Cardoso government preserved certain nuclei of technical and bureaucratic excellence and maintained development institutions such as the National Development Bank (BNDES), which had been created in the early 1950s as an agency to promote and finance development. During that government, while it was in charge of implementing privatisation, the BNDES clearly demonstrated that it was playing a role as prominent as during the developmentalism phase. Despite an apparent interruption in the agency's mission, as it was responsible for carrying out neoliberal privatisation, the continuity of its trajectory is explained by the strict adherence of the constitutional precepts defined when it was created during the second Vargas government in 1952 – namely the support of projects that encouraged job creation. Guided by principles of career promotion and flexible adaptation to governmental priorities, the BNDES then equipped itself and broadened its scope, especially after Lula took office in 2003. In addition to the BNDES, where exceptionally few positions are politically appointed and where strictly Weberian criteria of performance evaluation are in practice, other bureaucracies can be mentioned: the Ministry of External Relations (*Itamaraty*), the Central Bank and Petrobrás.

This result can be traced back to the government's decisive initiative to give the BNDES a prominent role, rendering it the nucleus of an institutional network that coordinates development activities, finances private investment, sets up industrial policies and acts to promote counter-cyclical policies in times of crisis. The Lula government sought to redefine the BNDES role, to turn it into a promoter of stimulus for the private sector with a magnitude and reach without parallel in Latin America, in terms of significance, size and diversity of function. This redefinition sought, on the one hand, the implementation of an industrial, technological and trade policy (PITCE), which innovated in terms of a series of new credit lines available to small and medium-sized enterprises, and also increasing support to export activities.[4] The second phase of industrial policy was adopted more recently, in 2008, and was geared towards the development of the productive structure (PDP).[5]

Highlighting the role of the BNDES in Brazilian capitalism would mean questioning the current idea that the trade and capital market dynamics explain, by themselves, the country's recent economic performance (Almeida 2011). In a similar direction, Santana (2011) also shows the role of the BNDES and of the pension funds of both public banks and state companies that have been crucial for the stabilisation of macroeconomic variables that nowadays affect the labour market and important sectors of Brazilian industry. In turn, these actors secure an advantage in the capacity to innovate and compete in the global market and establish a space in which their interests can be intermediated and guided towards the formation of new productive coalitions. Last, but not least, the Development Bank has enacted a number of counter-cyclical measures to neutralise the negative effects of the international financial crisis.[6]

As to state structures, continuity of trajectory can be best expressed in terms of the maintenance of strong and efficient niches of bureaucracy. A number of administrative reforms occurred after the creation of interventionist capacities in the early 1930s, and the expansion of cadres only halted during the period of market reforms, when there was an indiscriminate shrinking of the state apparatus. The number of personnel recruited into the state bureaucracy decreases dramatically from 1995 to 2002: from a total of 19,675 people down to 660 in 2001, and only 30 in 2002. The recovery occurred just after 2003, when again state capacities were reinforced through recruitment processes aimed at restoring intervention: back to 7,220, up to 22,112 in 2006 and 19,360 new personnel in 2008. A total of 154,671 new administrative cadres were added to state bureaucracy in order to meet new needs in the 2003–08 period (see the preliminary data in Souza 2011). Sousa also shows that new personnel were added especially in strategic ministries such as finance, planning, budget and management.

6.4 The rise of labour through institutions of electoral democracy and changes in state–society relations

In the previous sections, we have already seen that the timing of the market reforms together with resistance towards new frames of reference helped to preserve the state *structure* and that much of the recovery of the state *capacity* to intervene occurred when the Workers Party came to power with the election of President Lula in 2003. It is worth mentioning, in addition, that the nature of capitalist relations changed with the increasing inclusion of labour in the financial circuits, new modes of regulation and the progressive opening of the state apparatus to labour-related segments. Lula can be said to be the craftsman of a new mode of capitalist development in Brazil. Three aspects of the new characteristics of the state and its relations with society are worthy of attention: first, the creation or reactivation of broad corporatist forums for the formulation of political guidelines in different spheres; second, elite executive positions in state enterprises being awarded to groups with a union background; and finally, the fact that the union sectors become partners of the capitalist model due to the increasing role that pension funds play in financial dynamics and in the support of development projects. These tendencies indicate, on the one hand, a movement towards the democratisation of the access to the state apparatus in many of its areas, and, on the other, a possible inclusion of labour interests in the workings of the productive regime. Altogether, institutional mechanisms connecting major economic actors to the state also make up for new forms of extra-market coordination in Brazilian capitalism.

Regarding the first aspect cited above, it is worth pointing out the forums involving civil society participation in the identification of public policy priorities and the formulation of directives in many areas. We can mention the arenas that have been more strongly institutionalised since the beginning of the Workers Party government, sometimes seen as a return to authoritarian practices, but which do not replicate in any way the type of corporatist arrangements established during the *Estado Novo*, even though they follow the same consultative tradition that was the basis of corporatism during the Vargas period. These initiatives combined with the central role played by the business interest representation structures developed through time in the direction of economic coordination.

In line with the earlier participation forums created by the Workers Party with the introduction of participatory budgets, we can notice the reactivation of public policy conferences, a mechanism existing since the 1940s but little used, geared towards the establishment of policy-making guidelines in several areas through public consultation. The national public policy conferences are a second activity where state and civil society meet. As a channel of participation as well as by producing consensus and setting substantive priorities, they attenuate the limitations of representative democracy with its electoral intervals. The proposals originating in these forums, moreover, seem to influence legislative activity.[7]

In the same vein of gaining comparative institutional advantages in terms of articulation between the state and the private sector, the Council of Economic and Social Development (CDES) was created in 2003. This institute did not replicate the formulas and characteristics of the period of authoritarian corporatism. At the service of the presidency and reflecting the necessity for more wide-ranging mechanisms of interlocution with civil society, it became a consultancy with the goal to formulate directives for development policies. The CDES is composed of 103 members, 90 of whom are members of civil society organisations and 13 of whom are ministers, plus the president. Like other agencies that are part of a network of institutions, the CDES differs from the corporatist councils of the developmentalist period. It is not a representative body of specific categories and is much less focused on the regulation of business conflicts. Instead, it focuses on the creation of overall consensus and the establishment of guidelines for development, providing guiding principles for the different spheres of government (see Boschi and Lima 2002).

Besides the CDES, we also have to mention the National Council of Industrial Development (CNDI). It was created in April 2004 and put in charge of implementing the main points of the Development Agenda. The CNDI is also a consultative agency. It is responsible for defining the directives for the industrial development of the country. It has a formative role in the formulation of public policies focused on industrial development, infrastructure activities, the creation of legal measures that allow for greater competitiveness of enterprises, and the financing of entrepreneurial activities. Linked to the presidency, the Council is composed of 13 ministers, the president of the BNDES and 14 representatives of capital and labour. CNDI development activities are the enhancement of investment and systemic innovation in the durable consumer goods industries, as well as the linking of governmental agencies, universities and research institutions for partnerships utilising sectoral funds from the Ministry of Science and Technology. Finally, in December 2004, an executive agency was created – the Brazilian Agency of Industrial Development, or ABDI – with the objective to implement industrial development policies. This agency seeks to 'execute and articulate actions and strategies of industrial policy by supporting innovation and development in order to improve the competitiveness of the productive sector'.

In another vein, recent studies (d'Araujo 2009) suggest a progressive occupation of elite positions in the state apparatus by unionists. Other studies argue for the importance of pension funds in the new dynamics of Brazilian capitalism, for these have become essential resources for the state to count on for investing in productive activities and development (Santana 2008a, 2008b). Pension funds have also become relevant in the sense of transforming unionised sectors into partners in financial dynamics (Jardim 2009). Based on data from this literature, one can conclude that there is a considerable tendency towards the democratisation of the state through the effective incorporation of unions and worker entities. From the bi-partite corporatist model of the 1930s and 1940s, they were excluded until the 1980s.

In this new context, it can be said that Brazilian capitalism, through the dimension of politics and access to the state apparatus by a democratically elected, union-based government, ended up acquiring a social democrat character. Furthermore, the democratisation of political life by the creation of consultation facilities and broad neo-corporatist forums shows that the country is heading in a direction of societal corporatism, in contrast to the state corporatism that existed during the developmentalist period that lasted until the 1980s.

6.5 Crisis, a statist shift in trajectory and policies of social inclusion

In this section, I will focus on the reactions of the Brazilian economy to the financial crisis of 2008, with the objective of highlighting the effect of trajectory and previous institutional characteristics on the performance and characteristics of the variety of capitalism in point. As opposed to other crises that have struck the worldwide capitalist system in recent years, the recession that began at the end of 2008 as a result of the deregulation of financial markets did not drastically affect the emerging economies (except Russia). What happened could be described as a dip. This was true for Latin America in general as well as Brazil in particular. Moreover, recovery was relatively quick in Brazil, as employment rates surged along with considerable GDP growth. This positive development continued until and including 2010, but then became more temperate and rendered Brazil the slowest-growing BRIC (IMF 2012).

It is true that a set of emergency counter-cyclical policies were adopted in several countries including Brazil, serving as evidence of a revival of an active role of the state in economic regulation and intervention. In the 2000s, some emerging economies in Latin America, and specifically Brazil, have been pioneers in this role as they had already favoured the adoption of interventionist policies in the wake of the market-oriented reforms guided by the Washington Consensus. In Brazil, Chile and Argentina, centre-left governments have implemented policies that revived statism. They signalled a return to, redefined as well as readapted certain principles of developmentalism that had been more typical of the pre-liberal period (Boschi 2008; Boschi and Gaitán 2008a, 2008b, 2009b). In Argentina, the drastic measures taken to deal with previous crises, such as in 2002, were an early sign of the need to break with the neoliberal orthodoxy at the macroeconomic level, a step considered crucial for the reactivation of growth in the lines of a neo-developmentalist model (Bresser Pereira 2009). In other countries, leftist governments re-enacted their own versions of national revolutions as they adopted more radical measures resulting in re-nationalisation or re-privatisation, as in Bolivia, Venezuela and Ecuador.

In Brazilian capitalism, the positive role of state intervention is well known. In the course of time, it has become more coordinated and articulated. Beginning with the modernising revolution implemented by Vargas in the 1930s, followed by the brand of developmentalism of the Kubitschek presidency in the 1950s – promoted industrialisation based on ISI – and completed by the enhancement of the state-led economic model and its expansion in the productive sphere during the years of military rule, an active role of the state as supportive of capitalist development was a crucial element.

The forms of social protection implemented at different points in time evolved from modest yet important social policies aimed at wage earners in the formal labour market. They were gradually redesigned and expanded to what can be called the 'expansion of social frontier' by means of a set of targeted policies aimed at eradicating poverty and reducing inequalities in more recent years. Accentuated by policies that resulted in income concentration throughout the developmentalist period, especially under military governments, structural inequality has been a defining trait in the configuration of Brazilian capitalism. This is a consequence of several factors including a top-to-bottom model of transition that neglected agrarian reform, rapid urbanisation as a result of rural emigration, and social exclusion due to the aforementioned social incorporation via labour corporatism.

In innovative fashion and, in this sense, in contrast to the concentrating tendencies of the latter-day developmentalist matrix, the social inclusion policies to fight poverty and reduce social inequality implemented since the Lula government are a watershed. They opened up a development alternative geared towards the domestic market. The ensemble of counter-cyclical measures were put in place in the wake of these processes and as a follow-up to stabilisation, which, in its turn, was based on the regulation of the financial system established during the presidency of Cardoso from the mid-1990s to the early 2000s.

The option for targeted policies aimed at the reduction of poverty and social inequality had already been an issue on Cardoso's agenda, but it had to wait until the Lula government in 2003 before being elevated to a development priority. This shift epitomises the strategy of development based on social incorporation and expansion of the domestic market. It comprises an array of policies centred around, yet not limited to, the *Bolsa Família*. This is a means-tested income support programme created by the Lula government for poor families to keep their children in school. Bolsa Família is complemented by other initiatives aimed at expanding access to citizenship and to the consumer market. The most recent of this shift is the inclusion of low-income groups in the financial market by giving them access to the banking system via the doorway to micro-credit lines.

Some effects of this policy redirection can already be fully assessed by the data from the National Household Sample Survey 2007 (*Pesquisa Nacional por Amostra de Domicílios*; IBGE 2008). According to a report by the Applied Economic Research Institute (IPEA 2008), which analyses the data produced by the survey, the degree of inequality in Brazil dropped sharply and constantly from the beginning of this century. The exact figure is 7 per cent, meaning that the Gini coefficient dropped from 0.593 in 2001 to 0.552 in 2007, at an annual rate of 1.2 per cent. Nonetheless, for a country with social democratic ambitions, the Gini coefficient is still very high. The Scandinavian countries, traditionally social democratic, have half the Brazilian level of inequality. The trend has been turned around, however, and continued this way (according to Wikipedia, in 2012 the Gini was 0.519), while it is heading upwards in the other BRICs (see the Introduction to this volume). Figure 6.1 illustrates the downward trend in Brazil.

The previously mentioned survey also employed other indicators: the ratio between the average income of the highest decile and the four lowest deciles, as well as the ratio of the richest and poorest quintiles. In both cases, the indicators show an accentuated decline in the inequality in income distribution from 2001 to 2007: the first ratio declined by 5.2 per cent (IPEA 2008). In addition, the study shows that this accentuated drop, which has been observed since 2001, is the longest-lasting one in the last three decades. There have been six continuous years of declining rates of inequality. From 2001 to 2007, the income of those in

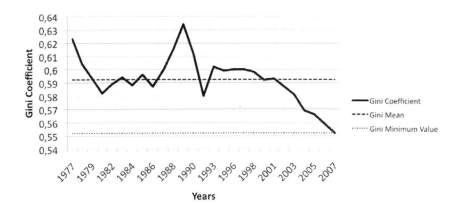

Figure 6.1 Family income inequality rates per capita: Gini coefficient, 1977–2007
Source: (IBGE 2010)

the lowest income bracket has grown significantly and therefore levels of poverty and extreme poverty have lowered. The analysis estimates that the recent decline in extreme poverty occurred at a rate three times faster than would be necessary in order to achieve the Millennium Development Goal, set for 2015, which had already been reached in 2006 (ibid.).

A more recent study by IPEA (2010) reveals that, between 1995 and 2008, 12.8 million people were lifted from absolute poverty (per capita family incomes not greater than half the value of the minimum wage of 415 Reales[8]), meaning that the fraction of the population in this category dropped from 43.4 to 28.8 per cent. In the case of the figure for extreme poverty (per capita family incomes not greater than one quarter the value of the minimum wage), 13.1 million Brazilians have left this condition. The percentage dropped from 20.9 of the population in 1995 to 10.5 per cent in 2008. According to this study, the overall decrease of the levels of absolute and extreme poverty did not occur in a geographically even fashion. In the most modern and industrialised southern region, the decline of both absolute and extreme poverty was strongest with levels of 50 and 60 per cent, respectively. In the poorer agrarian and rainforest centre-west (Mato Grosso), north (Amazon, among other provinces) and coastal north-east, the decline was weakest, with average levels between 20 and 35 per cent. The south-east, the richest region including Rio de Janeiro and São Paulo, was located in between.

According to this same source, regarding social mobility, the 2007 survey contains surprisingly revealing data. First of all, it is evident that there has been significant change in Brazil, as the fraction of the population at the minimum wage level in 2007 comprised less than 30 per cent of the population (IPEA 2008). Some 13.8 million people were moving up the social ladder. The most significant change is concentrated in the transition from the lowest quintile to the second lowest: 74 per cent of all income mobility took place there. Geographically, this upwards mobility has been highly concentrated in the north-east, north and central-west regions. Concerning the transition from the second to the third quintile, the concentration clearly shifts towards the south-east and south regions of Brazil. These two regions account for two thirds (2.7 million people) of those who made the transition.

Based on the positive bias of the drop of poverty rates during the period of monetary stability, the projections indicate the possibility that Brazil will eventually overcome extreme poverty and drastically reduce absolute poverty in the coming years. This is quite promising. When recent rates of poverty decline are projected into the future and supposed GDP growth accelerates again, one can assume that in the near future Brazil will have overcome misery and the rate of absolute poverty will not exceed 4 per cent (IPEA 2010). Figure 6.2 illustrates these projections.

In terms of employment, the development was also positive in the 2000s with annual increases of 1 per cent until 2010 and thereafter a slight downturn that corresponded to the slowing of GDP growth from 7.6 per cent in 2010 to 1.5 per cent in 2012 (OECD 2012b: 270). According to the National

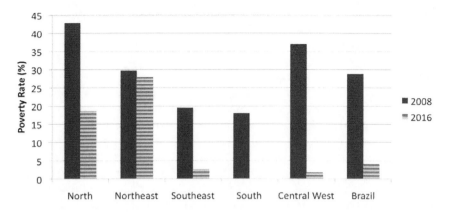

Figure 6.2 Absolute poverty rate in 2008 and projection for 2016 (in %)
Source: (IBGE 2010)

Household Survey 2007 and 2011 (IBGE 2008, 2012), measuring employment of persons 10 (*ten!*) years and older, the formal employment rate was 51 per cent in 2007 and 56 per cent in 2011 (57 per cent in 2009). In the *World Development Indicators* (World Bank 2012b), the rate circles around a level of 65 per cent, but these percentages include informal jobs and are restricted to ages 15–64. Given the huge but only estimated size of the informal sector, these data have to be taken with a pinch of salt, however. The same is true for unemployment, which, according to IBGE as well as World Bank data, has been reduced to currently about 6 per cent.

Nonetheless, the positive employment development fits into the picture of the improved social conditions of life in Brazil during the successive Labour Party governments. In sectoral terms, the outstanding performance of the Brazilian labour market in recent years is due to a great extent to industry and civil construction and has to be related, notably in the latter case, to the projects and works of the Growth Acceleration Plan (PAC). A positive effect also seems to have come from the reduction of the tax on industrialised products (IPI), which sectors such as household appliances, civil construction and automobile industry were responsible for preserving, directly and indirectly (Ministry of Planning 2009). In its entirety, the employment development shows that the counter-cyclical policies worked effectively as they stimulated spending, increased sales, energised the economy and made the consumer spend savings at a time when looming uncertainties provoked by the crisis suggested otherwise. State initiative, not the market, has been crucial here.

Since 2007, the government has concentrated efforts in a new development programme, of which PAC has already been mentioned. Furthermore, illustrating political activity characteristic of the Workers Party government are the National Plan of Science and Technology (2007) and National Plan of Education (2008), with their long-term perspective. Focused on the need to bring industrial production closer to research programmes carried out by academic institutions and other agencies, innovation has been given attention in a number of governmental programmes as well. As compared to the 1990s, when very few initiatives existed on this score, the years since 2003 have witnessed a number of new policy initiatives in innovation. Particularly worth mentioning are the concern with science and technology since 2007, new forms of regulation and new institutions focusing on aspects such as venture capital, and the creation of National Institutes of Science and Technology (INCTs).

6.6 Conclusions

Emphasising the importance of trajectory in the configuration of concrete cases of varieties of capitalism does not imply that each case is unique, thus denying the possibility of framing them according to ideal types. Given the heterogeneity and inequalities present in the configuration of the Brazilian model of capitalism, partly due to the magnitude and complexity of its economy and the size of its population, I hoped to demonstrate that it is in fact possible analytically to privilege certain characteristics over others to come up with an approximation of one ideal-typical configuration. Of course, capitalism is more or less liberal, because the market is one of its essential features. Brazil is a market economy, and Brazilian capitalism is patrimonial to some degree – as has comparatively been exercised in Chapter 2 of this volume. *Specifically*, however, the modality of capitalism that has prevailed in Brazil is a combination of statism and corporatism. This has been highlighted in this chapter. Considering the latter type, it is possible to identify contours of a social-democrat model in the recent past, due to the increased importance of interests linked to labour unions in the dynamics of the productive regime and as a function of neo-corporatist or societal institutional arrangements. Finally, with respect to complementarities, one can notice the presence of apparently contradictory traits, which nevertheless succeed in articulating with each other to produce a result that apparently works.

On the other hand, as the label of an *emerging economy* adequately indicates for some cases, the general direction of the trajectory is clearly ascendant, even if low growth rates and economic performance slowdowns occurred in the period being analysed here. Capitalist development in Brazil is for the most part a continuous and upward process. A comparison with other Latin American cases indicates discontinuous trajectories and downward tendencies, contrasting with the case of Argentina, for example, if we compare the beginning of the development cycle to the more recent period.

Development involves long-term processes that are best analysed in hindsight, at times introducing strong uncertainties about the sense and direction of change in a certain state of affairs. In some aspects, especially those pertaining to structural dimensions, we can truly speak of path dependency in terms of institutional choices taken at the outset of any process and which begin to generate increasing returns as is the case with bureaucracies, and political institutions capable of ensuring governability to enhance the executive's effectiveness. In other aspects, as in the case of the types of social security associated with a certain productive regime, it would be more appropriate to speak of a trajectory that is influenced by changes or reorientations in policies, even in a radical fashion, according to changes in the elite's reference frames.

In the Brazilian case, as I have attempted to show, the long-term analysis indicates path dependency of state institutions in terms of their role as the coordinator of economic activities. At the same time, it indicates the continuation of a trajectory that has undergone adjustments in terms of contested frames of reference concerning social and inclusion policies. Finally, a factor such as the size of the population can shift from being considered an obstacle to development, as it indeed was not too long ago, to becoming a facilitator for development within a new outlook, as it seems to be at this moment.

The present moment seems to indicate the establishment of a virtuous circle due to a unique confluence of factors that combines political choice and luck, starting with the late build-up process of the state apparatus in the 1930s – actually the result of a political rupture with the oligarchic agro-exporting model – and continuing with the progressive and deepening import substitution industrialisation combined with a process of social exclusion and income concentration. Under authoritarian governments and democratic interregna, this logic was pushed forward by the ruling elites in an outlook of growing foreign debit and high inflation that ended up exhausting this type of development model, which remained the predominant one until the end of the 1970s. Concurrently, the transition to a competitive and pluralist democracy, characterised by the expansion of the political universe and the simultaneous emergence of a working-class party, both prior to the economic transition, opened up the possibility of an inward-oriented and more inclusive pattern of capitalist development in the long run. The financial system, which had undergone reforms in the 1970s, was improved and regulated during the implementation of the Real plan. However, previous structures and models, especially those relating to the articulation of the state with the private sector and those related to development and productive activities, remained in place.

A party with roots in the labour movement emerged democratically in the political scene and, after reaching the presidency, implemented developmentalist policies, while maintaining the principles of monetary stability established by the previous government through the administration of interest rates and public spending. The main thrust of this government is the priority given to poverty and inequality reduction through social policies. What can appropriately be labelled the 'expansion of the social frontier' opened up the doorway to a new development model based on the possibility of domestic market expansion, without overlooking the insertion in foreign markets, ensured by an extremely diversified and complex export portfolio, of which primary goods and agro-exports are but a few of its components. Combining these tendencies with an incisive foreign policy in the global scenario, characterised by a strong orientation towards regional integration, it is possible to foresee a positive context for development in Brazil. Also, the rich, energetic potential that opens up with the exploration of the *pré-sal* (the oil-containing geological formation on the continental shelf off the coast) constitutes a fortuitous element in these dynamics. This scenario not only further empowers the state as the central actor in a new development model, but also makes it the nucleus of the productive regime.

Accentuated by income-concentrating policies implemented during the developmentalist period, especially during military rule, structural inequality was a defining force in the configuration of Brazilian capitalism, the result of a top-to-bottom pattern of transition, which occurred without agrarian reform and with urban growth resulting from rural migration and social exclusion. Thus, politics geared towards the reduction of these outcomes is a necessary prerequisite in order to break the vicious cycle or the 'negative complementarities' often highlighted in the organisation of the Brazilian productive regime when perceived exclusively from the perspective of enterprises, as they entail the fulfilment of the basic conditions for the inclusion of a vast portion of the population in the labour and consumption market.

In addition to its importance in shaping a project of national development, the role of labour is decisive in terms of its participation in the process of democratisation through electoral institutions. The commitment to democratic institutions guides the political struggle of the working class and frames it within the logic of alliances and strategic coalitions, while at the same time legitimating its incorporation into politics, in much the same way as in the case of European social democracy. Unlike the paternalistic format that characterised the incorporation of segments of the working class in the bi-partite corporatist model of the early stages of industrialisation, the new situation guarantees workers the exercise of power in order to implement an independent government platform – for this very reason, one that is more effective from the perspective of structural and social transformations.

Ultimately, here I have dealt with legacies, trajectories and distinct moments that have led to the present-day configuration of the Brazilian variety of capitalism and the possibilities of development and growth in the context of post-neoliberal globalisation. The rhythm and shape of market-oriented reforms were drastic in the cases of Chile and Argentina, while in Brazil the late implementation and social resistance to them served to preserve elements of the country's developmentalist past, especially in terms of state capacities. Yet Brazil, despite this tradition of greater state interventionism, has operated under great competitive pressure, with a type of capitalism that has been adequate for the functioning of financial markets, increasingly based on open capital enterprises, which tend to be internationalised and, above all, with macroeconomic policies that have quite strictly protected the foundations of stability and functioning of the market.

The role of politics in shaping the Varieties of Capitalism (VoC) stems from the need to knit and maintain coalitions of support to a developmental project involving potentially conflicting interests in the long run. Problems will certainly exist and can be envisaged vis-à-vis the China factor from the point of view of negative impacts in the domestic productive structure (specialisation in primary products for exports to the detriment of industrial production), furthering a delicate balance between interests of large agribusiness, the primary goods export sector and local industry backed up by a powerful financial sector on one hand and labour on the other.

A final word with regard to the fact that upward trends are in principle capable of suffering reversals, thus leading to further redefinitions in the nature of the Brazilian VoC, or any other for that matter. As already mentioned, the challenge posed by China as to the reconfiguration of the international capitalist system indeed may constitute a decisive factor in this respect. If negative complementarities exist as to some segments of business, the vicious circles entailed in low productivity traps, lack of investment in innovation at the level of firms and lack of interest by the private sector in furthering educational reform and training programmes can only be broken by an active role by the state aiming to reshape domestic capitalism, either through incentives or strong, effective industrial policies. Investment in education, innovation and infrastructure are key elements in this respect. As I tried to show, there are positive endogenous dynamics underway, although the risks of de-industrialisation are far from being neutralised. In spite of a positive demographic scenario, the possibilities of sustaining a model of growth based on the expansion of the middle classes via social policies and, therefore, centred on the consumption of these segments are not unlimited. Some sort of redefinition based on neo-Keynesian alternatives for expansion of infrastructure, together with a more competitive industrial sector based on innovation and a more skilled labour force, are essential aspects for the continuity of what has been referred to as a neo-developmentalist project of capitalist growth in Brazil.

Notes

1 An alternative view is that of Latin American capitalism characterised by a co-existence of hierarchical, non-competitive, family-owned companies with enterprises in cutting-edge fields, which innovate, go international and are likely to be active in capital markets (see Doctor 2010; Schneider 2009).

2 Comparing Brazil to Mexico is interesting. The trajectories of both countries were originally similar in terms of their accumulation and political regimes. Marques Pereira and Théret (2009) show how the positions adopted by these two countries headed in divergent directions after the crisis of the 1970s.

3 This acknowlededgement does not need to obscure the role of social actors in the configuration of institutional arrangements nor the variable dynamic of the relationship between the executive and legislative branches. In the context of re-democratisation and in the period of reform in the late 20th century, the legislative branch gained a more active role (Diniz and Boschi 2004) despite the acceptance of the executive's supremacy (Figueiredo 2001; Figueiredo and Limongi 1999).

4 The function of the BNDES is determined by its provision of credit for long-term investments with lower annual interest rates, particularly for small and medium-sized businesses. Three main directives guided its actions in the last few years, especially after 2004, with improvements of management routines and procedures, reduction of loan costs and the democratisation of credit access. The amounts the BNDES transferred to

businesses increased, and from 2004 to 2005 rose by 17.5 per cent to 47 billion Reales – a record level for project financing. In the industrial sector, BNDES financing even increased by 48 per cent as compared to 2004 (Boschi 2008).

5 The strategic role of the BNDES is fundamental in order to understand the logic of the productive regime. It could be criticised, however, for its lack of transparency and of clear disbursement criteria (Delgado *et al.* 2008).

6 According to Santana (2011), the BNDES plays a strategic role as a provider of credit precisely at times of financial crisis. This way it provides adjustment mechanisms helping to stave off the harmful effects of crisis on investment rates, employment and growth. BNDES-backed credit lines accounted for 20 per cent of the total credit offered by banks to the private sector. In 2009, the sum of credit offered by the BNDES and by other public banks accounted for 38 per cent of the total credit offered by the banking system. Santana concludes that these investment and credit institutions have become interpreted as an ideological force against the hegemonic liberal assessment regarding bank independence.

7 Preliminary data from an ongoing study (Santos and Pogrebinschi 2009) confirm the indicated role of the conferences for the recent period that corresponds to the Labour Party government, while a more than weak link between conferences and legislation has still to be sustained.

8 In 2013, the minimum wage was 678 Reales (about 335–340 Reales in February 2013). Corrected for inflation, this is a rise of nearly 30 per cent since 2008.

7 The South African variety of capitalism

Nicoli Nattrass

7.1 Introduction

This chapter argues that attempts were made in the early post-apartheid period to forge a more social-democratic and coordinated form of capitalism in South Africa but that this floundered as the government adopted neoliberal macro-economic policies. Black economic empowerment (BEE) policies subsequently undermined an already racially fraught business sector and opened the door to growing patrimonialism and corruption. Organised labour achieved gains in the post-apartheid period in terms of improved labour standards and the extension of industrial-level wage bargaining, but this came at the cost of growing policy inconsistency. Notably, trade liberalisation in the presence of strong labour-market protection and rising real wages exacerbated South Africa's unemployment crisis.

The problem of policy inconsistency is highlighted by the Varieties of Capitalism (VoC) approach, its key insight being that economic growth is shaped by the institutional/policy context and promoted most effectively when these are consistent with either liberal-market or coordinated ideal type 'varieties' of capitalism. We argue that South Africa has elements of both ideal types and is plagued by policy inconsistencies at the heart of the state. Although many of the ideas and practices during South Africa's democratic transition suggested the possibility of a post-apartheid political economy shaped by social accords/tripartite negotiation, this impetus floundered because the state preferred to act unilaterally with regard to macroeconomic policy, business was divided and preferred bilateral engagement with government, and organised labour had a strong ideological preference for managing capitalism through a developmental state tasked with promoting wage and productivity growth.

7.2 South Africa in comparative context

The VoC approach draws a key distinction between two ideal types: the liberal market economy (LME) and the coordinated market economy (CME) (e.g. Hall and Soskice 2001; Hall and Gingerich 2009). In an LME, seen as approximated most closely by North America, the United Kingdom, Australia and New Zealand, firm strategies are mediated by competitive markets: large stock markets and regulatory regimes facilitate hostile take-overs, thus encouraging managers to be particularly sensitive to current profitability, while fluid labour markets with limited employment protection incentivise workers to invest in general skills that can be transported to other jobs. By contrast, firms in a CME (seen as approximated most closely by Germany and the Scandinavian social democracies) operate in an institutional environment that provides greater 'voice' for organised labour and favours incremental innovation and strategic collaboration between firms. Generous welfare and retraining policies on the part of government incentivise workers to make the necessary investments in firm-specific skills. Firms in countries approximating the CME accept higher labour costs (and taxation) as long as the system delivers the necessary skills, productivity growth and long-term finance needed to operate profitably in this institutional and policy context. Where these synergies are not evidenced, economic growth has been slower than in countries approximating either the CME or the LME (Hall and Gingerich 2009).

The strong policy implication is that institutions matter for the type and pace of economic growth. As Hall and Soskice note, firms face a set of institutions that are not 'fully under their control' and companies can be expected to gravitate towards strategies that take advantage of the opportunities provided by these institutions (Hall and Soskice 2001: 15). This raises the tantalising prospect of government being able to affect their national 'variety' of capitalism and its related growth path by changing the institutional environment. For example, in the 1950s when Germany introduced legislation to enhance workers' rights on the shop floor, employers expressed strong opposition; however, once these institutions were in place, they developed production strategies oriented towards high value-added production, which made a virtue out of the necessity of greater worker voice (Streeck 1992). As discussed below, this idea, that governments can create such a 'win-win' situation through institutional design, is powerfully evident in South Africa today.

The VoC approach has been criticised for its tendency towards static and functionalist analysis (e.g. Boyer 2005a; Schmidt 2009; Becker 2012). One way to avoid this danger is to highlight the political processes shaping the nature of institutional configurations and coordination. As Hall and Thelen observe:

> active support for a specific mode of co-ordination must be mobilised on a relatively continuous basis from actors who are conscious of the limitations as well as the advantages of any particular course of action. Achieving and maintaining coordination usually involves the exercise of power, because forging and maintaining particular institutional arrangements creates winners and losers, notably on both sides of the class divide.
>
> (Hall and Thelen 2009: 13)

Politics is shaped not only by conflicts of interest and accordant mobilisation. The way these interests are framed in ideas and discourse by economic and state actors is of central importance, especially at critical junctures where policy makers and stakeholders are not sure how best to understand and pursue their interests. In this regard, discursive institutionalism is useful in that it 'calls attention to the ways in which political actors' ideas serve to (re)conceptualize interests and values as well as (re)shape institutions' (Schmidt 2009: 530). These ideas are, in turn, embedded in different discourses – notably 'communicative discourse' between the state and the general public, and 'coordinative discourse' within the state between policy actors (Schmidt 2008: 309–11). We touch on these issues below with reference to the South African policy debate in the post-apartheid period.

The usefulness of the VoC approach has also been challenged by the substantial institutional convergence – notably falling levels of wage bargaining – that has taken place in Europe since the mid-1990s. However, in a recent review of collective bargaining arrangements, Hayter *et al.* (2011: 235) observe that, with the exception of Germany, Spain and Greece, European wage bargaining systems are adapting rather than weakening. Even where the dominant level of wage bargaining has fallen in countries approximating the CMEs, multi-level bargaining is the norm and this has been consistent with fairly stable levels of coverage of collectively bargained agreements. In other words, bargains at industry or firm level often take place within a floor or framework set at higher levels, or through national initiatives. Like the countries approximating the LME, South Africa has relatively high levels of market capitalisation and inequality (cf. Chapters 1 and 2 of this volume), but, as discussed below, it also shares some characteristics with countries approximating the CME (labour regulation) and has the attendant problem of policy incoherence.

7.3 The South African case

South Africa clearly approximates neither an ideal type CME nor LME. Schneider (2009) suggests that South Africa is more like a Latin American 'hierarchical market economy' characterised by vertically integrated dominant firms, multinational enterprises and weak trade unions. However, while this may have been so under apartheid, the post-apartheid political economy is characterised by politically and institutionally powerful trade unions and much lower levels of vertical integration. In 1994, the gold-mining giant Anglo American controlled 43 per cent of the entire Johannesburg Securities Exchange (JSE) capitalisation, and the top five groups controlled 84 per cent through complex cross-holdings and preferential shares. This apartheid-era concentration had been driven by exchange controls that prevented firms from divesting abroad, so, when exchange controls were liberalised in the mid-1990s, it had a dramatic impact on economic concentration. By 1998, Anglo's share had plummeted to 17 per cent as it 'unbundled' (selling off part of the business to a BEE consortium), listed on the London Stock Exchange and moved its head office to London.

One of the consequences of such unbundling and deregulation has been increased investment volatility. As can be seen in Figure 7.1, portfolio investment has come to play the dominant role in financing South Africa's current account

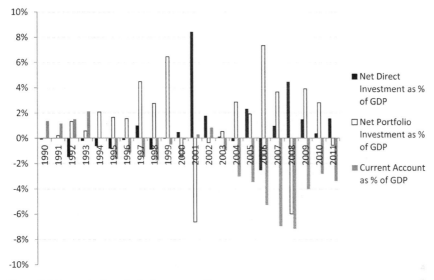

Figure 7.1 Increasingly volatile investment flows
Source: (South African Reserve Bank 2011)

deficit – and these flows are easily reversed. The only significant inflow of foreign direct investment in the post-apartheid period was in 2001 when De Beers mining company was sold to a foreign financial holding company causing both a spike in foreign direct investment and an outflow of portfolio investment capital. Increased reliance on volatile portfolio capital flows, privatisation of state assets and the abolition of apartheid-era agricultural marketing boards has fundamentally transformed the South African business environment in the direction of an ideal type LME, but economic collusion remains a problem (Competition Commission 2008) and South Africa's labour-market regime looks more like an ideal-typical CME.

South Africa is an interesting case for scholars of political economy because there was significant impetus from above (institutional formation at national level) and below (regional accord processes) to create a more coordinated and social-democratic post-apartheid political economy. As argued below, this CME-like vision was subsequently undermined by government when it unilaterally adopted orthodox macroeconomic policies and divided the business sector through BEE and other preferential procurement policies. It was also undermined at the ideological level by an alternative vision put forward by organised labour in favour of a developmental state and which down-played class compromise.

South Africa today contains elements of the ideal types LME and CME. Macroeconomic, trade and investment policy is economically liberal, but, while it is relatively easy to retrench workers for economic reasons, labour legislation is protective in other respects, raising costs to employers (Barker 1999: 19;

Bhorat and van der Westhuizen 2009). South Africa's welfare system is also more akin to the ideal type CME: in 1994, the post-apartheid government inherited a system of social grants that reached 2.9 million recipients (7 per cent of the population) at a cost of 2.1 per cent of gross domestic product (GDP); as of 2010, it reached 14 million people (28 per cent of the population) at a cost of 3.3 per cent of GDP.[1] But unlike the ideal type CME, no significant nor sustained support is provided for the unemployed.

South Africa has relatively high coverage of collective bargaining and routine involvement of trade unions and business in government policy. It also has by far the highest unemployment rate. Between a quarter and a third (depending on the measure) of the labour force is unemployed and less than half of working-age adults have jobs (Nattrass 2011). This is partly because the state has strong regulatory capacity – particularly with regard to tax and labour legislation – and there is thus no significant informal sector to provide jobs for those who cannot find work in the formal sector. This is the crucial difference between South Africa and other middle-income countries – especially in Latin America – where informal employment provides a safety net of sorts.

Unemployment is *the* central economic dilemma facing the country – and one which poses different challenges for economic policy- and wage-setting institutions than is evident in the Eurocentric CME/LME-like paths to growth. In the European CME-like countries, labour-market protection is associated with lower inequality because the wage distribution is compressed and because the unemployed get generous welfare assistance. In South Africa, however, where so many working-age adults are without work or government grants, inequality is driven primarily by the gap between those with some work, and those with none (Seekings and Nattrass 2005). Creating jobs, even at low wages, thus would have a positive impact in terms of poverty alleviation and narrowing inequality. However, for the trade union movement, the priority is protecting and raising real wages, boosting productivity and advocating for 'decent work' for the employed.

Figure 7.2 shows that employment growth was positive in the mid-2000s but that it has been typically lower than that of real output, resulting in a trend increase in aggregate labour productivity. Rising labour productivity is a positive sign in so far as it indicates that the economy is becoming more efficient, but the serious downside of rising labour productivity for a labour-surplus economy like South Africa is that ever-fewer jobs are being created for each additional unit of output.

South Africa's employment problem has strong historical roots. Mining and agriculture were the major employers of unskilled labour under apartheid, but their relative and absolute contribution to employment has fallen over the past four decades. As the manufacturing and services sectors expanded, the apartheid institutional infrastructure was revealed to be a major fetter on development. Business responded to shortages of skilled labour and to the incentives provided by government (e.g. tax breaks for capital investment and negative real interest rates) by becoming more capital intensive. The tragedy of this growth path is

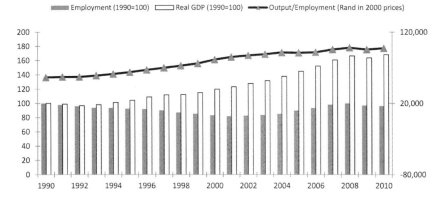

Figure 7.2 Output, employment and aggregate labour productivity in South Africa
Source: (South African Reserve Bank 2011)

that, just as the economy switched from labour shortage to labour surplus in the 1970s, economic growth became steadily less labour-demanding. High and rising unemployment was the inevitable result (Seekings and Nattrass 2005).

7.4 The democratic transition: the rise and fall of a CME-like vision in South Africa

When South Africa made the transition to democracy, it did so under the long shadow of apartheid. Racial discriminatory policies had left the economy with persistent skills shortages and a business community divided on sectoral, cultural and racial lines (Nattrass 1997b). Some labour-market reforms had been undertaken in the 1970s, notably the ending of job reservation for whites only, and from 1979 the system of collective bargaining was de-racialised. This effectively legalised black trade unions, allowing black workers to participate in industry-level bargaining, and this system persists, fundamentally unchanged, today.

Representative employer organisations and trade unions set wages in bargaining councils and these are typically extended to non-parties on request by the minister of labour. Where no bargaining council exists, the government's Employment Conditions Commission sets minimum wages. This amounts to a relatively strong level of wage coordination.

As political opposition to, and protests against, apartheid mounted during the 1980s, key figures within South Africa's business elite held secret meetings with the African National Congress (ANC) in exile, and started engaging with opposition leaders inside the country (van Wyk 2009: 9–10; Handley 2008: 53–54). These consultations continued after 1990 when the ANC was allowed to operate legally in the country and South Africa began the transition to democracy. Nelson Mandela, who became South Africa's first president, received regular briefings from the business leaders and often dined with Anglo American patriarch Harry Oppenheimer (Waldmeir 1994: 256–57).

When Mandela was released from prison in 1990, his first speech called for nationalisation of the mines and monopoly industry. This was a long-standing demand of the anti-apartheid movement – as embodied in the 1955 Freedom Charter.[2] However, ANC economic policy changed sharply during the early 1990s. In 1991, Mandela attended the Davos conference where he met with Li Peng, the new premier of China, who said to him: 'I don't understand why you are talking about nationalisation. You're not even a communist party. I am the leader of the communist party in China and I'm talking privatisation.' Mandela subsequently repeated this conversation at every ANC discussion on the economy and sought to assure investors that their investments would not be endangered by nationalisation (Green 2008: 345–46). Davos proved to be a pivotal moment, laden with different meanings and interpretation. According to Pallo Jordan, an ANC cabinet minister from 1994 to 1999, 'those who wield power in the West told Nelson Mandela in no uncertain terms that any actions that threatened property rights would invite their wrath', and that 'a chastened Mandela returned to South Africa from Davos ready to drop the nationalisation of the mines' (Jordan 2012). Tito Mboweni, Mandela's minister of labour and subsequently Reserve Bank governor, disagrees. Noting that he was at Davos with Mandela and helped him rewrite the plenary address that was drafted 'by well-meaning folks at the ANC office in Joberg', Mboweni argues that Mandela's decision to drop nationalisation was sparked by his discussions with communist party leaders in China and Vietnam and that 'It was not Western capitalists. Not at all. I bore witness to that' (Mboweni 2012).

As ANC policy documents became increasingly market friendly and liberal (Nattrass 1994), left critics started accusing it of forging an elite pact that would leave existing power structures intact (e.g. Bond 2000; McKinley 1997). However, as Cyril Ramaphosa, a leading ANC architect of the transition to democracy, noted of the time, an ideological groundswell was evident and 'many people were beginning to feel more and more comfortable with a mixed type of economy' (quoted in Green 2008: 339). Even the South African Communist Party (SACP – a long-standing ally of the ANC) engaged in some soul searching as its secretary-general penned an influential piece titled 'Has Socialism Failed?' (Slovo 1990), criticising Stalinism and asserting the importance of democratic freedoms. The stage thus seemed set for the adoption of a more social democratic or coordinated variety of capitalism in South Africa.

Further impetus was provided by spontaneous regional accord processes. In the Eastern Cape Province, business organisations, labour and government came together to form the Eastern Cape Socio-Economic Consultative Council. This helped to foster more cooperative relations between business and the state (in one initiative, private-sector advisers were seconded to local government to help with public infrastructure revitalisation), but was less successful with regard to capital–labour relations. Whereas business wanted organised labour to 'put the region first', i.e. to negotiate regionally specific wages and not to participate in national strikes, this was resisted by organised labour (Nattrass 1997a). In other respects, however, organised labour started cutting productivity-related pay deals with employers in order to save jobs (Nattrass 1995). In 1991, mining employers and the National Union of Mineworkers (NUM) entered into agreements where workers accepted wage restraint and various forms of profit sharing. The NUM acting general secretary noted: 'The choice we had to make was whether to drive a higher wage increase with less employment in the industry as a real prospect – or whether we try to achieve maximum employment, and at the same time augment wages and win social rights.'[3] Although these innovative wage-setting agreements fell apart three years later (because there were concerns about the process of profit sharing and union officials were concerned about the potentially divisive effect of having the more profitable mines pay workers relatively higher wages[4]), they demonstrated that even South Africa's militant trade unions were capable of concluding agreements that recognised the trade-offs between wages, employment and profitability. The possibility that South Africa could move towards CME-type coordinated wage setting seemed very real during the early 1990s and substantial energy was put into developing regional- and national-level social democratic institutions.

In 1990, organised business and labour agreed, in principle, to create a national forum to discuss the impact of labour relations on the economy. This resulted in the National Economic Forum being set up in 1992 – a body that was subsequently transformed into the National Economic Development and Labour Council (Nedlac) by one of the first pieces of legislation passed by the new democratic government in 1994. According to the leading business representative, Nedlac was intended to 'inaugurate a new era of inclusive consensus-seeking and ultimately decision-making in the economic and social arenas' (Parsons 2007: 9). Unfortunately, this hoped-for vision failed to materialise.

The first problem was that attempts to create the kind of peak-level business organisation necessary for national coordination were plagued by racial divisions. An organisation called Business South Africa (BSA) was formed to represent South Africa at the International Organisation of Employers conference in 1994, and it subsequently went on to represent business in Nedlac. However, this unity was fragile and tensions soon arose and the organisation fragmented between the predominantly black and white business organisations. It took eight years before a new umbrella body – Business Unity South Africa (BUSA) – was created, but even then racial divisions continued to simmer. These were exacerbated by the government's BEE policies (discussed more below), which further undermined the incentives for black and white business to work together. Eventually, in 2011, the major black organisations left BUSA to form the Black Business Council.

The second problem was that the government referred some, but not all, of its economic policies to Nedlac. Thus, while the post-apartheid Labour Relations Act was negotiated in Nedlac prior to reaching parliament, this was not the case with the infamous 1996 Growth, Employment and Redistribution (GEAR) macroeconomic framework, which sought to restrain government spending (to deal with a debt crisis), boost private investment and liberalise aspects of the labour laws to promote job creation (DOF 1996). Although GEAR also called for a social accord, this aspect was drowned out in the public debate by condemnation – especially from organised labour – of its supposedly 'neoliberal' macroeconomic and labour policy proposals (Nattrass 1996).

The discursive problem for the ANC was that, when it fought its first election, it had in its Reconstruction and Development Programme (RDP) promised to boost employment creation through demand-driven growth and state-facilitated infrastructural and housing programmes (ANC 1994). This vision had been supported by a group of ANC-aligned economists calling for expansionary fiscal and macroeconomic policies (MERG 1993). However, this option was rendered unworkable by the sharp increase in the government deficit (from 1.5 per cent of GDP in 1990 to 7.3 per cent in 1993) that took place during the transitional period. By 1996, when the ANC first obtained full control of government, controlling the debt burden and stabilising the economy had become a priority – and even more so in 1998 after the Asian currency crisis. The Ministry of Finance (now known as the National Treasury) responded with GEAR – a document intended to boost private investment by emphasising 'fiscal discipline' and to pave the way for greater 'regulated flexibility' in the labour market (Nattrass 1996). Left trade unionists, however, saw it as the beginning of the '1996 Class Project' – i.e. the 'co-optation by White monopoly capital to weaken the National Democratic Revolution and reverse the gains of the 1994 democratic breakthrough'.[5]

The public debate and protests over GEAR involved both communicative discourse (with the public) and coordinative discourse between the ANC and its alliance partner – the Congress of South African Trade Unions (Cosatu). In both cases, the National Treasury lost the rhetorical battle. Cosatu attacked government for imposing these policies unilaterally, for reneging on its electoral promises, by proposing changes to the labour legislation (by appearing to be supporting a 'two-tier' labour market) and selling out to business. The ANC responded by maintaining its stance on fiscal discipline and continuing with trade liberalisation, but it backed away from any changes to labour-market policy and effectively ceded the Ministry of Labour to Cosatu.

While this served the ANC's immediate political needs by offering an olive branch to its alliance partner, the result was an entrenched oppositional relationship between macroeconomic and labour market policy making at the heart of the state. Whereas the National Treasury was and continues to be staffed by mainstream economists, the director-general of labour and the deputy director-general in charge of labour policy and industrial relations are both long-standing trade unionists, and the current and previous ministers of labour were a former chair of the Cosatu Women's Forum and head of the teacher's union, respectively.

The result of this institutionalised ideological mismatch between two crucial organs of economic policy making has been an uncoordinated set of economic and labour-market policies inimical to employment growth. While labour-market

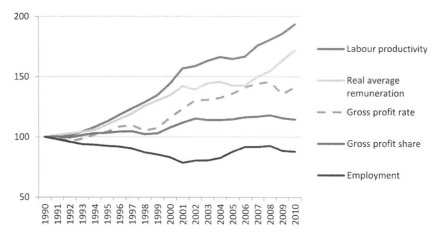

Figure 7.3 Trends in profitability
Source: (South African Reserve Bank 2011)

policies sought to raise and extend the coverage of the minimum wage while increasing non-wage costs of employment for business, tariffs on imported manufactured goods were reduced sharply, from 23 per cent in 1994 to 8.6 per cent in 2004 (Edwards 2005). As was the case in other countries attempting trade liberalisation under rigid labour-market conditions and fiscal austerity (OECD 1999: 156–59), the results were costly in terms of employment, especially of unskilled labour. Figure 7.3 shows that employment fell as real average remuneration rose during the 1990s (and that this trend is evident in more recent years too). Note that labour productivity rose faster on average than real wages, thereby enabling the gross profit share and rate to rise. The winners were thus the employers who remained in business and those workers who kept their jobs. Some of these workers, notably the most skilled, enjoyed substantial wage increases, but for the most part average real wages rose because relatively unskilled low-wage jobs were shed (see also Seekings and Nattrass 2005).

Many factors contributed to the shedding of unskilled labour. These included the impact of labour legislation, which raised the cost of employing labour, and the operation of the wage-bargaining system, which set wage floors by industry (binding predominantly unskilled labour), all of which provided strong incentives for firms to substitute machinery for workers, and to have a smaller, better-skilled, better-paid and more manageable workforce (see Moll 1996; Nattrass 2000). Even policies designed to improve the machinery of labour dispute resolution, notably the introduction of the Commission for Conciliation, Mediation and Arbitration, had the unintended effect of burdening employers further by operating in an unnecessarily legalistic way, thereby increasing the risks to employers of hiring labour (Bhorat and van der Westhuizen 2009). This, in conjunction with the trade liberalisation, put substantial pressure on firms, especially those in the more labour-intensive tradable sectors such as clothing (Anstey 2004: 1842).

Other policies, notably industrial policy, with its focus on recapitalisation contributed further to rising capital intensity (Kaplan 2003, 2007). Although the post-apartheid economic planners had hoped that recapitalisation would provide a strong basis for growth – thereby expanding employment opportunities in the future, industrial policy proved disappointing. As Kaplan (2007: 98–99) points out, industrial policy was never consolidated under one arm of the state, but remained scattered and even 'hidden' – such as support for arms production. Industrial policy was also bedevilled by having to address too many strategic concerns, including regional development, small-business development, racial transformation in hiring, skills development, moving up the value chain, promoting labour-intensive growth, and BEE. The result was that industrial policy as a whole became less well targeted and effective. Attempts to create structured forms of engagement with business (including national investment summits and regional forums as part of the spatial development initiative) failed to build the necessary trust and information flows required for effective industrial policy.

The key institutional casualty was Nedlac. According to a representative from the presidency (during Mbeki's term of office), Nedlac failed because Cosatu was fearful that business was bypassing Nedlac and influencing the state directly – as it was believed to have done with regard to GEAR. Others argue that government was primarily to blame and that its failure to discuss GEAR in Nedlac was symptomatic of a broader desire to maintain control over policy.[6] However, according to Jayendra Naidoo, Nedlac's first executive director, the key issue was that organised labour was never comfortable with the tripartite aspect of Nedlac, preferring instead to have bilateral engagement with business over wages/working conditions and with the ANC over policy.[7] This, in turn, was facilitated by an alternative policy discourse emanating from the trade union movement in favour of a strong developmental state designed to assist and discipline capital while promoting productivity growth and 'decent' work.

7.5 The contrasting growth vision from organised labour

During the early 1990s, intellectuals aligned with the trade union movement grappled with how to engage with capitalism. Constrained by the collapse of socialism in Europe to accept market-oriented policies, they nevertheless saw themselves as radical socialists engaging with both state and business on a strategic level to establish a basis for socialism in the future (Gall 1997). Arguments by visiting social democrats and Australian trade unionists for class compromise and linking wage increases to productivity growth failed to resonate within Cosatu (Nattrass 1999). According to Harcourt and Wood, this reflected deep historical antagonisms: 'Years of intense conflict, precipitated, at least in part, by a system of "Racial Fordism" at the workplace, have radicalised workers, so that calls for wage moderation and cooperation with management would probably be perceived as signs of co-optation' (Harcourt and Wood 2003: 95–96). Thus, even those unionists who accepted the need for class compromise may have felt themselves discursively trapped by this history.

Instead, the trade union position eventually coalesced into support for a capitalist system shaped and managed by a 'developmental' state, which would support a high-wage, high-productivity growth path through complementary labour-market and industrial policies (e.g. Vavi 2008a, 2008b). This 'high productivity now' strategy assumes that even in a labour-surplus country like South Africa it is necessary to increase labour productivity today in order to project the economy onto a more 'dynamic' growth path tomorrow (Nattrass 2001). It adopts aspects of the East Asian development experience – notably a role for active industrial policy (Wade 1990) – while disregarding the central characteristic of the East Asian growth experience: that surplus labour was drawn initially into low-wage, labour-intensive sectors, and that the economies were only projected onto a more capital- and skill-intensive labour demand growth path once that surplus labour had been absorbed and average skill levels improved (Birdsall and Jaspersen 1997). Instead, it asserts the need for 'living wages' and 'decent work', thereby employing a rhetorical strategy inimical to low-wage, low-productivity employment strategies. Precisely because it prioritises 'decent' high-wage jobs for the employed, it is, ironically, a reincarnation of the old trickle-down story: increases in productivity supposedly drive the rising tide of economic growth; the unemployed must get trained and wait for the employment waters to rise.

This approach has strong echoes of Porter (1990), in that it assumes national competitive advantage rests primarily (if not solely) on the adoption of 'best practice technology' and on active state involvement in support of innovation and otherwise generally encouraging structural change in favour of higher value-added activities. In the hands of trade union intellectuals, this approach was adapted to include the use of wage pressure to 'force' South African capitalism onto the cutting edge and up the value chain (Nattrass 2001).

An early influential statement of this vision was articulated by the Industrial Strategy Project (Joffe *et al.* 1995), a trade union-linked think tank that favoured using wage growth and employment protection to 'encourage restructuring up the value chain rather than restructuring towards low-wage, low-productivity forms of production' (ibid.: 213). They situated the South African labour movement's approach to industrial restructuring within this particular logic, pointing out that it was 'premised on the need to move South African firms out of their low-wage, low-skill, low-productivity vicious circle in which they are out-competed by the second tier, newly industrialising countries' (ibid.: 214). In other words, not only does it take it as a given that South Africa's wage structure is too high to compete with the newly industrialising countries and that the appropriate response is for the state to assist firms to become more productive (which typically implies more capital-intensive production) in order to compete on a higher-wage, high-productivity trajectory, but it assumes that destroying existing (competitive) low-wage production is part of the strategy. This resonates with popular notions that, if low-wage production is allowed to exist, there will be a 'race to the bottom'. Such ideas serve to denigrate low-wage, labour-intensive jobs and deflect attention away from the fact that high- and low-productivity operations can co-exist where they compete in different product markets.

In 2009, in the cabinet reshuffle following Thabo Mbeki's replacement as president by Jacob Zuma, Ebrahim Patel was appointed to the newly created Ministry of Economic Development, tasked with coordinating and planning the government's economic policies. Patel, who had been general secretary of the South African Clothing and Textile Workers Union in 1999–2009 and national labour convenor for Nedlac, is deeply committed to using government resources and policies to promote high-wage, high value-added forms of production. The first policy document produced by the Ministry of Economic Development, the New Growth Path plan, is centred on this vision (Nattrass 2011), as is industrial policy with its Porter-like emphasis on 'world-class manufacturing', upgrading, etc. (see e.g. DTI 2011).

Cosatu's vision thus appears to be at the centre of the government's growth strategy, but there are signs that it is not necessarily a hegemonic position. For example, the Minister of Finance Pravin Gordhan recently suggested that changes to South Africa's labour dispensation may be necessary to prevent further job losses in the clothing sector – a view subsequently endorsed by Trevor Manuel, a previous minister of finance.[8] There appears to be major differences of opinion within government about economic policy, but, under Jacob Zuma's political leadership, there have never been any serious attempts to resolve them. Certainly since Rob Davies (a member of the SACP) became minister of trade and industry, there has been better coordination between trade and labour policy in the sense that there have been no further unilateral decreases in tariffs, and government assistance to industry has been conditional on firms complying with labour legislation. However, tensions remain between the Department of Trade and Industry (DTI) and Labour on the one hand and the Ministry of Finance and the Reserve Bank on the other (both of which are regarded by the left as pursuing unnecessarily restrictive fiscal and monetary policies).

7.6 Race, business and the state

The potential for economic coordination has been undermined further by racialised and increasingly clientalistic relations between business and the state. The cordial relationship between the ANC and the white business elite that had been evident during the transition to democracy unravelled in early 1997 when the head of Standard Bank offered to assist government with its 'capacity' problems by suggesting that senior executives be seconded to government as 'part of their commitment to transformation' (Gevisser 2007: 686–87). Thabo Mbeki, then deputy president and increasingly responsible for economic affairs, was apparently offended by the suggestion that the new government needed assistance from white business. It was only once the white corporate sector created the 'Business Trust' in 1998 to raise money for job creation and education that he re-opened lines of communication by creating a working group through which he would meet with big business leaders (Handley 2008: 90–91).

The situation for black business, however, was very different. The ANC government, especially after Mbeki became president in 1999, championed BEE to encourage rapid redistribution of share ownership from white to black hands. This had a significant impact. Just as the old white corporate sector had maintained power and control over vast swaths of the apartheid economy through interlocking directorships and shareholdings, a now tightly connected new black elite serve on each other's boards and are closely connected to the national government (Calland 2006: 265; van Wyk 2009; Seekings and Nattrass 2011). This is justified by an unabashed ideology that frames the promotion of a black business elite as both just and good for South Africa (Seekings and Nattrass 2011). SACP critics, however, regard this as a justification for cronyism and as a betrayal of the revolution (Turok 2008; SACP 2006). Ironically, though, beneficiaries of BEE include the politically connected black elite and trade unions, which, by virtue of their largely black membership, are able to invest pension funds and debt in BEE deals. Notable amongst these have been the Mineworkers Investment Company (owned by the NUM), Kapanao ke Matla (owned by Cosatu), Sactwu Investment Group (owned by Sactwu) and the Union Alliance Holdings (owned jointly by Cosatu and other trade union groupings).

The first major BEE legislation was the 2000 Preferential Procurement Framework Act, which required that government favour tenders from black-owned companies. Further BEE legislation was promulgated in 2003 to promote sector-specific 'charters' specifying targets in terms of BEE deals (Hirsch 2005; Gqubule 2006; Turok 2008: 155–57). This was backed up by legislation, for example the Minerals and Petroleum Development Resources Act of 2004, which required mining houses to become BEE compliant if they wanted to renew their mining licences. The basic model for a BEE deal is that black investors buy a discounted stake in a company (sometimes through holding companies or Trusts), financed through a combination of bank loans (sometimes underwritten by the company involved), expected dividend flows and increases in share price.[9] In return, the company is able to gain informal access to the black political elite, lucrative government contracts, mining licences and the like.

In February 2007, the government gazetted new 'Codes of Good Practice' for so-called 'broad-based' BEE in an attempt to spread the benefits more widely.[10] It widened the range of business practices, such as affirmative action, employee share ownership for which firms could earn BEE 'points'.[11] As the BEE status of supplier firms affects the BEE status of contracting firms, BEE compliance is now being strongly transmitted through value chains. In the process, the business environment has become fundamentally re-racialised, although this time to the advantage of (especially politically connected) black rather than white people.

Increasingly, the interconnections between the ruling elite and BEE beneficiaries have raised the spectre of corruption and nepotism, with the attendant
worry that South Africa may be moving towards a more patrimonial variety of
capitalism. In the mid-1990s, the Treasurer of the ANC Thomas Nkobi
favoured the creation of a party-aligned business structure. Although this was
never endorsed as official policy, Jacob Zuma's adviser Shabir Shaik went on to
create Nkobi Holdings (of which the ANC had a 10 per cent stake), a conduit
later shown to have received payments from companies in return for lucrative
contracts mostly in the arms industry, but also government contracts such as the
supply of South African driver's licences (KPMG 2012: 27). Other similar
shady investment vehicles were created and South African newspapers regularly
carry stories and exposés of corruption, where tender processes are abused
and contracts awarded to individuals close to the state. As Robinson and
Brummer concluded in 2006, 'the murky relationship between money
and politics has been at the heart of almost every major scandal faced by political parties and the government since 1994' (Robinson and Brummer 2006: 2).
Most infamously, there has been a steady drip of revelations in the media about
the corrupt arms deal, in which *inter alia* millions of Rands were channelled
through Nkobi Holdings to Jacob Zuma. Schabir Shaik was found guilty in
2005 on two counts of fraud and corruption for his profiteering in the arms
deal through Nkobi Holdings. Jacob Zuma (now president) was depicted by
the judge as having a 'generally corrupt' relationship with Shaik. Subsequent
attempts to prosecute Zuma failed as the prosecuting authority folded in the
face of political pressure and influence.

The arms deal is one of the most contentious issues of post-apartheid South
Africa. It has resulted in civil society mobilisation in favour of full disclosure, in
resignations from parliament by disgusted ANC members of parliament, and
various public interest lawsuits. Part of the justification for the arms deal was
that the firms awarded the armaments contracts would deliver 'offset' investments – i.e. would promise to invest in other parts of the economy, thereby
creating jobs. Alec Erwin, the erstwhile minister for trade and industry, was one
of the most fervent supporters of the arms deal, supposedly because the offset
deals could boost South Africa's industrial policy (Green 2008: 474–75; Feinstein 2007: 232). However, less than a quarter of the paltry 12,000 offset-related jobs
were actually delivered (Feinstein 2007: 232).

The growing number of examples of graft, corruption and the abuse of state
power in the allocation of contracts has harmed South Africa's reputation in the
business and international communities. So, too, has the erosion of trust in
South Africa's police services. Jackie Selebi, the national police commissioner
from 2000 until 2008, was convicted of corruption and sentenced to 15 years
in jail (though he was released on supposedly medical grounds after serving
less than a year), and South Africa's criminal investigation and prosecutions authorities have been plagued for more than a decade by political intrigue. Figure 7.4 plots
the Heritage Foundation's changing index of perceived corruption and other
aspects of 'business freedom'.[12] Perceived freedom from corruption improved

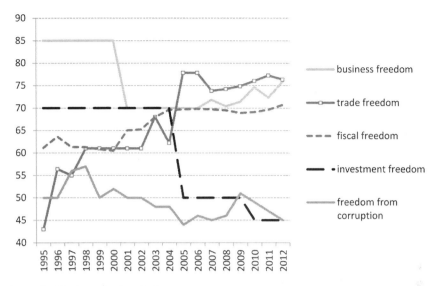

Figure 7.4 Business freedom indices
Source: (Heritage Foundation database 2012)

in the late 1990s, but has been on a sharp trend decline since 1998. Thus, while fiscal and trade 'freedom' (basically a measure of trade liberalisation and orthodox fiscal policy, both of which shape the macro environment) trend upwards, the micro business environment (corruption, controls on investment, BEE, labour laws barriers to entrepreneurship) have trended the other way. The World Bank governance indicators are even more negative about post-apartheid South Africa's ability to control corruption. As shown in Figure 7.5, perceived regulatory quality and especially control of corruption have been trending sharply downwards in the 2000s.

The rational strategy for white business, in this environment, is to act defensively and for individual capitalists to look after their own narrow interests, perhaps through continued unbundling and disinvestment, and otherwise by engaging in BEE deals and the like in order to obtain government patronage through the back door. The rational strategy for black business is to accumulate capital on a parasitic basis (by obtaining shares in return for political favours and connections), rather than participating in the productive sector of the economy where conflict with labour is inevitable. Those that do venture into the productive sector are likely to lobby the government for additional support, such as tariff protection and even bail-outs.

In short, there are strong indications that a form of crony capitalism is developing with a peculiarly South African twist in which organised labour lobbies government on behalf of employed workers and its investment interests. However, unlike in Zambia and Ghana where this is a serious problem (Handley 2008), the South African economy is large enough for there to be many other routes

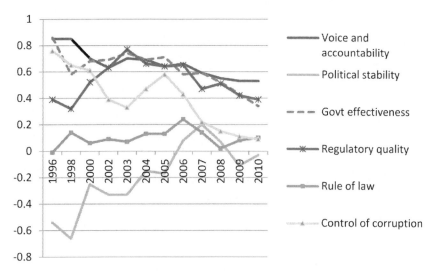

Figure 7.5 Governance indicators, 1996–2010 (scale -2.5 to 2.5)
Source: (World Bank 2011)

for aspirant capitalists to make money, even though BEE regulations may act as a tax on that effort. Furthermore, there exists a dynamic civil society that has resisted the government, notably on AIDS, poor education delivery and corruption in the arms deal. Neo-patrimonialism thus may grow, but as long as civil society remains strong, and the economy reasonably diverse, it is unlikely to become the key defining feature of the post-apartheid variety of capitalism.

The rational strategy for organised labour is to continue lobbying the government for pro-labour policies and to involve itself in BEE deals. What this means for the prospects of a more coordinated variety of capitalism emerging in South Africa is an open question. Iheduru (2002) points out that organised labour's involvement in business deals (so-called 'comrade capitalism' or 'business unionism') blurs the lines between workers and owners, thereby giving workers a 'material stake' in the economy and helping to build a black business class. He argues that this will make cross-class compromises more likely and be good for 'social concertation'. However, as long as unions continue to reject wage restraint and insist that it is the job of government to mobilise development state-type policies to boost productivity and move firms up the value chain, then class compromise is unlikely. Indeed, one would expect unions to demand industrial policy support when companies run into trouble. For example, in 2011/12, 66.7 million Rand was provided by the DTI to Seardell, a clothing and textile producer part owned by Sactwu, for modernisation, upgrading and the financing of additional capacity. Ironically, though, this large injection failed to stem the tide of job losses as Sactwu continued to push for higher wages.

7.7 Conclusion

Post-apartheid South Africa thus appears to have CME-like labour regulations entrenched alongside growing neo-patrimonialism, but it also, somewhat paradoxically, operates in a more liberal economic environment – at least on some dimensions. For example, Figure 7.4 shows that South Africa's 'fiscal' and 'trade' freedom increased between the 1990s and 2000s, largely because of trade liberalisation and the country's fairly orthodox fiscal and monetary policies. The problem for businesses – especially those in the internationally competitive labour-intensive product markets – is that the combination of high and rising labour costs and trade liberalisation places a serious squeeze on profitability (Nattrass and Seekings 2012). The situation, as depicted in Figure 7.2, may benefit firms operating in higher-wage, higher-productivity niches, but it comes at the cost of growing capital intensity and persistently high unemployment. Racial inequality has declined sharply in the post-apartheid era, but unemployment coupled with no support for the unemployed has resulted in the persistence of both poverty and inequality, albeit in new, class-based forms (Seekings and Nattrass 2005). It is a variety of capitalism that provides CME-like support for the employed, patrimonial and increasingly corrupt support for sections of black business, while effectively excluding the predominantly unskilled, unemployed from the fruits of growth.

South Africa's failure to create sufficient jobs to address the unemployment crisis is posing serious challenges for economic policy and social policy. Recent attempts to boost youth employment through a wage subsidy scheme met with strong resistance from organised labour, which has remained implacably opposed to the idea that jobs should be created through lowering the cost of employment. Despite growing concern about job losses (notably in clothing), bargaining councils continue to use the legal system and local sheriffs to shut down firms that fail to pay the negotiated minimum wage. Calls by the minister of finance and the head of South Africa's Planning Commission for a more employment-friendly labour-relations system reflect a growing disquiet in government circles about the role of institutions in exacerbating unemployment.

One option is to move more in the direction of an ideal type CME and introduce social welfare for the unemployed, which will lower inequality but increase the tax burden. However, this is resisted by business and organised labour because South Africa's relatively narrow tax base means that all income earners would have to pay higher taxes. Another option is to move more in the direction of an ideal type LME with regard to labour laws while retaining statist components (e.g. industrial policy) where they are effective. This, however, is strongly resisted by organised labour. The framing of those who propose labour-market reforms as 'neoliberal' and as 'sell-outs' makes it very difficult to have a productive discourse about how best to build an inclusive political economy in South Africa.

Finally, South Africa's adversarial labour relations pose major challenges for any coordinated solutions involving class compromise. Most worryingly, violent strikes disrupted the mining industry in 2012 – most notoriously in August when over 47 miners were killed by the police. The once powerful NUM, which had brokered profit-sharing deals in the gold mining industry in the early 1990s, appears to have lost ground to a rival union, with a particularly adversarial approach to wage setting. This has all but stalled investment in South African mining. The Western Cape wine industry has also suffered from spontaneous and organised protests and demands that the minimum wage in agriculture be doubled. In neither the mining nor the agricultural wage disputes have any efforts been made to link wage demands to profit-sharing arrangements or job retention. Although there are some employee share ownership schemes in mining and agriculture, these are rare. Overall, there appears to be no immediate prospect for a more coordinated, social-democratic variety of capitalism in South Africa.

Notes

1 The increase is attributable to the introduction of a child support grant and extensions in eligibility criteria for the old age pension. See South African Reserve Bank *Quarterly Bulletin*, September 2011: 52–53.
2 See scnc.ukzn.ac.za/doc/HIST/freedomchart/freedomch.html.
3 Interviewed in *The South African Labour Bulletin* 16(2), 1991: 19.
4 Personal communication with NUM officials in 1994.
5 www.cosatu.org.za/show.php?ID=2534.
6 Interviews with business representatives and the spokesman for, and executive director of, Nedlac (May–October 2008).
7 Discussion, 16 October 2008.
8 For a report on this, see: mg.co.za/article/2011-08-25-cabinet-no-pravin-we-wont-relax-sas-labour-laws.
9 Interview with a broker of BEE deals, February 2009.
10 Government Gazette 29,617, 9 February 2007.
11 Information on legislation, charters, BEE scorecards, etc. can be found on the Department of Trade and Industry website: www.thedti.gov.za/bee/beecodes.htm.
12 See www.heritage.org/index/book/chapter-1.

8 Emerging on an illiberal path

The Turkish variety of capitalism

Işık Özel

8.1 Introduction

The Turkish market economy has gone through major transformations in the last few decades. In this emerging country with daring aspirations to be placed in the *first league* of advanced countries and to play a significant role in world politics, the encounter between the institutional legacies and the newly transplanted institutions has caused considerable tension, at times, endangering the effectiveness of the latter. Despite such aspirations and substantial changes that have taken place in the recent past, institutional characteristics of the Turkish market economy display major differences from those of the advanced countries. This chapter suggests that some of the key institutions and patterns of governance inherited from the *old regime* persist, bestowing on the Turkish market economy an illiberal character. By and large, market liberalisation coexists with old institutions and norms, while the former is often moulded by the latter. Demonstrating the coupled processes of change and continuity with respect to recent transformations in Turkey, the chapter asserts that the Turkish Variety of Capitalism (VoC) is situated between patrimonial, statist and liberal varieties construed as ideal types for emerging countries (see Becker's Introduction to this volume). The following sections of this chapter will examine the major transformations that have taken place with regard to institutions and policy making throughout the multifaceted market transitions since the 1980s. Following an introduction on such transformations, particularly with respect to state–economy relations, the chapter will focus on several dimensions that help delineate the VoC, including corporate governance and state–capital relations; labour–capital and labour–state relations; social policy; and privatisation.

Despite the drastic changes that have taken place in the last few decades, market economies in emerging countries diverge from those of the advanced countries. In their canonical study, Hall and Soskice (2001: 19) construct two ideal types of VoC for advanced countries, liberal and coordinated market economies, while clustering several countries, including France, Italy, Greece, as well as Turkey, into the 'Mediterranean' variety, where different forms of non-market coordination prevail in the existence of extensive state intervention and a large agrarian sector. The dominant role of the state in the emerging countries is a well-known characteristic. In cases where capitalism has prevailed without interruption – but in varying shades – this feature has been inherited from the state-led development era, which prevailed between the 1930s and the 1980s in most of these cases. Although the experience of these countries that implemented a state-led import substitution industrialisation strategy (ISI) is considered rather common, a state's control and/or influence in multifarious processes including market dynamics, interest representation, wage bargaining and corporate governance reigned to different extents in all emerging countries.

The Turkish market economy, which has gone through an extensive liberalisation following more than half a century of state-led development, provides a good example to demonstrate the coexistence of drastic change and significant continuity. It carries many aspects of the ideal types explicated in the Introduction, mainly falling into the types of statist, patrimonial and liberal. Although statism has declined substantially, particularly with respect to state ownership of the means of production, political regulation over the market still prevails, along with the persistence of the hierarchical organisation of firms. In general, the Turkish state mostly let go of its grip on production, but it has kept its intervention in the market mechanisms and players, a process that has been intensified in the 2000s and early 2010s. Patrimonialism is also persistent as the patron–client relationship and favouritism between the state and the key players in the market continue, accompanied by clientelistic networks and widespread patronage distribution (Sayarı 2011).

An interesting pattern in Turkish state–business relations gives clientelism a vibrant approach that each government creates its own clientele with whom it nourishes cosy ties in exchange for hefty incentives and/or rents. This pattern inevitably fosters the emergence of new players, thus power struggles between the old and the new, which in turn affects institutional development and collapse (Mahoney and Thelen 2009). After all, the state's domination over society embellished by the patriarchal notion of the 'father state' was inherited from the Ottoman Empire, kept throughout the state-led development era, and eventually was mostly sustained in the context of market transition, despite the (practical and discursive) retreat of the state from the economic realm. Such continuity is fairly similar to that in some of the BRICs, but mostly in Russia (see Vasileva's chapter in this volume). Hence, the Turkish market economy carries important characteristics of statist and patrimonial types of VoC, while it evidently has some key features of the liberal type as well, based on long experience with private property and the market, which has increasingly been freed of restrictions since the 1980s.

Amongst the emerging countries, the Turkish market economy displays striking similarities to that of Brazil in the BRICs group, especially regarding its relatively longer capitalistic experience marked by state-led development strategies as well as market transitions still manoeuvred by the respective states (Boschi in this volume; Özel 2014). Akin to many middle-income countries, Turkey went through junctures throughout the 20th century with respect to development strategies and transitions as well as structural transformations from agrarian to largely industrialised market economies. After having implemented ISI for about five decades, in the 1980s, these countries began to open up, coupled with the process of re-democratisation, often referred to as *dual transitions*, as the next section will explicate.

8.2 The transformation of state–economy relations

Swinging on a pendulum as a developing country involved in some of the major clubs of the advanced countries, such as the Organisation for Economic Co-operation and Development (OECD), Turkey is now considered an upper-middle-income country, one of the G20, with a fairly developed industrial base akin to those in the BRICs and other emerging countries. In fact, this indicates a substantial transformation, as the Turkish economy was predominantly agrarian a few decades ago. Although the initial efforts in industrialisation began in the 1930s, the major surge was undertaken from the 1960s, the period when the ISI regime was institutionalised. The share of agriculture in gross domestic product (GDP) diminished from 52.8 per cent in 1961 to 18.1 per cent in 1990 and 9.1 per cent in 2011. Despite such a major decline in the overall value added of the agricultural sector, the rural population still constitutes about 35 per cent of the overall population (a decline from 69 per cent in the 1960s), indicating concerns over productivity. The share of industry in GDP has increased since the 1960s (from 17.6 per cent in 1961 to 27.9 per cent in 2011), but the share of services increased further (from 29.6 per cent in 1961 to 63 per cent in 2011), congruent with the worldwide trends (World Bank 2013a).

The 1980s are widely considered a turning point for the Turkish political economy due to the launching of a substantial market liberalisation programme in 1980. Up until then, the Turkish economy was highly protected under the strong grip of the state, exemplifying statist and patrimonial VoC. Although Turkey was one of the pioneers in the emerging countries with respect to launching liberalisation, its market transitions have taken a protracted form, coupled with backlashes. Following a belated *lost decade* in the 1990s, the Turkish economy has shown a striking performance in the first decade of the 21st century. Institutional reforms carried out in the aftermath of severe economic crises under the tutelage of the European Union (EU) in the context of Turkey's protracted accession process, as well as international organisations such as the International Monetary Fund (IMF), have played a central role in facilitating the recent performance and relative resilience of the economy to the current global crisis (Öniş 2010: 56). By attaining an annual growth rate of 7.2 per cent between 2002 and 2007, the GDP reached US$775 billion, making Turkey the 16th largest economy in the world and the 6th largest in Europe, although it is still situated in the ranks of an upper-middle-income economy with a GDP per capita of $10,410 by 2011 (World Bank 2013a).

One of the most drastic transformations in the Turkish economy since the 1980s is the increasing openness – from 9.1 per cent in 1979 to 52.2 per cent in

2008, signifying substantial trade liberalisation (Central Bank of Turkey 2010). Following the change in the economic development strategy in the 1980s, a considerable surge in exports occurred, paving the way for an export-led growth path which thrived especially in the 2000s. The export volume has increased more than tenfold since 1990, from $13 billion in 1990 to $135 billion in 2011. Interestingly, the ongoing global crisis has not halted this trend, except for a sizeable decline only in 2009 when the volume of exports diminished by 27 per cent, but almost recovered in the two following years (Turkish Statistical Institute 2013a).

The composition of exports also changed similar to those in other emerging countries. Manufacturing exports, most importantly in the automotive, consumer electronics and home appliances, textiles and clothing sectors, increasingly constitute the overwhelming majority of Turkish exports − a major change when the previous composition of exports, mostly agricultural, is considered. Particularly in the last decade, income growth began to be highly correlated with export growth, exemplifying the establishment of an export-led growth trajectory. Another major trend of the last decade in terms of foreign trade is the diversification of the exports market towards outlets outside Europe, which helped to recover the export volume after the first impact of the 2008 financial crisis (Kirişçi 2009).

Antecedents of market liberalisation

As in several other emerging countries, particularly those in Latin America, state-led development in Turkey began in the 1930s and further institutionalised in the 1950s, and lasted until the 1980s. Although the new republic mostly pursued liberal economic policies following its foundation in 1923, it then embarked upon a state-led development path in the 1930s in line with the responses of most developing countries when encountering the impact of the Great Depression (Pamuk 2008). Akin to other emerging countries, this period signified the emergence of a model where protectionism and state interventionism in the markets were accompanied by increasing authoritarianism and shades of corporatism, legitimised by the nationalist ideology as well as the aspirations to *catch up* with the advanced world, in line with the modernisation rhetoric of the early republican era (Özel 2014).

Turkey's close alliance with the market economies of the capitalistic Western bloc in the Cold War era did not impede state intervention coupled with price controls, a protectionist international trade regime, and strict barriers to international capital movements until the 1980s. Turkish *etatism* was placed in the Constitution in 1937, engendering large state investment. Turkey's experience with the ISI was initially positive, with a high rate of growth in GDP (5–6 per cent) until the early 1970s when the resource-dependent economy was severely hit first by the oil crisis, and then the debt crisis (Turkish Statistical Institute 2013b). The second phase of the ISI, which entailed heavy industries, was launched in the 1970s, increased the debt burden to an unsustainable level by the late 1970s. These shocks bolstered a devastating inflationary cycle and recession, with the Turkish economy succumbing to a foreign exchange crisis, hobbling its import capacity and resulting in a triple-digit inflation rate rising to 100 per cent in 1980 (Turkish Statistical Institute 2013c).

In the midst of these crises, Turkey launched a thorough market reform programme in 1980 under the auspices of the international financial institutions (IFIs), making the country one of the forerunners of the market reform process in the emerging countries. Yet the Turkish market economy is remote from the liberal ideal type. Although the state has mostly retreated from the owner-ship of means of production, it often intervenes in the market as well as in institutions, organisations and actors, and distributes selective incentives. Thus, the Turkish case denotes a large space of intersection between patrimonial, statist and liberal varieties of the market economies, entailing tensions between institutional legacies and the newly transplanted institutions, at times impairing the effectiveness of new institutions.

Institutional legacies of the developmental state 'à la Turca'

The process of economic reforms in Turkey has taken a zigzagging path given the legacy of an interventionist-cum-authoritarian state and resistance by the existing institutions along with the interests entrenched in those. Both the institutional legacies and the size of the anti-reform coalition made the process a rather protracted one marked by major zigzagging wherein discretionary policy making, populism and de-institutionalisation were central (Eder 2004). The most important of those institutional legacies that affect economic gov-ernance are centralisation, executive discretion and bureaucratic fragmentation, while interventionism and authoritarianism in varying shades impinge on the making and implementation of rules. In the process of transition from state-led development to *free market* economy, then, to an illiberal regulatory state, the Turkish state has carried along some of its key characteristics that previously defined its functioning as a particular developmental state with low capacity to steer economic development and negotiate with societal actors (Waldner 1999). It preserved its provision of selective incentives, though the clientele has shifted over time.

In the initial phases of transition, politicians who encountered increasing political competition usually undermined the necessity of establishing a solid institutional framework for reforms. They opted to proceed through bypassing the existing institutions based on a short-cut pragmatic stance by means of dis-cretionary tools, leading to liberalisation accompanied by de-institutionalisation. One of the most significant examples of undermining institutional frameworks was the privatisation process, initiated and conducted in the absence of an apt legal framework up until the mid-1990s (Atiyas 2009).

The widespread use of executive discretion has become common practice since the beginning of the market transition process. It was, indeed, facilitated by a major institutional change granted by the 1982 Constitution, which institutionalised the executive bypassing the legislature.[1] The 1982 amendments enable the executive to 'share' legislative power, although the 7th Article of the Constitution strictly prohibits the delegation of legislative power. Strikingly, many important changes in institutions and policies that have marked the process of transformation since the 1980s have been established by executive decree. The decrees provided the executive with the means to bypass actual or potential opposition to changes in rules and policies, and they have been widely used throughout the market transition process, akin to the process in Russia (see Vasileva's chapter in this volume). The thin base of the pro-reform coalition, particularly at the beginning of the reforms, along with the available ground provided by the Constitution escorted reforming governments into this pragmatic path partly bypassing democratic processes. In fact, prevalent use of executive discretion and its recent intensification has led to a system nearly hosting de facto presidentialism, despite the existent parliamentary system.

The legacy of short-cut problem solving includes bypassing constraints and resistance by making new rules and organisations whenever the old ones do not cooperate in the manner desired by the executive (Özel 2003, 2012a). Combined with the legacy of politicisation of bureaucracy, such pragmatism resulted in an oscillating pattern between institutionalisation and de-institutionalisation in Turkey by a constant change of rules and procedures, which has marked the market reforms. The distrust between politicians and bureaucrats that has persisted since the 1950s provided an apt ground for de-institutionalisation. While the so-called bureaucracy's hegemony has been challenged incessantly by politicians, the politicisation of bureaucracy became prevalent to divest bureaucrats' resistance to policy implementation (Heper 1987). Throughout the market transition process, authority constellations were often changed, bureaucratic agents were fragmented, and new agencies were created in order to overcome resistance.

Contrary to the common discourse that depicts the Turkish state as strong, I argue that strength tends to be conflated with interventionism and, at times, with authoritarianism. Although it maintained heavy interventionism in the respective market, the Turkish state suffered from limited capacities throughout most of the 20th century with respect to steering economic development, implementing policies and negotiating with societal actors. Although the state capacity increased in the last decade when compared to increases in certain emerging countries like Brazil, it has been limited (Boschi in this volume).

Transitions in the Turkish market economy

In the group of emerging countries, Turkey was one of the first to launch market reforms, but later followed a vacillating track. The state sustained its control over the market as well as its role as a 'patron', offering new incentives to new 'clients' in different phases of the transition, meanwhile creating new allies as the transition proceeded.

The milestone of Turkish transformation was the reform programme popularly known as 'January 24 decisions', a comprehensive policy bundle entailing a wide range of liberalisation in the areas of financial markets, foreign trade, capital markets and privatisation of public enterprises. However, the realisation of these ambitious goals not only took a long time, but also diverged from the initial orthodox rhetoric. Although the 1980 package announced the opening of the Turkish economy to the world, the implementation of trade liberalisation in its initial phases emphasised export promotion rather than overall liberalisation, turning *de jure* Washington Consensus into de facto mercantilism in the initial phases of liberalisation. Import liberalisation gained new momentum with the initiation of the customs union process in 1989. Albeit launched in 1985, privatisation mostly stalled until the 2000s.

Resonating with Latin America in the 1980s, the 1990s are usually referred to as 'the lost decade' in Turkey as macroeconomic indicators worsened, privatisation stalled, stabilisation efforts stumbled, and expansionary fiscal policies shaped economic policy making. The credibility of the government's policies diminished in this period and populism marked the policy-making process (Eder 2004). The critical changes were the capital account liberalisation (1989) and launching the customs union agreement with the EU (1995) in the midst of severe instability. Widely referred to as 'premature', capital account liberalisation enabled arbitrage-seeking short-term capital inflows and made high interest rates sticky, triggering a vicious cycle between governments, commercial banks and individual investors (Rodrik 1991; Yeldan 2006). Successive governments exacerbated this cycle by increasing indebtedness and interest rates to attract short-term capital flow in order to finance their expansionary fiscal policies and debt. Hence, the Turkish economy was trapped in debt and sticky rates of interest and inflation, impairing investment. Between 1989 and 2000, fixed private investment increased only 5.2 per cent on average, while changes in private stock (contribution to growth) averaged 0.17 per cent (based on 1988 prices) (Turkish Republic Undersecretariat of Treasury 2004: 5). The culprit behind the disastrous spiral was not only the governments that financed deficits by further borrowing, but business also contributed by transferring its resources to debt instruments and securities, engendering a 'speculative rentier accumulation' (Yeldan 2006: 208). Such a spiral gave rise to three major financial crises emerging in 1994, 2000 and 2001, the latter being the most severe in Turkish history.

The crisis of 2000–01 became an important milestone in Turkey, spawning major institutional reforms along with macroeconomic stabilisation. The crisis caused a drastic downturn in the Turkish economy, signified by a 6–7 per cent annual drop in GDP. Political stability also followed course as the unstable short-termed coalition governments came to an end in 2002, replaced by a strong one-party government that has recently started its third term. In accordance with the 'post-Washington Consensus' and emerging belief in good governance, the Turkish economy has gone through a process of institution building and reform mostly fostered by international and regional actors, such as the IMF and the EU, usually referred to as a 'double external anchor', the conditionalities of which have played a major role in policy change and institutional reform (Öniş and Şenses 2009: 4). Turkey's official candidacy to the EU in 1999 and the launch of accession negotiations in 2005 became critical turning points, pushing Turkey to undertake a broad range of reforms to fulfil the Helsinki criteria, engendering a Europeanisation process in several policy areas and institutions (Müftüler-Baç 2005).

The most important institutional reforms introduced in the post-2001 governance are the independence of the Central Bank, the rise of an illiberal *regulatory state*, social policy reforms and fiscal discipline. The independence of the Central Bank has been a major institutional reform and it played a key role in macroeconomic stability attained after decades of turbulent instability (Alper and Hatipoğlu 2009: 59–60). The often-acknowledged resilience of the Turkish economy in the context of the current financial crisis is mainly provided by a regulatory framework and fiscal discipline, which have worked as filters against the crisis.

In the context of instituting regulatory reforms, nine independent regulatory agencies were established, mostly under the aegis of IFIs and the EU.[2] Although regulatory frameworks in some policy areas, including finance and competition, have mostly converged with international standards, some others suffer from a broad range of constraints particularly in the implementation stage. Moreover, a process of dismantling the regulatory agencies began in 2012: the Tobacco and Alcohol Market Regulatory Agency was closed down, while some other agencies were stripped of their power in terms of regulating and supervising their respective sectors (Özel 2013).

A major paradox is that the Turkish state has been in the process of endangering some of the most essential institutions, which facilitated such resilience against the crisis. Some of the rules that enhanced the Turkish market economy's capacity to resist against the crisis have been established by the regulatory agencies endowed with substantial authority and independence. Although the regulatory state, which mostly works through independent agencies is on the rise throughout the world, the current government in Turkey has curtailed the independence of those agencies, as political control, already prevalent at the de facto level, is now granted by recent *de jure* changes entailed by decree no. KHK/649, signifying a process of de-delegation of authority by the executive, concomitant with the legacy of de-institutionalisation (Özel 2012a). This indicates the reluctance of the executive authority to delegate power, justified by its objective to enhance its capacity to respond more flexibly to the ongoing global crisis. Overall, the Turkish regulatory state has espoused an increasingly more illiberal character and the deadlock in EU negotiations accelerated this trend.

One of the most important institutional changes in the political realm since the 1990s has been the curtailing of the role of the military in Turkish politics. As a self-acclaimed guarantor of stability, territorial integrity and secularism, in line with the official ideology of Kemalism, the Turkish military used to play a substantial role in politics, based on what is granted by the constitution. During the reform process bolstered by the EU accession process, the structure and sphere of authority of the National Security Council (NSC), which was one of the central apparatuses through which the military maintained its power in policy making, were redefined (Jenkins 2007). Additionally, the share of military expenditure in the budget dwindled from 3.89 per cent in 2002 to 2.08 per cent in 2012 (Kamu Harcamaları İzleme Platformu n.d.). The alleged coup plots by some military officers and their exposure by the government and the media since 2007 have challenged the military's role in politics further, followed by the enactment of additional amendments eradicating the remaining power of the military in politics (Gürsoy 2012). Nevertheless, the decades-long prevalence of the military in political and economic realm will not disappear immediately and one of the most important marks of this is the powerful conglomerate owned by the Turkish Armed Forces Assistance and Pension Fund, which has 268,112 members (OYAK 2012).

The Turkish case generally exemplifies how reforms might be impaired or sometimes invalidated by previous institutional settings and the entrenched interests in those. Even the recent EU accession process and its strict conditions has not been a panacea for this, because *de jure* formation and existence of institutions in order to fulfil the necessary criteria does not necessarily guarantee their de facto operation. The discrepancies between *de jure* design and de facto operation of various institutions in Turkey can be easily observed through the governance indicators such as the rule of law, control of corruption and voice and accountability. Turkey usually scores in the middle-range category when the BRICS are considered, but is certainly a poor performer compared to most Eastern and Southern European countries. Its governance scores are comparable to those of Brazil, and usually higher than those of China, India and Russia (World Bank 2013b).

Increasing confidence and losing steam for reforms

The political will that emerged in the context of a severe crisis in order to undertake reforms began to dwindle recently, as the executive lost steam for furthering the reform process, accompanied by the resentment about a deadlock in the EU accession process. Such will was initially appropriated by the current incumbent, the Justice and Development Party (JDP), which effectively combined their anti-establishment stance (particularly against the secularist civilian and military bureaucracy) with pro-market ideology, mostly representing 'conservative globalists' (Öniş 2007: 248). Amongst all the political parties, the JDP is so far considered to have the highest levels of commitment to the ideals of liberal economy, the state's withdrawal from the economic realm – even compared to the Motherland Party, the pioneer of market reform in Turkey (Düşkün 2009). Nevertheless, the JDP governments have increased state control over markets in several realms, while maintaining patrimonial patterns and clientelistic mechanisms by means of constructing novel forms of give and take with their allies amongst varying social groups.

The JDP came to power in 2002, forming a one-party government following successive coalition governments between 1991 and 2002. The party's commitment to reforms was more striking in its first term (2002–07), when major institutional reforms were carried out and stabilisation was achieved. Before the global financial crisis emerged, the Turkish economy was one of the fastest growing in Europe and the Middle East, as it expanded at an average rate of 7.2 per cent between 2002 and 2006, coupled with stabilisation as the inflation rate dropped from 35 per cent in 2002 to 6.5 per cent (Central Bank of Turkey 2011). As in other emerging markets, the global liquidity boom of 2000–07 helped such high growth rates in the Turkish economy.

The global financial crisis that emerged in 2007 halted this upward trend. The Turkish economy encountered the crisis in a relatively weak position, with a high current account deficit, low savings rate and resulting dependency on short-term capital inflows. In the presence of such obstacles along with high unemployment and institutional flaws, macroeconomic indicators began to worsen in the second term of the JDP government (2007–11). A persistent – and the most important – problem facing the Turkish economy is the current account deficit, which rose from $22.1 billion in 2005 up to $47.7 billion in 2010, constituting 6.6 per cent of GDP (Central Bank of Turkey 2012). Turkey is particularly similar to South Africa in this respect. For both countries, an alarming outcome of expanding current account deficit is the dependence on short-term capital inflows, which introduces considerable volatility. Figure 8.1 displays the recent increase in the current account deficit.

The decline in the current account deficit in 2009 correlated with the decline in GDP in that year. However, growth resumed again from 2009. An

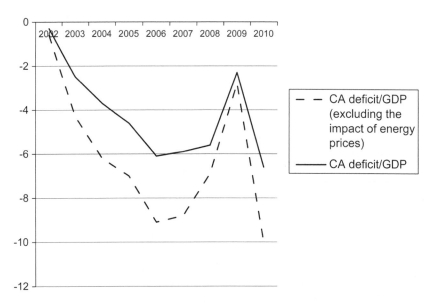

Figure 8.1 Current account deficit in Turkey in %
Source: (Central Bank of Turkey 2012)

important issue to underline is that the 'success' of the JDP governments regarding the recovery from the 2001 crisis, as well as the relatively slight damage by the 2008 global financial crisis, was mainly based on the 'strong economy programme' designed and implemented by the previous coalition government. Yet, this cannot undermine the commitment by both the JDP governments and the Central Bank to implement sound macroeconomic policies. Such a record undoubtedly contributed to the JDP's electoral success based on a cross-class coalition since 2002.

An important dynamic that emerged through the JDP's economic record and consequent electoral success is the emergence of a one-party dominant regime in Turkey. Fortified by its majority in the parliament and the weakness of the opposition, along with the discretionary power of the executive granted by the constitution, the JDP has increasingly ruled as the incumbent of a one-party, dominant regime. After having lost its reformist zeal of the early 2000s, which was bolstered by the EU accession process, the JDP government not only brought the democratic reforms to a standstill, but also increased its interventionism, while expanding selective access to state resources. Thus, certain aspects of patrimonial and statist types of VoC, along with the liberal type, continue to mark the Turkish market economy, while certain communitarian aspects also prevail based on the increasing role of identity-based networks in economic transactions (Özel 2010, 2012b).

8.3 Privatisation and foreign direct investment (FDI) in Turkey

The privatisation process was launched in Turkey much earlier than in most other emerging countries, but its progression has lagged behind those countries. For two decades after its launching in 1985, the cumulative privatisation revenue only reached $9.4 billion, while it was $5.7 billion between 1985 and 1999. The average annual privatisation revenue was about $500–600 million in the 1990s and rose up to $8 billion in 2005–06 (Atiyas 2009: 1, 4). Thus, despite its relatively long history, privatisation only gained momentum within the last decade, particularly after 2004. Additionally, privatisation has moved to infrastructure industries such as telecommunications and electricity, though the divestiture in some segments of the latter is still problematic. Since 2000, the cumulative divestiture totalled $37.3 billion, while the overall total since 1985 is $41.9 billion (PMT 2011). Some of the giant state-owned enterprises (SOEs) have been privatised since 2004 including Turkish Airlines, Turkish Telecom, Tüpraş (refinery), Erdemir (steel), although the privatisation of the last three was launched in the early 1990s but they were all subject to legal obstacles and strong opposition as they were deemed highly strategic.

State-owned enterprises had a major share in the Turkish economy. Between 1950 and 1960, the SOEs already constituted about 60 per cent of total value added in manufacturing, and this ratio went down to 40 per cent at the launch of privatisation in 1985, and then further declined to 18.5 per cent in 2000

(OECD 2011e). There are still SOEs (some to be privatised) and prominent public banks, which constitute about 35 per cent of all those active in the Turkish banking sector, compared to 32 per cent in Brazil and 35.5 per cent in Russia (BRSA 2012: 9).

One of the major factors behind such a protracted implementation was the absence of a legal framework for privatisation in Turkey, as the divestiture of SOEs was deemed a violation of the constitution, and the existing legal framework lacked coherence as it was complex and disorganised, while the agencies and the rules to which they were subject changed constantly up until the late 1990s (Atiyas 2009: 2–4). In line with the legacy of bypassing existing institutions rather than reforming them, successive governments since the 1980s have opted for short cuts to circumvent the laws rather than creating a solid legal framework for the privatisation process.

The argument that 'privatisation was unconstitutional' was broadly used by the anti-privatisation coalition, usually led by the opposition parties and statist intellectuals. Interestingly enough, all parties variably situated from left to right attacked privatisation whenever they were in opposition, but owned and promoted it whenever they came to power, indicating the lack of demarcation between economic policies across political parties throughout the 1980s and 1990s (Düşkün 2009). Starting from the late 1980s, several privatisation attempts were brought to the Constitutional Court of Turkey by the opposition parties and the Court invalidated those cases that had been launched by means of several decree-laws issued to bypass the legal constraints in a pragmatic fashion. A legal framework that thwarted such unconstitutionality of privatisation was established in 1994 by the Privatisation Law, No. 4046, setting out the principles, procedures, authorised agencies and other issues regarding privatisation. Following a series of revisions, the legal framework was finalised in 1997, and began to contain established rules about international arbitration as late as 1999. Later, in 2003, an amendment was issued to accelerate the privatisation process by Law No. 4971, entitled Law Regarding Making Amendments in Some Laws and in the Decrees with the Force of Law Dealing with Establishment and Duties of the General Directorate Turkish National Lottery.

In addition to the legal constraints, the small size of the pro-privatisation coalition and accordingly the lack/inadequacy of a political will to privatise also played a role in the protracted nature of the process (Atiyas 2009; Ökten 2006). The broad coalition against privatisation not only consisted of workers in the SOEs, but also included bureaucrats (not only of the SOEs), public employees, certain segments of the intelligentsia as well as the general public (Ercan and Öniş 2001). In this process of opposition, the internalised statist ideology was effectively used by the opposition parties for which the absence of a legal framework provided a large legitimisation space. The privatisation in strategic sectors proved particularly difficult, as has been observed in the case of Turkish Telecom, the privatisation of which was initiated in 1994, and finalised in 2005.

The JDP has been the most committed incumbent regarding privatisation, which can be assessed based on its party programmes compared to those of other parties since the early 1980s (Düşkün 2009). The widespread scepticism toward privatisation and particularly about divestiture to foreign capital, which has been owned by all parties across different ideological stances, has not existed in the case of the JDP, the governments of which have played an important role in changing the prevalent discourse against privatisation and foreign capital inflows, as the section below demonstrates. However, expansion of privatisation process in the 2000s can also be explained by strong incentives for the JDP governments to privatise, given the rigid fiscal adjustment programmes in the context of the post-2001 conditionalities imposed by the creditors (Atiyas 2009).

Although the privatisation process has not been completed and there are still 25 companies in the privatisation portfolio besides those not included, the state withdrew entirely from some sectors such as cement, dairy production, forest products and petroleum distribution, while more than 50 per cent of its shares have been privatised in sectors such as tourism, iron and steel, textiles and sea freight. A few of the public banks have been privatised and some of the largest banks in Turkey are still public.

One of the most remarkable changes in the Turkish economy is the increase in FDI inflows since the 2000s, partially tied to the recent surge in the privatisation process. Turkey went through an extremely sluggish path regarding FDI inflows and it was identified as a country with low FDI attraction throughout the 1990s. It received drastically lower inflows compared to the BRICs and other emerging countries' averages (see Becker's Introduction to this volume). However, there has been a remarkable upward trend in FDI inflows into the Turkish market, increasing from $684 million in 1990 and $1 billion in 2000, to $22 billion in 2007, catching up with some of the BRICs, like Brazil (UNCTAD 2010). In line with the global trend, FDI inflows showed a substantial decline after the emergence of the global financial crisis in 2008, dropping to $9 billion in 2010. FDI outflows from Turkey also followed a similar trend, declining from $3 billion in 2008 to $2 billion in 2009 (ibid.: 43).

A significant cause of such discrepancy between Turkey and the BRICs in the 1990s was the weak institutional framework to attract FDI along with economic and political instabilities including high inflation, high interest rates and high public debt along with an unstable political environment in which nine different governments came to power. In a business environment where the state crowded out the market by becoming the rival of the corporate sector in the financial markets, foreign capital hesitated to invest in Turkey. With the existence of such severe instability, a protracted process of start-stop reforms marked by weak commitments of the incumbents and scepticism towards foreign capital fed by populist policy making curtailed potential FDI inflows to the Turkish market. An insolvent and indebted state, chronic inflation, credit difficulties and insider credit transactions accumulated and triggered the 2001 crisis in Turkey, which provided another backlash against the FDI inflows. Nonetheless, fast recovery after the 2001 crisis led to a spurt of FDI inflows. Recent improvements in public finances, which helped economic stabilisation, the EU accession process and recent improvements in the legal, administrative and regulatory framework including the new law on FDI legislated in 2003 (Law No. 25141), the establishment of the Advisory Council, the abolition of the Treasury's authority in providing permits, the easing of the process of starting business, and the privatisation programme all facilitated positive signals to investors, prompting FDI inflows. Another important institutional change in this regard was the establishment of the Coordination Council for the Improvement of Investment Environment (YOIKK) in 2001 (restructured in 2012), in the charge of the Ministry of Economy. YOIKK has helped to reduce red tape and implement a reform programme to rationalise regulations and policies regarding investment, domestic and foreign alike, while facilitating coordination between private and public actors, which in turn played an important role in fostering economic growth in general and increasing FDI volume in particular. Platforms like the Investment Advisory Council, established in association with YOIKK, help to foster information flow between multiple actors, public and private, national and international alike. Such institutional innovations settled in the 2000s have played important roles in (relatively) sustained economic growth.

8.4 Social policy

Concomitant with institutional reforms of the last two decades, social policy and its central institutions have also gone through important changes. Despite the expansion of social security regarding both its share in GDP and coverage of population, social protection in Turkey is still limited, in line with the common characteristics of the statist VoC. On the path of the EU accession process, Turkey has had to adopt and implement the *acquis* of the European Community with respect to several areas in social policy, labour-market regulations and employment policies. Recent reforms changed the institutional framework that had served since the 1950s, which had been highly fragmented in the existence of three major public institutions: the Public Employees' Retirement Fund (ES, founded in 1950, covering civil servants including the civilian and military bureaucracy); the Social Insurance Institution (SSK, established in 1964, covering blue-collar workers); and the Social Insurance Institution for the Self-Employed (Bağkur, established in 1971, covering the artisans, farmers, voluntarily insured in agriculture and home makers, as well as the self-employed). These all entailed different conditions for eligibility and benefits. The fragmentation generated significant distributional consequences along with fairness issues amongst the contributors (Adaman *et al.* 2007: 28).

In 2006, these individual institutions were merged into a new umbrella agency, the Social Security Institution (SGK), which was established by Law No. 5502, based on the goal of maintaining a financially sustainable retirement, easier access to health care and harmonising eligibility conditions and benefits across beneficiaries of the previous institutions. In addition, health and social assistance have been separated from retirement benefits. Some of the articles of the reform package were at first invalidated by the Constitutional Court and the law was later enacted in 2008. A parametric reform was introduced in order to decrease substantial deficits in the social security system and a health care reform was carried out to offer universal coverage, currently covering more than 90 per cent of the population. A programme called Transformation in Health was introduced in 2003, based on a referral system and a health insurance fund integrating the functions and collections within the former agencies, strengthening the role of the Ministry of Health in the provision of health care. In the reform process, the share of social expenditures (education, health and social protection combined) in GDP rose from 15.1 per cent to 19 per cent between 1999 and 2006, while the budgetary transfer to the Social Security Institution increased from 2.81 per cent of GDP (combined transfers to the previous three institutions) in 2000 to 5.56 per cent in 2009 (SSI 2011). Another important component of recent reforms has been the detachment of social assistance from social insurance.

The populist policy making of the 1990s caused major inefficiencies in the social security system, the most important of which was the change allowing employees to collect retirement benefits as early as aged 38 and 43 (for women and men, respectively), after paying contributions for 20 years. Thus, this made the median retirement age in Turkey much lower than those in the OECD and other countries. The Social Security Act of 1999 (Law No. 4447) first introduced a new scheme to increase the retirement age to 58 and 60 (for women and men, respectively), following a transition period of 20 years (amended in 2002) and the 2007 Law (No. 5502) complemented this by gradually increasing the retirement age further to 65 by 2036 for both men and women (Adaman *et al.* 2007).

In spite of these changes in the direction of increasing social security expenses and schemes, the presence of a large informal sector jeopardises the availability of social security for a considerable portion of the population. Eligibility in most programmes is based on formal employment, thus a substantial portion of the workforce does not even have access to these, except for health. Hence, social networks (including those based on religious orders, movements, etc.), family and more extended kinship ties provide a broad range of assistance (Buğra and Keyder 2003).

8.5 Corporate governance and state–capital relations

Corporate governance and state–capital relations in Turkey entail most of the aspects associated with statist and patrimonial market economies. Indeed, Turkey displays striking similarities to its Latin American counterparts in this dimension, as highly diversified large conglomerates – mostly controlled by families, like the grupos – dominate the Turkish market economy (Buğra 1994; Schneider 2009). Commonly referred to as 'groups', these concentrated conglomerates have access to multi-sectoral investment and inter-firm proprietary structures, and they are the very products of state-led capitalism, which explicitly encouraged conglomerates to specialise in distinct fields, partitioning the production of consumer products, and providing major incentives towards monopolisation. Additionally, varying forms of state interventionism in the market persist as an important feature of statism, and clientelistic patterns between the state actors and businesses continue, signifying patrimonialism (see Becker's Introduction to this volume).

Although a history of a state-nurtured business in Turkey is similar to those in other late developers, Turkish state-led development – coinciding with nation building – began after the business actors of the late Ottoman Empire were all but eliminated. Business elements, which had overwhelmingly been constituted of non-Muslim elements, were mostly eliminated in the dissolution of the empire at the beginning of the 20th century through wars, the massacre and deportation, and the convention of compulsory population exchange (Aktar 2006; Gocek 1996). State leaders were eager to replace them with a so-called 'national bourgeoisie', which had to be 'created' from scratch (Buğra 1994; Keyder 1987). This newly created business community's dependence on the domestic market was exacerbated by a law ruling out the 'exit option' – the law on Protecting the Value of the Turkish Lira, which restricted capital outflows until 1983 (Özel 2014).

For a business sector that emerged under the auspices of an interventionist state and was highly dependent on it, the ISI regime and its adjoining arrangements (overall an 'ISI pact') were lucrative for several decades. The state's protectionist trade regime, the subsidised large population with inflated purchasing power, and a repressed financial system with negative real interest rates all particularly favoured big business and created diverse tools for the generation and distribution of rents (Krueger 1974; Özel 2003). The result of such nurturing has been a high level of capital concentration and large conglomerates with multi-sectoral investment as the dominant corporate structure within big business. Implicit pacts between the states and industrialists – particularly the large conglomerates – were formed in several countries that implemented state-led development strategies, where the state provided major rents to the industrialists through personal or organisational contacts and the latter avoided challenging the regime (Barkey 1990; Heredia 2002; Schneider 2004), and these pacts were sustained up until the 1980s. The state's control of societal interests – including those of business – mostly prevailed as a common practice for decades, but this control was accompanied by a tactful use of redistributive strategies, including the formation of large patronage networks through which varying degrees and forms of rent were distributed.

This pact, which ruled in most countries with ISI regimes, had another component in the Turkish case: secularism. The alliance between big business and the state establishment (including the military) throughout the state-led development was based on staunch support for secularism, which remained unchallenged until the rise of conservative parties with roots in political Islam and the rise of religiously conservative businesses challenging strict secularist practices in the 1990s. Commonly referred to as 'Anatolian tigers' based on their eager export drive, these medium-size enterprises formed a new alliance with pro-Islamist parties, carrying the ruling JDP to power (Özel 2010). Despite the withdrawal of the state from the economy since the 1980s, particularistic clientele ties with the firms still prevail in different forms. Recently, there has been a new layer in such ties that business actors who share a common religious identity (individuals and organisations alike) with the incumbent JDP might have better access to a wide range of resources (Öniş 2010).

Although the processes of market opening were expected to change the dominance of conglomerates, considered the very outcome of the ISI phase, the empirical reality has proven this expectation wrong. The adjustment capability of conglomerates to market opening was facilitated by their shifting resources across sectors (Özel 2014). However, such resilience has not necessarily thwarted increasing competition in the Turkish market particularly generated by *tigers*, some of which have recently become giant conglomerates, benefiting from a wide range of selective incentives provided by the successive governments that aligned with these newly emerging businesses based on various affinities, the most important of which being religious identity. Hence, increased competition has certainly added new players into the market, but has not transformed corporate governance structures.

Turkish corporate governance entails characteristics of the 'insider system' such as few listed companies, a large number of substantial share stakes and large inter-corporate shareholdings, concentrated in mostly family-based ownership with a pyramidal structure (Yurtoğlu 2000; Ararat and Uğur 2003). A pyramidal ownership structure, family control, diversification, high levels of concentration and bloc holding, as well as limited investment in research and development and labour training, prevail in Turkish corporate governance practices, akin to those prevalent in market economies in most Latin American countries (Schneider 2009). The concentration level is very high, as the average percentage of shares held by the largest shareholder is 45 per cent in the 100 largest traded companies in Turkey, while 28 per cent have one shareholder with an ownership stake of at least 50 per cent, and the largest five shareholders hold 64.5 per cent on average (Demirağ and Serter 2003: 43). Families tend to be the ultimate owners in Turkish companies, since they control 68 of the top 94 traded companies, and 37 of those 68 companies are controlled through pyramids. The pyramidal structure has been fostered through incentives such as tax advantages provided for holding companies (avoiding double taxation in multiple firms, abolished as late as 1986) and transfer pricing mechanisms. Still in line with the Latin American experience, the Turkish capital market used to be marked by significant problems including low levels of capital formation and liquidity, high volatility and high cost of capital, as well as a weak legal and regulatory framework.

Turkish corporate governance practices are subject to challenges including difficulties regarding enforcement of law and regulations, minority shareholders' and creditors' rights, uncertainties arising from legal and regulatory frameworks, and the dismantling of privileged oligopolistic coalitions that operate as corporate insiders. The state's lengthy heavy involvement in the market led to the emergence of various rents but also private risks, which then generated pressure on state actors to compensate for such risks (Ararat and Uğur 2003: 64).

8.6 Turkish labour: squeezed between state and capital

The Turkish variety of capitalism fits into the ideal type of statist VoC based on the presence of weak unions with limited rights, state control over labour and a low unionisation rate. Although the weakening of labour unions is a world-wide phenomenon, the interesting aspect of the Turkish case is that centralisation prevails as the major strategy of the state to restrain labour, depicted as a strategy of 'unite and restrain' by Kuş and Özel (2010). The Turkish state created a more centralised union movement with fewer players to enhance its control while breaking the power of large unions and de-politicising the union movement. The labour movement, which had been strong but fragmented and highly politicised before 1980, was first annihilated by the military coup in 1980, and later revitalised in the late 1980s, but has never re-acquired its power of the 1970s. Currently, not only the unionisation rate is much smaller (10 per cent overall, public and private included), but also severe limits on unions' activities along with widespread repression are imposed both by the state and capital to weaken the unions further.[3] Between 1979 and 2010, the number of labour unions in Turkey dropped from 800 to 100, and currently there are three labour confederations (Ministry of Labour and Social Security 2012).

As in most other emerging countries, atomistic employee–labour relations characterise labour–capital relations in Turkey, where informality poses a significant problem and millions of unregistered workers do not have any legal protection and access to unionisation. In this respect, another characteristic of the Turkish market economy is the discrepancy between *de jure* institutions (laws, regulations and procedures alike), and their de facto implementation. Although Turkey is known as a country with rigid labour regulations, they are often overlooked in practice as the actors are used to bypassing the rules.

State and employers, control over the unions has increasingly intensified since the beginning of the market transition, which was almost in sync with the rise of authoritarianism in Turkey. Indeed, Turkish labour had become strong on the eve of the transition, although it had never gained as much power as in the corporatist settings in several Latin American cases where labour had maintained a close, co-dependent and often co-opted relationship with governments.

The legacy of authoritarianism in the state's relationship with labour still abounds. Despite the transition to (semi-)democracy in 1983, the 1982 Constitution and the subsequent legal changes on union organisation, collective bargaining, strikes and lockouts mostly institutionalised state control over the unions. Thus, the 1982 Constitution took away most of the labour rights that had been granted by the 1961 Constitution and resulted in labour becoming a powerful actor in Turkish politics in the 1960s and 1970s (Mello 2010). Most of the changes enacted by the 1982 Constitution are still intact and include rules such that unions must have the support of at least 10 per cent of union membership within that industry, as well as 50 per cent at a particular workplace to represent workers. Political strikes, work slowdowns and picketing are prohibited and those who strike may be subject to the loss of their financial claims (including their pension, or even their job) or imprisonment (Önder 1999).

Like its counterparts, the Turkish state considered labour a major challenge to market reforms as well as the political stability of the country based on widespread labour activism of the 1970s. After the military coup in 1980, two pieces of legislation that entailed particularly important provisions regulating union activities were adopted: Acts 2821 (Trade Unions Act) and 2822 (the Collective Bargaining Strike and Lockout Act). These laws did not forbid workers from joining unions but forbade membership to more than one union and restricted the right to strike. According to these laws, only those unions that obtained a certificate of competence from the Ministry of Labour could negotiate a collective agreement.[4] Aiming to control membership, the state restricted the power and resources of unions vis-à-vis the state and employers, envisaging a centralised union movement with very narrowly defined objectives monitored by the state (Önder 1999: 234).

Despite increasing state control, unions began to take on a political tone in the 1990s. The three confederations − namely, Türk-İş, DISK and Hak-İş − and independent unions are in rivalry with one another. An interesting one among these is Hak-İş, a confederation emphasising religious values as well as the 'common ground' regarding employer and employee interests on the basis of these values. Hak-İş has been in close alliance with the successive JDP governments since 2002 and does not allow any unions 'in opposition' under its umbrella, while its membership base has expanded via rather repressive mechanisms (Duran and Yildirim 2005: 231).

Throughout the market transition process, labour has been considerably marginalised in the formal policy-making process, while real wages diminished and social benefits and associational rights have been restricted. Rigid legal restrictions to unionisation have been adopted, only allowing industrial unions operating at the national level and confederations. By and large, political unionism − of the leftist brand represented by DISK[5] − has been restrained for the sake of the unity of the state and society (Özbudun 1991). In the 1990s, Türk-İş, dominated by conservative unions, was the only confederation that was engaged in large-scale collective bargaining. Representing several unions representing the workers in the public sector, it established committees to participate in the collective bargaining process. Nevertheless, given the detached link between the union members and the shop floor, such participation does not usually represent the workers, but signifies arrangements between the largely co-opted union bosses and state actors.

The co-optation of the union leaders by the state and the capital along with the absence of intra-union democracy have been prominent characteristics of Turkish union movement, exacerbated further since the 1980s. The workers' representatives are now appointed by the union administration (the only exception being the independent 'lefty' unions), rather than being elected by the workers, which was the practice before 1980. In this context, the link between the workers and the shop floor is extremely weak and hierarchical structures prevail in most unions, including those represented by the allegedly 'revolutionary' confederations. Hence, state–labour and capital–labour relations, through which labour's rights are increasingly limited, situate the Turkish market economy in the statist and hierarchical varieties.

8.7 Concluding remarks

This study explored the ways in which the Turkish market economy has evolved into a form situated between liberal, patrimonial and statist market economies. Emphasising the coexistence of continuity and change through the transformation of the Turkish market economy, it delineated the tensions between the old and the new institutions as well as vested interests entrenched in those. It examined the resistance of some of the former patterns in which the Turkish state interacted with society, while state intervention and patronage distribution has prevailed in new forms. It then pointed out the processes where the Turkish market economy has sustained its statist and patrimonial character, particularly through persistent state interventionism in market dynamics and adaption of new forms of patron–client relations, despite the retreat of the state from the markets in terms of ownership.

Although major institutional reforms were undertaken – mostly under the aegis of international and supranational actors – during severe economic crises, which functioned as external shocks, the study underlined that the effectiveness of newly established institutions is usually at stake in Turkey, as many actors (the most important of whom are the politicians, particularly the executive) with various forms of power and discretion find ways to undermine those institutions, spawning constant vacillations between institutionalisation and de-institutionalisation.

Notes

1 Initial amendments to the 1961 Constitution regarding the power of decrees were made in 1971 following the military intervention, but no significant decrees were issued until 1980.
2 Currently, there are eight independent regulatory agencies (IRAs) in Turkey: the Capital Markets Board (established in 1982), the Higher Board for Radio and TV (1994), the Competition Authority (1994 and 1997), the Banking Regulation and Supervision Agency (1999), the Information and Communications Technologies Authority (2000), the Energy Markets Regulatory Agency (2001), the Sugar Agency (2001) and the Public Procurement Agency (2002).
3 Accurate data on unionisation in Turkey are not available and there are major contradictions between the data presented by the Turkish state (which go up to 68 per cent) and those presented by various unions and confederations. Source: interviews with union leaders in Deri-İş and DISK.
4 It required a trade union to represent a minimum of 10 per cent of all workers in a particular industry, and 50 per cent + 1 of all the workers in an individual establishment, in order to be eligible for collective bargaining.
5 Indeed, although the activities of both left- and right-wing unions were suspended in the context of military intervention, the measures taken against DISK were exceptional (see Adaman *et al.* 2007).

9 Prospects and politics

A sketch

Uwe Becker[1]

The BRICs have become an eminent economic force, and generally emerging economies have recently taken a big share of world production and trade. What will happen in the short- and medium-term future? It seems clear that the BRICs together with other emerging economies will continue their rise – at least many of them, particularly China and India – and that the world will continue to change relatively quickly, in terms of the global economy and, probably, geo-politically. The environmental and social prospects are less clear, and the same is true for the future of individual countries such as Russia and perhaps Brazil. What will happen in the fields of *political* economy and politics? Will the BRICs, on which I wish to focus here, not only become richer but also more liberal? Will Russia leave its path towards increasing authoritarianism? Might China democratise to some extent? Is there a chance for corruption to decline? Very often the correct answer to these questions is that we do not know, yet we can circumscribe some of the factors that will be important in the years to come. That is what I briefly want to do here.

9.1 Prospects

Gross domestic product (GDP) growth has become an obsession in the advanced economies; no politically relevant group continues to put question marks against the ongoing focus on economic growth, or more and more production and consumption – not even the major green parties do so. No doubt, technological progress can improve life, competitiveness is required to keep up with the global division of labour, but politics and civil society organisations have to think again about its fundamental goals. For emerging economies, GDP growth has a different meaning, of course. There it is the basis for poverty reduction and the improvement of the basic quality of material life, particularly health. First of all, we have to think here about most African countries and South Asia, including Bangladesh, Pakistan, the smaller Bhutan, Nepal and Sri Lanka, and India. The dramatic conditions of life of hundreds of millions of people are stressed by Mazumdar in his contribution (cf. Banik 2011). The problems are also still very pressing in most of Latin America and in South-East Asian countries like Indonesia, Laos and the Philippines.

The forecast for the emerging countries as a whole is – not corrected for population growth – 5.5 to 6 per cent growth in 2013 and 2014, for China about 8 per cent, for India 6 per cent, and for Brazil and Russia about 4 per cent (the projected South African percentages are even a bit lower). In Brazil and Russia, this is considerably lower than in the first decade of the millennium, but still more than twice as high as the forecast for the advanced economies (IMF 2013: 2). Brazil, Russia and South Africa are richer than the giant China and India, and the richer a country becomes, the lower GDP growth tends to be. Brazil and Russia are furthermore highly dependent on the export of oil, gas and basic materials, for which demand in the advanced economies has somewhat declined in the wake of the recent crisis. In the case of Brazil, for which exports constitute only about 10 per cent of its GDP, a political factor might have to be considered: according to the Economist Intelligence Unit (EIU, 4 March 2013), both domestic and foreign investors have become cautious through their 'fear of excessive interventionism' by the leftist government. This seems to imply that parts of the business community use an investment strike against the re-distributional policies as described by Boschi in Chapter 6.

Looking at longer-term projections, we receive a similar picture that shows Chinese and Indian GDP growth decline to an average rate of about 5 per cent for the period from 2005 to 2030 (World Bank 2012c: 9; OECD 2008a: 3). Russia's figure is 4 per cent and that of Brazil is 3 per cent (OECD 2008a: 3). If this projection is roughly correct, then it implies that these countries will not return to their high growth rates of the early 2000s. Such forecasts tend to be highly speculative, however. Many years have still to pass until 2030 or even 2050 (Dadush and Shaw 2011), a time during which political eruptions might take place, smaller countries in Asia or Africa might take over parts of the international markets of Chinese and Indian goods and services, and new technological inventions or climate catastrophes might bring about fundamental change of a sort we cannot even describe now. A dangerous, often overlooked but potentially extremely disruptive possibility is the intensification of the conflict between China and India over the water supply from the Himalayas, which is 'essential to the economic growth, prosperity and the very survival of the countries' vast populations' (APDF 2012).

A change that is already taking shape is in the world energy scene, driven by the sharply rising extraction of shale gas and oil, notably in the USA. The global reserves are huge but the extraction is contested because of its environmental effects – the poisoning of the ground by the fracking process and the rise of methane emissions. The discussion (the internet is full of reports and opinions) has not come to a conclusion yet, not even a preliminary one. If the production of shale gas and oil continues to increase, it will probably deprive the Arab countries and Russia of their dominant position in the energy market. Will Russia be able to develop alternative sources of economic growth? In the past twenty years it has not. As touched upon in the Introduction and Vasileva's chapter, the non-oil and gas sector in fact deteriorated. It seems that this is related to predatory corruption, to the absence of a tradition of individual initiative, and the state structure with its suffocating bureaucracy. In this context, it does not help to tell the Russians, as the European Bank of Reconstruction and Development has done (EBRD 2012), that they have to innovate and to improve skills as well as the financial support of start-ups. The obstacles to do this have to be removed first.

What are the chances for the environment in the context of the rise of emerging economies and possibly the large-scale production of shale gas and oil? In recent years, emissions of most relevant polluters fell in the advanced economies (see Table 1.3), but the Kyoto targets – not signed by the USA – were not reached. In the BRICs and other emerging countries, emissions went up. Environmental news from Chinese and Indian megacities is often dramatic, but this is also true for some African cities. About 2 billion people, of whom hundreds of millions live in India and Africa, still have to make their way from a very poor to a modestly decent living standard. Theoretically, as the OECD (2008a: 2ff) has calculated, this move could be combined with a reduction in CO_2, SO_2, NO_2 and PM (particulate matter, or fine dust).

From a practical point of view, the question is: who will do this job? The public acceptance of slightly lower income growth coupled with a political system capable of asserting this goal are required, but this is not easy against the background of a dominant economic ideology that abides by the market and of a majority in US politics that does not care about the environment. If the USA is not doing its best, why should an emerging economy do so? Without politically created incentives – here we are back to the aspects of support and capacity – the market will not lower pollution. The OECD (2008a) is therefore sceptical. The World Bank (2012c) has, regarding China, a more optimistic view, also with respect to the reduction of inequality. The title of its report illustrates this: *China 2030: Building a Modern, Harmonious, and Creative High-Income Society*. Its advice is to go innovative, go green, go social. The condition it mentions is continuing liberalisation. Is this a viable formula, for China as well as the other BRICs?

Perhaps to some degree. More liberalisation of trade and investment generally in the BRICs, more privatisation in China and Russia – at least as long as it does not affect statist control of core businesses. Analysing the past two decades, we only saw India liberalise, though modestly. Given that India lacks a strong liberal party, future liberalisation will be limited. China liberalised in the 1980s, but became cautious then, and liberalisation moved forward very slowly, while Brazil and Russia reversed the liberalisation trend of the 1990s in the 2000s. The Chinese Communist Party (CCP) wants to maintain its authoritarian rule, the Russian government is keen to keep control over the country's treasures of the soil, and both governments consider it necessary to guide their country. The incumbent Brazilian left-wing government principally and very explicitly distrusts the market and wants the state to 'tame' capitalism. Perhaps, however, the Brazilians will vote against the Labour Party's etatism in a future election. Although elections do not automatically bring about certain legislation, the possibility of change by elections is an aspect that distinguishes Brazil, as well as India, from China and at the moment also from Russia, where election results seem to be pre-determined.

On the world stage, China and the other BRICs (whether or not including Russia as well as a number of other rising countries like Indonesia, Pakistan and Iran) will probably gain influence. It would be nothing more than a reflection of the altered balance of economic strength. In twenty years, China will probably have the biggest economy in the world in terms of total GDP (GDP per capita is a different story) and the global top ten economies will only include the USA, the European Union (EU) and Japan as advanced cases (which in terms of income per head will still be ahead in 2030). Three to four hundred years of Western dominance in the world will come to an end. Will the USA nonetheless survive as the sole superpower? Will it join forces with China and/or more than ever with the EU? Will new alliances emerge, and what will happen to Russia if it sticks to its gas/oil dependence in a disadvantageously changing energy market? Will the so-called realism in international relations, according to which (some) world orders at the last resort have to be secured by United Nations (UN)-approved (military) power, work in the context of fundamentally changed power relations? What countries will have a seat in the Security Council in 2030? There are many intriguing questions.

9.2 A chance for democracy in Russia and China?

The political system is not without relevance for political-economic development. Democracies are more open than autocracies and at the same time tend to facilitate gradual development, while autocracies at a certain moment might be overthrown by a revolution. India and Brazil are, just as South Africa and Turkey, democracies in formal terms. They are more or less working democracies: in the Combined Index of Democracy, scaled 0 to 10 (see Table 9.1), they had scores between 5.42 (India) and 7.20 (South Africa) in 2010. This

Table 9.1 Democracy scores of the BRICs, South Africa and Turkey plus, as contrasts, France, Sweden and the USA, 1996 and 2010 (scale 0–10)

	1996	2010
Brazil	6.07	7.09
China	0	0
India	5.73	5.42
Russia	4.38	3.15
South Africa	5.64	7.20
Turkey	4.37	5.62
France	9.10	8.89
Sweden	9.77	9.64
USA	9.34	8.59

Source: (Lauth and Kauff 2012: 48ff)

index distinguishes between autocratic regimes (0–5), defective democracies (5–7) and functioning democracies (7–10), and is based on data on freedom and equality (including the (non-)existence of free, universal elections), freedom of expression and organisation, the level of the rule of law as well as that of corruption (Lauth and Kauff 2012: 19ff).

The figures, which have to be taken with some reservation regarding precision, tell us that the quality of democracy in Brazil has strongly improved since 1996 and has recently lifted the country over the threshold of a 'functioning democracy'. Indian democracy, by contrast, has slightly eroded to a level not so far from autocracy. Both countries, just as Turkey and, somewhat less, South Africa, will only improve their democracies when they reduce corruption (cf. the data in Chapter 2, Tables 2.1 and 2.4) and improve the human rights situation. Apart from India, they seem to be on their way, although reversals are always possible: think about Islamism in Turkey and the history of democratic ups and downs in Brazil.

As said, I do not intend to provide an overview here, but want to say something on the Russian and Chinese prospects. China and Russia are the least democratic and geo-politically the most important BRICs. Do any pre-conditions for improvement exist? Are there any prerequisites for improvement? From the literature on democratisation processes elsewhere (for example, O'Donnell and Schmitter 1986; Linz and Stepan 1996), we know that apart from economic development it is crucial that:

- social cleavages are bridgeable;
- a political culture prevails where elites are willing to find compromises and accept electoral defeats; and
- civil society has developed to a level where democracy becomes an existential condition for organisations and associations as well as for professions like journalists.

Of course, a strong force supporting democratisation also needs to exist. In an evolutionary process, it can only be successful when the authoritarian rulers ultimately, perhaps after a long period of struggle, gradually allow for the erosion of their power (examples are the Perestroika in Russia, in Brazil the Geisel presidency during the second half of the 1970s, and recently the military leaders of Myanmar).

The social cleavages do not seem to pose a challenge to democratisation, either in China or in Russia. Potentially there could be a deep cleavage between the countryside and the big cities, but at the moment the possibility of democratisation primarily depends on political-cultural conditions and on power relations.

Russia is formally a presidential democracy and has a *trias politica*. Under Putin, it became highly centralised again. As is reflected in the low scores in Table 9.1, it is only a façade democracy. Election fraud is widespread – although it is not clear whether presidential elections would have had decisively different results without manipulation – and the climate of intimidation is destroying the independence of the courts and the media. Anna Politkovskaya (2007: 10f, 103) has forcefully described this. Police impunity and even political murder, whoever gives the order, are part of this climate. Politkovskaya herself became a victim of it in late 2006. On top of that, the freedom of demonstration and speech is judicially restricted – remember Pussy Riot.

A basic condition of this grim picture is a weak civil society and the lack of a democratic tradition. A tradition of the rule of law also does not exist (Shevtsova 2010: 153). In 1917, a poor, overwhelmingly agricultural society with a dependent peasantry still a prominent feature and an absolutist political regime became communist – repressively communist with the rise of Stalin in the mid-1920s. Sixty years later, Gorbachev's Perestroika was the beginning of a liberal turn which put an end to communism and continued into the first Yeltsin years. The weak civil society, lack of a culture of compromise and of fair political contest in combination with a high level of corruption resulted in this period in a disaster. During this period, a small group of bureaucrats and adventurers – later known as the oligarchs – plundered the national wealth, decentralisation resulted in fragmentation, and the standard of living of the majority rapidly declined: it was a big bribe-and-enrich-yourself party including national and local politicians (see the concise overview in Rutland 2008b).

Putin's reversal of this development (echoed by public sentiments), the recentralisation of Russia and the subjugation of the oligarchs is often described as necessary for the survival of the country (for instance, by Gudkov and Zaslavsky 2011: 91f). In any case, the disempowerment of the oligarchs was a sort of revolutionary act, and 'Putinism' developed a regime akin to revolutionary, with the fear of being overthrown by a counter-revolution and subsequently by rising control, intimidation, when required repression, and the recruitment of a group of faithful. In Putin's case, the latter are the *siloviki* (see Vasileva, this volume) – comrades or congenial people from the secret service and the military, of whom a few became new oligarchs or more precisely 'silovarchs', not through ownership but through control of companies.

There is still some freedom of the media in Russia, critical scientists publish their articles and books there, and the internet is not or is only marginally censored – one way in which Russia is much freer than China (Shevtsova 2013). This does no harm to the Putin regime, which appears to be relatively stable. However, as the public protests since the late 2011 Duma elections have demonstrated, an active minority among the Russians is no longer prepared to put up with fraud and increased authoritarianism. The reaction of the regime to the protest wave has been a clear indication of increasing nervousness. Repression and intimidation of activists is continuing (one example is the arrest of Alexey Navalny, a prominent figure of the protest movement), while campaigns against foreign-funded non-governmental organisations (NGOs), notably Western ones (labelled 'foreign agents') have become a new aspect. In March 2013, this escalated when there were a large number[2] of raids on NGOs such as Amnesty International, Human Rights Watch, Transparency International and the foundations of German political parties. Time will show the effects of these events in the longer term.

The basic anchor of the relative stability of the regime is the improved well-being and at the same time the apathy of large parts of the Russian population. The 'whole system', Politkovskaya (2007: 107) wrote in 2005, 'of thieving judges, rigged elections, presidents who have only contempt for the needs of their people can operate only if nobody protests. That is the Kremlin's secret weapon and the most striking feature of life in Russia today'. She furthermore speaks of apathy and elsewhere of opportunism (ibid.: 11, 21). It is an attitude that does not facilitate democratisation.

The results of the PEW Survey conducted in spring 2012 support this interpretation. Asked what was more important, democracy or a strong leader, 57 against 32 per cent opted for the latter (in 2009, the respective percentages were 60 and 29). To the question of whether they preferred a good democracy or a strong economy, 75 per cent voted for the economy. Esteem for democratic values and rights was also rather low. While 71 per cent supported a free judiciary, honest elections were deemed important by only 52 per cent, uncensored media by 49 per cent and free speech by 44 per cent. The positive thing is that these values are higher than in 2002, with respectively 68, 37, 31 and 30 per cent approval. A democratic culture will require a higher value given to democracy and a more critical stance towards Putin, whose approval rate was 72 per cent (PEW 2012).

In short, democratisation does not seem to be the near future for Russia. Civil society organisations and institutions with a vital interest in democracy are intimidated (media, foreign-funded NGOs), are feeble (for example, liberal or social democratic political parties and independent trade unions) or have, perhaps grudgingly, adapted to the regime (such as the post-communist unions and the associations of small companies, which are highly state-dependent). Social trust is low (PEW 2012) and a relevant force that would unite and lead a democratic opposition movement is not yet visible. The majority of the middle class – half of which works for the state – seems primarily to enjoy its new wealth (Kotkin 2007).

Will Putinism survive Putin? Much will depend on economic development in the years to come as well as on unpredictable developments in civil society. Nobody knew in 2009 what would happen a year later in the Arab countries, just as we do not know what will occur in Russia.

What about China? China is not a democracy at all – by Western standards, Chinese leaders would reply. It no longer has a communist economy, but the CCP still rules. The political system is that of Leninist 'democratic centralism' where the word democracy is the sole democratic detail. Somewhat strange, the ideology is still 'socialist'. Strange, because the country's capitalism is an engine of the world economy, inequality is rising and the party leaders enrich themselves and their families as do Russian oligarchs (according to *The Economist*, 3 November 2012, Prime Minister Wen's family owns US$2.3 billion and the wealth of Xi Jinping is comparable). In this context, socialism has become reduced to the claim that the party has ultimate wisdom on the basis of 'scientific socialism'. Traditionally, the party acting in the 'objective interest of the working class' was a central element of this construction, but it has lost significance. The centralism points to the central committee of the 'Politbureau' of the CCP, but does not exclude a certain decentralisation of China and the sub-division of the sometimes very large provinces into sub-units.

What is specific and increasingly stressed – for example, on 5 January 2013 in an address by the new Party Leader Xi Jinping (*NRC Handelblad*, 11 February 2013) – is that it is 'socialism with Chinese characteristics'. This is open to adjustment and deployable for the leaders' interests. It explicitly allows private property and includes entrepreneurs and managers into the class basis of the CCP as the then Party Leader Zhiang Zemin pointed out in a number of speeches in the early 2000s (cf. Zemin 2002). To 'socialism with Chinese characteristics' belongs 'democracy with Chinese characteristics'. When the former Prime Minister Wen pointed to the necessity of democracy (Li 2008: 9), he spoke of course about the latter, not about Western, liberal democracy.

Important aspects of the Chinese characteristics are Confucianism, informal pragmatism and the 'mass line', a sort of petition system (Chen 2013: 60). Pragmatism comes to the fore when courts get the order not to judge strictly on the basis of CCP guidelines, but to mediate (ibid.). This reflects the *guanxi* culture as described by McNally (this volume). The 'mass line' means that bottom-up information about grievances and wishes has to be channelled to the top of the CCP, which has to take it into consideration. The petition system is indeed deeply 'Chinese' as it goes back to imperial times, with petitioners travelling to Beijing to launch complaints (and local governments trying to stop them from doing so). The 'mass line' now also involves public surveys and other means to gauge public opinion.

In a country of 1.33 billion inhabitants, the 'mass line' is technically impossible and therefore ineffective. Protest has to find other ways. Increasingly, it uses what is called 'mass incidents': demonstrations, blockades and strikes against land grabs by local party officials, housing problems, corruption, exploitation by companies, the *hukou* system that strongly privileges city-born people, poisoned rivers and sometimes very local problems. From 1993 to 2010, the number of these 'mass incidents' has increased annually from 9,000 to 280,000 – until now, however, without a snowball effect (Wang 2013: 50). Worth mentioning, in January 2013 there was even a (non-suppressed) 72-hour strike of *Southern Weekly* journalists for freedom of the press (*NRC Handelsblad*, 15 January 2013). Another new phenomenon is the rise of the 'new opinion class' or 'netizens' (citizens on the internet) (Qiang 2011: 52). They are active as critical bloggers and as readers of these blogs. The blogs are censored, sometimes selectively, but smart brains always find new ways to reach their communities. As a result, China is becoming increasingly transparent (ibid.: 60).

There is some dynamism in Chinese civil society and political culture. Censorship and repression are still very important instruments of the CCP, but an increasing number of people is losing fear (Su *et al.* 2013: 31), just as an ever-increasing number of peasants in the late 1970s and early 1980s lost their fear on their own initiative to explore and finally to conquer the urban markets (Gregory and Zhou 2009: 4f). It took time before this was legalised, but the number of peasants was too large to repress and the Deng fraction in the CCP saw the advantages of the movement.

What will happen next? Is China becoming politically unstable? Will the top of the CCP stay coherent, will it demonstrate a capacity to learn that is related to the concept of 'resilient authoritarianism' (Li 2008: 13; Pei 2012: 39; Chen 2013), or will it become divided and anxious and, as a consequence, intensify repression? According to Chen (2013: 62f), the regime already has become frightened and cracks have appeared on the façade of stability. This view is supported by *The Economist* (27 October 2012), which sees China as 'unstable at the grassroots, dejected at the middle strata and out of control at the top'. Wang (2013: 48) similarly writes that the costs of maintaining authoritarianism are, financially as well as organisationally, rising out of control.

If this interpretation is too dramatic and the upper echelons of the CCP are able to stay coherent (an aspect stressed by He and Feng 2008: 141), then resilient authoritarianism might continue to work for a while and gradually adjust the political system towards 'democracy with Chinese characteristics'. It would probably mean bringing in more inner party pluralism and stressing the Confucian principle of guardianship. Resembling Plato's ideas, Chinese democracy then is outcome-centred instead of procedure-centred, with the CCP elite as the wise guardian. It would be – and this process is going on – a soft reformulation of 'democratic centralism'. A majority of the Chinese supports such ideas as being democratic and also supports the CCP elite as guardians (Shi and Lui 2010: 123–26), but what happens when a significant group does not follow this line and wants to have a party of its own? Is it also democracy with Chinese characteristics if this group is suppressed?

If the interpretation of the CCP losing control is correct, then more dramatic events and developments might follow: more disruption and more repression, direction unknown. Perhaps there might come a 'triggering event' (Nathan 2013: 21), but this will not necessarily end with Western-style democracy. Civil society is developing quickly, but is there any significant force in China that could bring about democracy? As in Russia, 'the middle class is busy enjoying itself' (ibid.: 24), while netizens and protesters are fragmented. Perhaps the importance of the middle class is generally overstated, however. Organisations and movements are the relevant players. Their members and activists have a socio-economic basis, but this basis might be diffuse and include workers, intellectuals, entrepreneurs and those who are not a class at all: juveniles. So, the middle class in all its fuzziness might politically sleep, while the minorities of the groups just mentioned become increasingly active in organisations and movements. It seems that this process is occurring in China at the moment.

Let us hope that the CCP will be able to reduce corruption and the self-enrichment of its elite and that the Chinese economy will continue its path of growth in a way that really improves the conditions of life of the large majority of the population. Otherwise, an evolutionary democratisation process will become very difficult.

Notes

1 For critical comments and suggestions regarding China and Russia, I would like to thank Christopher McNally and Alexandra Vasileva.
2 About 2,000 people, according to the German television news of 27 March: www.tagesschau.de/ausland/russland-ngo-kontrollen100.html.

Bibliography

Newspapers

The Economist
Financial Times
The Guardian
Izvestiya
The New York Times
NRC Handelsblad
People's Daily Online (China)
Vremia Novostey
Wall Street Journal

Publications

Adaman, F. (2011) 'Is corruption a drawback to Turkey's accession to the European Union?', *South European Society & Politics* 16 (2): 309–21.

Adaman, F., Çarkoğlu, A. and Şenatalar, B. (2007) *Corruption from the Perspective of Turkish Business*, Istanbul: TESEV Publications.

Agoramoorthy, G. (2012) 'India's pollution nightmare: can it be tackled?', *Environmental Science & Technology* 46(3): 1305–6.

Aktar, A. (2006) *Türk Milliyetçiliği, Gayrımüslimler ve Ekonomik Dönüşüm*, Istanbul: İletişim.

Alam, G. (1985) 'India's technology policy and its influence on technology imports and technology development', *Economic and Political Weekly* 20(45–47): 2073–80.

Almeida, R. (2011) 'Entrando no clube: o BNDES e a inserção brasileira no capitalismo internacional', in R. Boschi (ed.) *Variedades de Capitalismo, Política e Desenvolvimento na América Latina*, Belo Horizonte: UFMG.

Alper, E. and Hatipoğlu, O. (2009) 'The conduct of monetary policy in Turkey: in the pre- and post-crisis period of 2001 in comparative perspective – a case for central bank independence', in Z. Öniş and F. Şenses (eds) *Turkey and the Global Economy, Neo-liberal Restructuring and Integration in the Post-Crisis Era*, London: Routledge, pp. 50–72.

Amann, E. and Baer, W. (2008) 'Neo-liberalism and market concentration in Brazil: the emergence of a contradiction?', *The Quarterly Review of Economics and Finance* 48(2): 252–62.

ANC (1994) *Reconstruction and Development Programme*, Johannesburg: ANC.

Anchordoguy, M. (2005) *Reprogramming Japan: The High Tech Crisis under Communitarian Capitalism*, Ithaca, NY: Cornell University Press.

Anstey, M. (2004) 'National bargaining in South Africa's clothing manufacturing industry: problems and prospects of multi-employer bargaining in an industry under siege', *Industrial Law Journal* 25, October: 1829–64.

APDF (2012) 'India, China face growing tensions over water', *Asia Pacific Defence Forum*, December 31.

Ararat, M. and Uğur, M. (2003) 'Corporate governance in Turkey: an overview and some policy recommendations', *Corporate Governance* 3(1): 58–75.

Arbix, G. and Negri, J.A. (2006) 'Uma nova competitividade da indústria e o novo empresariado: uma hipótese de trabalho', *São Paulo em Perspectiva* 19(2): 21–30.

Arndt, C. and Oman, C. (2006) *Uses and Abuses of Governance Indicators*, Paris: Development Centre of the Organization for Economic Cooperation and Development.

Arriola, L. (2009) 'Patronage and political stability in Africa', *Comparative Political Studies* 42: 1339–62.

Ashwin, S. and Clarke, S. (2002) *Russian Trade Unions and Industrial Relations in Transition*, Basingstoke: Palgrave Macmillan.

Aslund, A. (2007) *Russia's Capitalist Revolution. Why Market Reform Succeeded and Democracy Failed*, Washington, DC: Peterson Institute for International Economics.

Athukorala, P.-C. (2009) 'Outward foreign direct investment from India', *Asian Development Review* 26(2): 125–53.

Atiyas, I. (2009) 'Recent privatization experience in Turkey, a reappraisal', in Z. Öniş and F. Şenses (eds) *Turkey and the Global Economy, Neo-liberal Restructuring and Integration in the Post-Crisis Era*, London: Routledge, pp. 101–22.

Banik, D. (2011) 'Growth and hunger in India', *Journal of Democracy* 22(3): 90–104.

Bannister, J. and Cook, G. (2011) 'China's employment and compensation costs in manufacturing through 2008', *Monthly Labor Review* 134(3): 39–52.

Barker, F. (1999) 'On South Africa's labour policies', *South African Journal of Economics* 67(1): 1–14.

Barkey, H. (1990) *The State and the Industrialization Crisis in Turkey*, Boulder CO, San Francisco CA, Oxford: Westview Press.

Barry, M. (2009) 'Corruption in Russia: a model exploring its economic costs', *Caucasian Review of International Affairs* 3(4): 387–403.

Baum, R. and Shevchenko, A. (1999) 'The 'state of the state', in M. Goldman and R. MacFarquhar (eds) *The Paradox of China's Post-Mao Reforms*, Cambridge, MA: Harvard University Press.

Baumol, W.J. (2002) *The Free Market Innovation Machine. Analyzing the Growth Miracle of Capitalism*, Princeton NJ: Princeton University Press.

Beattie, A. (2012) 'IMF drops opposition to capital controls', *The Financial Times* (London), 3 December.

Becker, U. (1988) 'From social scientific functionalism to open functional logic', *Theory and Society* 17(6): 865–83.

——(2007) 'Open systemness and contested reference frames and change. a reformulation of the varieties of capitalism theory', *Socio-Economic Review* 5(2): 261–86.

——(2009) *Open Varieties of Capitalism. Continuity, Change and Performances*, Basingstoke: Palgrave Macmillan.

——(2011) 'Introduction', in U. Becker (ed.) *Change and Continuity in the Small West European Countries' Capitalisms*, Amsterdam: Amsterdam University Press, pp. 11–44.

——(2012) 'Measuring change of capitalist varieties: reflections on method, illustrations from the BRICs', *New Political Economy* (online), 31 October.

BEEPS (Business Environment and Enterprise Performance Survey) (2009) www. enterprisesurveys.org (accessed 10 December 2012).

Béja, J.-P. (2006) 'The changing aspects of civil society in China', *Social Research* 73(1): 53–76.

Bellin, E. (2000) 'Contingent democrats: industrialists, labor, and democratization in late developing countries', *World Politics* 52(2): 175–205.

Bergsten, C.F., Freeman, C., Lardy, N.R. and Mitchell, D.J. (2009) *China's Rise. Challenges and Opportunities*, Washington, DC: Petersen Institute for International Economics.

Bertelsmann Foundation (2010) *BTI 2010 – Russia Country Report*, Gütersloh: Bertelsmann Stiftung.

Bettelheim, C. (1977) *India Independent*, New Delhi: Khosla and Co.

Bhattacharya, S. (2007) 'The state and labour market reforms: vicissitudes of the changing relationship between state, labour and capital – an appraisal of the neo-liberal reforms in India', paper presented at the Global Labour University Conference, 1–3 April 2007, University of the Witwatersrand, Johannesburg.

Bhorat, H. and van der Westhuizen, C. (2009) *A Synthesis of Current Issues in the Labour Regulatory Environment*, DPRU Working Paper, 09/136.

Birdsall, K. (2000) '"Everyday crime" at the workplace: covert earning schemes in Russia's new commercial sector', in A. Ledeneva and M. Kurkchiyan (eds) *Economic Crime in Russia*, London: Kluwer Law International.

Birdsall, N. and Jaspersen, F. (eds) (1997) *Pathways to Growth: Comparing East Asia and Latin America*, Washington, DC: Inter-American Development Bank.

Blasi, J.R., Kroumova, M. and Kruse, D. (1997) *Kremlin Capitalism. Privatizing the Russian Economy*, Ithaca NY: Cornell University Press.

Blyn, G. (1966) *Agricultural Trends in India, 1891–1947: Output, Availability, and Productivity*, Philadelphia: University of Pennsylvania Press.

Bohle, D. and Greskovits, B. (2007) 'Neoliberalism, embedded neoliberalism, and neo-corporatism: towards transnational capitalismin Central-Eastern Europe', *West European Politics* 30(3): 443–66.

Boisot, M. and Child, J. (1996) 'From fiefs to clans and network capitalism: explaining China's emerging economic order', *Administrative Science Quarterly* 41(4): 600–28.

Bond, P. (2000) *Elite Transition: From Apartheid to Neoliberalism in South Africa*, London: Pluto Press.

Boschi, R. (2008) 'Capacidades estatales y políticas de desarrollo en Brasil: tendencias recientes', in M.A. Sáez and C.R. Melo (eds) *La Democracia Brasileña, Balance y Perspectivas para el Siglo XXI*, Salamanca: Ediciones Universidad de Salamanca.

——(2009) 'Elites parlamentares e a agenda pós-neoliberal: Brasil e Chile', in F. Anastasia, A.M. Díaz, M. Inácio and M.M. Da Rocha, *Elites Parlamentares na América Latina*, Belo Horizonte: Argvmentvm.

——(2011) *Variedades de Capitalismo, Política e Desenvolvimento na América Latina*, Belo Horizonte: UFMG.

Boschi, R. and Gaitán, F. (2008a) 'Gobiernos progresistas, agendas neodesarrollistas y capacidades etatales: la experiencia reciente en Argentina, Brasil y Chile', in M.R.S. Lima (ed.) *Desempenho de Governos Progressistas no Cone Sul*, Rio de Janeiro: Edições IUPERJ.

——(2008b) 'Intervencionismo estatal e políticas de desenvolvimento na América Latina', *Caderno CRH* 21(53): 301–17.

——(2009a) 'Outra volta no parafuso desenvolvimentista-um manifesto', *Insight Inteligência* 45: 130–45.

——(2009b) 'Politics and development: lessons from Latin America', *Brazilian Political Science Review* 3(2): 11–29

Boschi, R. and Lima, M.R.S. (2002) 'O executivo e a construção do estado no Brasil: do desmonte da era Vargas ao novo intervencionismo regulatório', in L. Werneck Vianna (ed.), *A Democracia e os Três Poderes no Brasil*, Belo Horizonte: UFMG/IUPERJ.

Boschi, R. and Santana, C.H. (eds) (2012) *Development and Semi-Periphery. Post-neoliberal Trajectories in South America and Central Eastern Europe*, New York: Anthem Press.

Boyer, R. (2005a) 'How and why capitalisms differ', *Economy and Society* 34(4): 509–57.

——(2005b) 'Complementarity in regulation theory', *Socio-Economic Review* 3: 366–71.

Bremmer, I. (2010) *The End of the Free Market: Who Wins the War Between States and Corporations?* New York: Portfolio.

Bresser Pereira, L.C. (2009) *Mondialisation et Competition: Pourquoi Certains Pays Émergents Réussissent et d'Autres Non*, Paris: Editions la Découverte.

BRICS (2012) *BRICs Joint Statistical Publication*, www.bricsindia.in/publication.html (accessed July 2012).

Brinkerhoff, D.W. and Goldsmith, A.A. (2002) *Clientelism, Patrimonialism and Democratic Governance: An Overview and Framework for Assessment and Programming*, Bethesda, MD: Abt Associates Inc.

Brinks, D.M. (2010) 'Institutional design and judicial effectiveness: lessons from the prosecution of rights violations for democratic governance and the rule of law', in S. Mainwaring and T.R. Scully (eds) *Democratic Governance in Latin America*, Stanford CA: Stanford University Press, pp. 210–44.

BRSA (2012) *Overall Panorama of the Banking Sector in Turkey*, Ankara: Banking Regulation and Supervision Agency, www.bddk.org.tr/WebSitesi/turkce/Raporlar/TBSGG/11350tbs_genel_gorunumu_eylul_2012.pdf (accessed 26 September 2012).

Bruff, I. (2011) 'What about the elephant in the room? varieties of capitalism, varieties in capitalism', *New Political Economy* 16(4): 481–500.

Buğra, A. (1994) *State and Business in Modern Turkey: A Comparative Study*, Albany, NY: State University of New York Press.

Buğra, A. and Keyder, C. (2003) 'New poverty and the changing welfare regime of Turkey', Ankara: UNDP.

Calland, R. (2006) *Anatomy of South Africa: Who Holds the Power?* Cape Town: Zebra.

Campbell, J.L. (2011) 'The US financial crisis: lessons for theories of institutional complementarity', *Socio-Economic Review* 9(2): 211–34.

Campbell, J.L. and Pedersen, O.K. (eds) (2001) *The Rise of Neoliberalism and Institutional Analysis*, Princeton NJ: Princeton University Press.

Cartledge, S. (2007) 'The power of corruption', *China Economic Quarterly* 11(1): 29–38.

Central Bank of Turkey (2010) 'Calisma tebligi', No: 10/01, Ankara: T.C. Merkez Bankasi, www.tcmb.gov.tr/research/discus/2010/WP1001.pdf (accessed 21 September 2011).

——(2011) 'Inflation report', Ankara: T.C. Merkez Bankasi, www.tcmb.gov.tr/yeni/eng/ (accessed 21 September 2011).

——(2012) 'Analytical balance sheet', Ankara: T.C. Merkez Bankasi, www.tcmb.gov.tr/yeni/eng/index.html (accessed 17 October 2012).

Chalapati Rao, K.S. and Dhar, B. (2011) *India's FDI Flows: Trends and Concepts*, New Delhi: Research and Information Systems on Developing Countries (RIS) and Institute for Studies in Industrial Development (ISID).

Chalapati Rao, K.S. and Guha, A. (2006) 'Ownership pattern of the Indian corporate sector: implications for corporate governance', *Institute for Studies in Industrial Development*, Working Paper No: 2006/09.

Chan, A. (2008) 'The evolution of China's industrial relations system – the Japanese-German model and China's workers congress', *Labour Relations Journal* 1: 52–65.

Chaudhuri, S. (2008) 'Ranbaxy sell-out: reversal of fortunes', *Economic and Political Weekly* 43(29): 11–13.

Chellaney, B. (2012) *The BRICS Grouping: A Brick by Brick Development*, Doha, Qatar: Al Jazeera Centre for Studies.

Chen, X. (2013) 'China at the tipping point? The rising cost of stability', *Journal of Democracy* 23(1): 57–64.

Chibber, V. (2004) *Locked in Place: State Building and Late Industrialization in India*, New Delhi: Tulika Books.

Choate, P. (2009) *Saving Capitalism: Keeping America Strong*, New York: Vintage Books.

Chu, Y. and So, A.Y. (2010) 'State neoliberalism: the Chinese road to capitalism', in Y. Chu (ed.) *Chinese Capitalisms – Historical Emergence and Political Implications*, Basingstoke: Palgrave Macmillan, pp. 46–72.

Commander, S. and Jackman, R. (1993) *Providing Social Benefits in Russia: Redefining the Roles of Firms and Government*, The World Bank, Policy Research Working Paper Series, No. 1184, Ideas, RePEc. Org.

Competition Commission (2008) *Review of Changes in Industrial Structure and Competition*, Pretoria: Competition Commission, Policy and Research Division, 18 March.

Constanzi, R.N. (2009) 'Crise global e impactos no Brasil: o problema da estabilidade da instabilidade financeira', *Informações FIPE*, Agosto: 14–19.

Cooper, W. (2009) 'Russia's economic performance and policies and their implications for the United States', a Congressional Report Service Report for Congress, fpc.state.gov/documents/organization/115956.pdf (accessed 10 December 2012).

Costa, W.M.R. (2006) 'Os conselhos do CDES: experimento sem conclusão', *Insight Inteligência* 32: 146–61.

Crouch, C. (2005a) *Capitalist Diversity and Change. Recombinant Governance and Institutional Entrepreneurs*, Oxford: Oxford University Press.

——(2005b) 'Models of capitalism', *New Political Economy* 10(4): 439–56.

——(2005c) 'Three meanings of complementarity', *Socio-Economic Review* 3(2): 359–63.

CSO (2008a) *National Accounts Statistics, Factor Incomes (base year 1999–2000) 1980–81 to 1999–2000*, New Delhi: Central Statistical Organization.

——(2008b) *National Accounts Statistics*, New Delhi: Central Statistical Organization.

——(2009) *National Accounts Statistics*, New Delhi: Central Statistical Organization.

——(2011a) *National Accounts Statistics, Back Series 1950–51 to 2004–05*, New Delhi: Central Statistical Organization.

——(2011b) *National Accounts Statistics*, New Delhi: Central Statistical Organization.

——(2012) *Annual Survey of Industries: Summary Results 2009–10*, New Delhi: Central Statistical Organization.

d'Araujo, M.C. (2009) *A Elite Dirigente do Governo Lula*, Rio de Janeiro: Fundação Getúlio Vargas/CPDOC.

Dadush, U. and Shaw, W. (2011) *Juggernaut: How Emerging Markets are Reshaping Globalization*, Washington DC: Carnegie Endowment for International Peace (PowerPoint presentation available at: Juggernaut: Event Slides – Carnegie Endowment for International Peace).

d'Costa, A.P. (2004) 'The Indian software industry in the global division of labor', in A.P. d'Costa and E. Sridharan (eds) *India in the Global Software Industry: Innovation, Firm Strategies and Development*, Basingstoke: Palgrave Macmillan, pp. 1–26.

Deeg, R. (2005) 'Path dependency, institutional complementarity and change in national business systems', in G. Morgan, R. Whitley and E. Moen (eds) *Changing Capitalisms? Internationalism, Institutional Change, and Systems of Economic Organisation*, Oxford: Oxford University Press, pp. 22–52.

Delgado, I.G., Condé, E, Ésther, A. and Salles, H.S. (2008) 'Estudo comparativo de política industrial: as trajetórias do Brasil, Argentina, México, Coréia do Sul, EUA, Espanha e Alemanha', ABDI-FUNDEP, Brasília, www.abdi.com.br/Paginas/estudo.aspx (accessed November 2010).

Demirağ, I. and Serter, M. (2003) 'Ownership patterns and control in Turkish listed companies', *Corporate Governance* 11(1): 40–52.

Department of Finance (DOF) (1996) *Growth, Employment and Redistribution: A Macroeconomic Strategy*, Pretoria: Department of Finance.

Dicken, P. (2011) *Global Shift. Mapping the Changing Contours of the World Economy*, sixth edn, Los Angeles CA: Sage.

Dickson, B. (2008) *Wealth into Power: The Communist Party's Embrace of China's Private Sector*, Cambridge: Cambridge University Press.

Diniz, E. and Boschi, R. (2004) *Empresários, Interesses e Mercado: Dilemas do Desenvolvimento no Brasil*, Belo Horizonte: UFMG.

——(2007) *A Difícil Rota do Desenvolvimento: Empresários e a Agenda Pós-neoliberal*, Belo Horizonte: UFMG.

Doctor, M. (2010) 'Is Brazilian capitalism at an institutional equilibrium? A varieties of capitalism approach', *Desenvolvimento em Debate* 1(1): 51–69.

dos Santos, T. (1978) 'The crisis of development theory and the problem of dependence in Latin America', in H. Bernstein (ed.) *Underdevelopment and Development: The Third World Today*, Harmondsworth: Penguin, pp. 57–80.

DTI (2011) *Industrial Policy Action Plan 2011/12 – 2013/14*, Pretoria: Republic of South Africa, Department of Trade and Industry, February.

Duran, B. and Yildirim, E. (2005) 'Islamism, trade unionism and civil society: the case of Hak-İş labour confederation in Turkey', *Middle Eastern Studies* 41(2): 227–47.

Düşkün, Y. (2009) *Party Positions and Privatization in Turkey*, unpublished masters project, Istanbul: Sabancı University.

EBRD (2012) *Harnessing Regional Diversity. Diversifying Russia*, London: European Bank of Reconstruction and Development.

——(n.d.) 'Structural change indicators', London: European Bank of Reconstruction and Development, www.ebrd.com (accessed 10 December 2012).

Eder, M. (2004) 'Populism as a barrier to integration with the EU: rethinking the Copenhagen criteria', in M. Uğur and N. Canefe (eds) *Turkey and European Integration: Accession Prospects and Issues*, New York and London: Routledge, pp. 49–74.

EDGAR (2012) *CO2 Time Series 1990–2011 per Capita for World Countries*, European Commission, Joint Research Centre, edgar.jrc.ec.europa.eu/overview.php?v=CO2ts_pc1990-2011 (accessed July 2012).

Edin, M. (2003) 'State capacity and local agent control in China: CCP cadre management from a township perspective', *China Quarterly* 173: 35–52.

Edmonds, C., La Croix, S.J. and Li, Y. (2008) 'China's rise as a trading power', in C.A. McNally (ed.) *China's Emergent Political Economy – Capitalism in the Dragon's Lair*, New York and London: Routledge, pp. 169–89.

Edwards, L. (2005) 'Has South Africa liberalised its trade?' *South African Journal of Economics* 73(4): 754–75.

Eichengreen, B. (2011) *Exorbitant Privilege: The Rise and Fall of the Dollar and the Future of the International Monetary System*, Oxford: Oxford University Press.

Elizondo Mayer-Serra, C. (2002) 'El estado Mexicano después de su reforma', in C. Elizondo Mayer-Serra and B. Nacif Hernandez (eds) *Lecturas Sobre el Cambio Político en México*, Mexico City: CIDE and Fondo de Cultura Económica, pp. 151–74.

Encarnation, D.J. (1989) *Dislodging Multinationals: India's Strategy in Comparative Perspective*, Ithaca NY: Cornell University Press.

Ercan, M. and Öniş, Z. (2001) 'Turkish privatization: institutions and dilemmas', *Turkish Studies* 2(1): 109–34.

Ernst, D. and Naughton, B. (2008) 'China's emerging industrial economy: insights from the IT industry', in C.A. McNally (ed.) *China's Emergent Political Economy – Capitalism in the Dragon's Lair*, New York and London: Routledge, pp. 39–59.

EU Commission (2012) *European Economic Forecast – Autumn 2011*, Brussels: European Commission.

Faure, D. (2006) *China and Capitalism: A History of Business Enterprise in Modern China*, Hong Kong: Hong Kong University Press.

Feinstein, A. (2007) *After the Party*, Jeppestown: Jonathan Ball.

Figueiredo, A.C. (2001) 'Instituições e política no controle do executivo', *Dados* 44(4): 689–727.

Figueiredo, A.C. and Limongi, F. (1999) *Executivo e Legislativo na Nova Ordem Constitucional*, Rio de Janeiro: Fundação Getulio Vargas Editora.

Fries, S., Lysenko, T. and Polanec, S. (2003) 'The 2002 business environment and enterprise performance survey: results from a survey of 6,100 firms', EBRD Working Paper No. 47.

Frye, T. (2011) 'Korrupcija i verhovenstvo zakona', in S. Guriev, A. Kuchins and A. Aslund (eds) *Rossija Posle Krizisa*, Moskva: Alpina Business Books.

Gall, G. (1997) 'Trade unions and the ANC in the "new" South Africa', *ROAPE* 24(72): 203–18.

Gallagher, M.E. (2005) *Contagious Capitalism: Globalization and the Politics of Labor in China*, Princeton NJ: Princeton University Press.

Gates, H. (1996) *China's Motor: A Thousand Years of Petty Capitalism*, Ithaca NY: Cornell University Press.

Gelman, V. and Tarusina, I. (2000) 'Studies of political elites in Russia. issues and alternatives', *Communist and Post-Communist Studies* 33(3): 311–29.

Gerschenkron, A. (1962) *Economic Backwardness in Historical Perspective: A Book of Essays*, Cambridge, MA: Harvard University Press.

Gevisser, M. (2007) *Thabo Mbeki: The Dream Deferred*, Johannesburg: Jonathan Ball.

Gocek, F.M. (1996) *Rise of the Bourgeoisie, Demise of Empire: Ottoman Westernization and Social Change*, Oxford: Oxford University Press.

GOI (2010) *Economic Survey 2009–10*, New Delhi: Government of India, Ministry of Finance.

——(2012) *Economic Survey 2011–12*, New Delhi: Government of India, Ministry of Finance.

Gold, T., Guthrie, D. and Wank, D. (eds) (2002) *Social Connections in China: Institutions, Culture, and the Changing Nature of Guanxi*, Cambridge and New York: Cambridge University Press.

Goldman, M.I. (2010) *Petrostate. Putin, Power and the New Russia*, New York: Oxford University Press.

Golovshinskii, K.I., Parkhomenko, S.A., Rimskii, V.L. and Satarov, G.A. (2004) 'Business and corruption: how to combat business participation in corruption', www.indem.ru (accessed 10 December 2012).

Gomes, A.V. and Prado, M.M. (2011) 'Flawed freedom of association in Brazil: how unions can become an obstacle to meaningful reforms in the labour law system', *Comparative Labor Law & Policy Journal* 32(4): 843–89.

Gordhan, P. (2011) *2011 Budget Speech by Minister of Finance Pravin Gordhan*, 23 February, Pretoria: South African Government Information.

Government of India (2007) *Report on Conditions of Work and Promotion of Livelihoods in the Unorganized Sector*, National Commission for Enterprises in the Unorganized Sector (NCEUS): New Delhi.

Goyal, S.K. (1979) *Monopoly Capital and Public Policy*, New Delhi: Allied Publishers Private Ltd.

Gqubule, D. (ed.) (2006) *Making Mistakes, Righting Wrongs: Insights into Black Economic Empowerment*, Johannesburg: Jonathan Ball.

Grant, C. (2012) *Russia, China and Global Governance*, London: Centre for European Reform.

Green, P. (2008) *Choice, Not Fate: The Life and Times of Trevor Manuel*, Johannesburg, South Africa: Penguin Books.

Gregory, P.R. and Zhou, K. (2009) 'How China won and Russia lost', *Policy Review* 158: 35–50.

Gudkov, L. and Zaslavsky, V. (2011) *Russland. Kein Weg aus dem postkommunistischen Übergang?* Berlin: Wagenbach.

Guriev, S. and Rachinsky, A. (2005) 'The role of oligarchs in Russian capitalism', *Journal of Economic Perspectives* 19(1): 131–50.

Gürsoy, Y.F. (2012) 'The changing role of the military in Turkish politics: democratization through coup plots?' *Democratization* 19(4): 735–60.

Gustafson, T. (1999) *Capitalism Russian-Style*, Cambridge: Cambridge University Press.

Hale, H.E. (2007) 'Correlates of clientelism: political economy, politicised ethnicity, and post-communist transition', in H. Kitschelt and S.I. Wilkenson (eds) *Patrons, Clients and Politics*, Cambridge: Cambridge University Press, pp. 227–50.

Hall, P. and Gingerich, D. (2009) 'Varieties of capitalism and institutional complementarities in the political economy: an empirical analysis', *British Journal of Political Science* 39(3): 449–82.

Hall, P.A. and Soskice, D. (2001) 'An introduction to varieties of capitalism', in P.A. Hall and D. Soskice (eds) *Varieties of Capitalism: Institutional Foundations of Comparative Advantage*, Cambridge: Cambridge University Press, pp. 1–78.

Hall, P.A. and Thelen, K. (2009) 'Institutional change in varieties of capitalism', *Socio-Economic Review* 7: 7–34.

Hall-Jones, P. (2007) *Unionism and Economic Performance*, New Unionism News Wire, www. newunionism.net (accessed 8 February 2012).

Hamilton, G.G. (ed.) (1996) 'The theoretical significance of Asian business networks', in G. G. Hamilton (ed.) *Asian Business Networks*, Berlin: Walter de Gruyter.

Hancke, B., Rhodes, M. and Thatcher, M. (2007) 'Introduction: beyond varieties of capitalism', in B. Hancke, M. Rhodes and M. Thatcher (eds) *Beyond Varieties of Capitalism: Contradictions, Complementarities & Change*, Oxford: Oxford University Press, pp. 3–38.

Handley, A. (2008) *Business and the State in Africa: Economic Policy-Making in the Neo-Liberal Era*, Cambridge: Cambridge University Press.

Harcourt, M. and Wood, G. (2003) 'Is there a future for a labour accord in South Africa?' *Capital and Class* 27(1): 81–106.

Hay, C. (2004) 'Common trajectories, variable [paces, divergent outcomes? models of European capitalism under conditions of complex economic interdependence', *Review of International Political Economy* 11(2): 231–62.

Hayter, S., Fashoyin, T. and Kochan, T. (2011) 'Review essay: collective bargaining for the 21st century', *Journal of Industrial Relations* 53(2): 225–47.

Hazari, R.K. (assisted by Oza, A.N.) (1966) *The Structure of the Private Corporate Sector, A Study of Concentration, Ownership and Control*, Bombay: Asia Publishing House.

He, K. and Feng, H. (2008) 'A path to democracy: in search of China's democratization model', *Asian Perspective* 32(3): 139–69.

Heilmann, S. (2010) 'Economic governance: authoritarian upgrading and innovation potential', in J. Fewsmith (ed.) *China Today, China Tomorrow: Domestic Politics, Economy and Society*, Lanham, MD: Rowman and Littlefield, pp. 109–26.

Hellman, J., Jones, G. and Kaufman, D. (2000) 'Seize the state, seize the day: state capture, corruption, and influence in transition economies', World Bank Policy Research Working Paper No. 2444.

Hendley, K. (2010) 'The law in post-Putin Russia', in S.K. Wegren and D.R. Herspring (eds) *After Putin's Russia. Past Imperfect, Future Uncertain*, Lanham, MD: Rowman and Littlefield Publishers, pp. 83–108.

Heper, M. (1987) 'State, democracy and bureaucracy in Turkey,' in M. Heper (ed.) *The State and Public Bureaucracies, A Comparative Perspective*, New York, Westport, London: Greenwood Press.

Heredia, B. (2002) 'Estructura política y reforma económica: el caso de México', in C. Elizondo Mayer-Serra, and B. Nacif-Hernández (eds) *Lecturas Sobre el Cambio Político en México*, Mexico City: CIDE and Fondo de Cultura Económica, pp. 175–228.

Herrigel, G. (2005) 'Institutionalists at the limits of institutionalism: a constructivist critique of the two edited volumes from Wolfgang Streeck and Kozo Yamamura', *Socio-Economic Review* 3(3): 559–67.

Higley, J., Pakulski, J. and Wesolowski, W. (1998) 'Introduction. elite change and democratic regimes in Eastern Europe', in J. Higley, J. Pakulski and W. Wesolowski (eds) *Post-communist Elites and Democracy in Eastern Europe*, Basingstoke: Palgrave Macmillan, pp. 1–33.

Hirsch, A. (2005) *Season of Hope: Economic Reform under Mandela and Mbeki*, Pietermaritzburg: University of KwaZulu-Natal Press.

Ho, P. (2001) 'Who owns China's land? policies, property rights and deliberate institutional ambiguity', *The China Quarterly* 166: 394–421.

Hodgson, G. and Knudsen, T. (2006) 'Why we need a generalized Darwinism and why a generalized Darwinism is not enough', *Journal of Economic Behavior & Organization* 6(1): 1–19.

Hoffman, D. (2007) *Oligarkhi. Bogatstvo i vlast v novoj Rossii*, Moskva: Kolibri.

Hopewell, K. (2013) 'New protagonists in global economic governance: Brazilian agribusiness at the WTO', *New Political Economy* (online), 9 January 2013.

Höpner, M. (2005) 'What connects industrial relations and corporate governance? explaining institutional complementarity', *Socio-Economic Review* 3(2): 331–58.

Howell, J. (2006) 'Reflections on the Chinese state', *Development and Change* 37(2): 273–97.

Hsing, Y. (1998) *Making Capitalism in China: the Taiwan Connection*, New York: Oxford University Press.

Huang, Y. (1996) *Inflation and Investment Controls in China: The Political Economy of Central-Local Relations During the Reform Era*, Cambridge: Cambridge University Press.

——(2008) *Capitalism with Chinese Characteristics: Entrepreneurship and the State*, Cambridge: Cambridge University Press.

IBGE (2008) *National Household Sample Survey 2007 (PNAD)*, Rio de Janeiro: Instituto Brasileiro de Geografia e Estatística.

——(2010) *National Household Sample Survey 2009 (PNAD)*, Rio de Janeiro: Instituto Brasileiro de Geografia e Estatística.

——(2012) *National Household Sample Survey 2011 (PNAD)*, Rio de Janeiro: Instituto Brasileiro de Geografia e Estatística.

IEDI (2009) 'Industrial production and jobs: more positive signs with distinct regional and sector characteristics', *IEDI Newsletter* 371, www.iedi.org.br (accessed December 2011).

Iheduru, O. (2002) 'Social concertation, labour unions and the creation of a black bourgeoisie in South Africa', *Commonwealth and Comparative Politics* 40(2): 47–85.

Ikenberry, G.J. (2008) 'The rise of China and the future of the West – can the liberal system survive?' *Foreign Affairs* 87(1): 23–37.

IMF (2012) *World Economic Outlook Update. Global Recovery Stalls, Downside Risks Intensify*, Washington DC: International Monetary Fund, 24 January, www.imf.org/external/pubs/ft/weo/2012/update/01/index.htm (accessed 9 February 2013).

——(2013) *World Economic Outlook, Update*, Washington, DC: International Monetary Fund, 23 January, www.imf.org/external/pubs/ft/weo/2013/update/01/pdf/0113.pdf (accessed 9 February 2013).

Incecik, S. and Im, U. (2012) 'Air pollution in mega cities: a case study of Istanbul', in M. Khare (ed.) *Air Pollution – Monitoring, Modeling and Health*, Rijeka and Shanghai: InTech, pp. 77–116.

INDEM (2005) 'Corruption process in Russia: level, structure, trends', www.indem.ru/en/publicat/2005diag_engV.htm (accessed 10 December 2012).

Intracen (2012) *Trade Competitiveness Map*, Washington: International Trade Center, legacy.intracen.org/appli1/TradeCom/TP_TP_CI.aspx?RP=008&yr=2010.

IPEA (2008) 'Pobreza e mudança social', PNAD 2007: Primeiras Análises, *Comunicado da Presidência*, no. 09.

——(2010) 'Pobreza, desigualdade e políticas públicas', *Comunicado da Presidência* no. 38 Brasília, www.ipea.gov.br/sites/000/2/comunicado_presidencia/100112Comunicado38.pdf (accessed December 2011).

Jackson, G. (2005) 'Modelling complementarity. multiple functions and different levels', *Socio-Economic Review* 3(2): 378–81.

Jardim, M.C. (2009) *Entre a Solidariedade e o Risco: Sindicatos e Fundos de Pensão em Tempos de Governo Lula*, São Paulo: Annablume.

Jefferson, G.H. and Rawski, T.G. (1994) 'Enterprise reform in Chinese industry', *Journal of Economic Perspectives* 8(2): 47–70.

Jenkins, G. (2007) 'Continuity and change: prospects for civil-military relations in Turkey', *International Affairs* 83(2): 339–55.

Jensen, D.N. (2001) 'How Russia is ruled', in P. Rutland (ed.) *Business and the State in Contemporary Russia*, Boulder CO: Westview, pp. 33–64.

Jha, R. (2007) 'Options for Indian pharmaceutical industry in the changing environment', *Economic and Political Weekly* 42(39): 3958–67.

Joffe, A., Kaplan, D., Kaplinsky, R. and Lewis, D. (1995) *Improving Manufacturing Performance in South Africa: Report of the Industrial Strategy Project*, Cape Town: University of Cape Town Press.

Johnson, C. (1982) *MITI and the Japanese Miracle: The Growth of Industrial Policy 1925–1975*, Stanford CA: Stanford University Press.

Jordan, P. (2012) 'Mbeki's vitriol evades Reason', *Sunday Independent*, 28 October, www.safpi.org/news/article/2012/pallo-jordan-mbekis-vitriol-evades-reason (accessed July 2012).

Kahler, M. (2010) 'Asia and the reform of global governance', *Asian Economic Policy Review* 5 (2): 178–93.

Kamu Harcamaları İzleme Platformu (Public Expenditures Monitoring Platform) (n.d.) www.kahip.org (accessed 19 November 2012).

Kapelushnikov, R. (1999) 'Rossiyskiy rynok truda: adaptaziya bes restrukturizacii', *Trud i Zanyatost*: 69–93.

——(2009) *Konez Rossiyskoy Modeli Rynka Truda?* Moskva: Visshaya Shkola Economiki.

Kaplan, D. (2003) 'Manufacturing performance and policy in South Africa', paper presented to the Trade and Industry Policy Secretariat (TIPS) and Development Policy Research Unit (DPRU) Forum, Johannesburg.

——(2007) 'The constraints and institutional challenges facing industrial policy in South Africa: a way forward', *Transformation* 64: 91–111.

Karackattu, J.T. (2011) 'BRICS: opportunities and challenges', *Idsa Issue Brief*, New Delhi: Institute for Defence Studies and Analysis.

Kasahara, Y. (2011) 'A Regulação do Setor Financeiro Brasileiro: Uma análise exploratória das relações entre Estado e setor privado', in R. Boschi *Variedades de Capitalismo, Política e Desenvolvimento na América Latin*, Belo Horizonte: UFMG.

Kaufmann, D., Kraay, A. and Mastruzzi, M. (2010) *The Worldwide Governance Indicators: Methodology and Analytical Issues*, Washington, DC: World Bank Research Policy Paper 5430.

Kazgan, G. (2004) *Tanzimat'tan 21. Yuzyila Turkiye Ekonomisi*, Istanbul: Bilgi Universitesi.

Kelliher, D. (1992) *Peasant Power in China*, New Haven CT: Yale University Press.

Kenworthy, L. (2006) 'Institutional coherence and macro-economic performance', *Socio-Economic Review* 4(1): 69–91.

Keyder, C. (1987) *State and Class in Turkey: A Study in Capitalist Development*, New York: Verso.

King, L. (2007) 'Central European capitalism in comparative perspective', in B. Hancke, M. Rhodes and M. Thatcher (eds) *Beyond Varieties of Capitalism: Contradictions, Complementarities & Change*, Oxford: Oxford University Press, pp. 307–27.

Kirişçi, K. (2009) 'The transformation of Turkish foreign policy: the rise of the trading state', *New Perspectives on Turkey* 40: 29–57.

Kliamkin, I. and Timofeev, L. (2000) *Tenevaya Rossiya*, Moskva: Rossiyskiy Gosudarstvenniy Gumanitarniy Universitet.

Kochanek, S.A. (1987) 'Briefcase politics in India: the congress party and the business elite', *Asian Survey* 27(12): 1278–301.

Kohli, A. (2006) 'Politics of growth in India 1980–2005', Part I ('The 1980s') and Part II ('The 1990s and Beyond'), *Economic and Political Weekly*, 1 April: 1251–59; and 8 April: 1361–70.

Kohli, A. and Shue, V. (1994) 'State power and social forces: on political contention and accommodation in the third world', in J.S. Migdal, A. Kohli and V. Shue (eds) *State Power and Social Forces – Domination and Transformation in the Third World*, Cambridge: Cambridge University Press, pp. 293–326.

Kornai, J. (1992) *The Socialist System – The Political Economy of Communism*, Princeton, NJ: Princeton University Press.

Kotkin, S. (2007) 'Russia under Putin. toward democracy or dictatorship?' *FPRI e-notes*, Philadelphia PA: Foreign Policy Research Institute.

KPMG (2012) *The State versus Jacob G. Zuma and others. Forensic Investigation*, draft report on factual findings, for review only; report undated and leaked by the *Mail and Guardian* newspaper, 6 December 2012 (online), cdn.mg.co.za/content/documents/2012/12/06/KPMG_report.pdf (accessed June 2012).

Krueger, A. (1974) 'The political economy of the rent-seeking society', *The American Economic Review* 64(3): 291–303.

——(1995) 'Partial adjustment and growth in the 1980s in Turkey', in R. Dornbush and S. Edwards (eds) *Reform, Recovery and Growth, Latin America and Middle East*, Chicago, IL and London: University of Chicago Press, pp. 343–68.

Kryshtanovskaya, O. (2005) *Anatomie der russischen Elite*, Köln: Kiepenheuer & Witsch.

Kryshtanovskaya, O. and White, S. (2005) 'The rise of the Russian business elite', *Communist and Post-Communist Studies* 38(3): 293–307.

Kudrov, V. (2009) 'Ekonomika rossii: sushnost i vidimost', *Mirovaya Economica i Mezhdunarodniye Otnosheniya* 2: 39–48.

Kuş, B. and Özel, I. (2010) 'United we restrain, divided we rule: neoliberal reforms and labor unions in Turkey and Mexico', *European Journal of Turkish Studies* 11, online 21 October 2010.

Kynev, A. (2012) 'Regionalniye reformi Putina pri presidente Medvedeve: zentralisaziya prodolzhayetsa', *Neprikosnovenniy Zapas* 81 (25–35), www.nlobooks.ru/node/1789 (accessed 20 February 2013).

Kynge, J. (2009) *China Shakes the World. The Rise of a Hungry Nation*, London: Phoenix.

Lane, D. (2006) 'Post-state socialism: a diversity of capitalisms?' in D. Lane and M. Myant (eds) *Varieties of Capitalism in Post-Communist Countries*, Basingstoke: Palgrave Macmillan, pp. 13–39.

Lauth, H.-J. and Kauff, O. (2012) *Demokratiemessung. Der KID als aggregiertes Maß für die komparative Forschung. Empirische Befunde der Regimeentwicklung von 1996 bis 2010*, Würzburger Arbeitspapiere für Politikwissenschaft und Sozialforschung, no. 2; Würzburg University.

Ledeneva, A. (1998) *Russia's Economy of Favours*, Cambridge: Cambridge University Press.

——(2001) *Unwritten Rules. How Russia Really Works*, London: Centre for European Studies.

——(2011) 'Telephone justice in Russia', *The EU-Russia Centre Review* 18: 4–22.

Lee, K., Hahn, D. and Lin, J. (2002) 'Is China following the East Asian model? a "comparative institutional analysis" perspective', *The China Review* 2(1): 85–120.

Levada Centre (n.d.) *Indeksi odobreniya deyatelnosti Vladimira Putina i Dmitriya Medvedeva*, www.levada.ru/indeksy (accessed 1 February 2013).

Levine, D.H. and Molina, J.E. (2007) 'The quality of democracy in Latin America', *Kellog Institute*, Working Paper 342.

Levitsky, S. (2007) 'From populism to clientelism? The transformation of labor-based party linkages in Latin America', in H. Kitschelt and S.I. Wilkenson (eds) *Patrons, Clients and Politics*, Cambridge: Cambridge University Press, pp. 206–26.

Li, C. (2008) *China's Changing Political Landscape. Prospects for Democracy*, Washington, DC: Brookings Institution.

Li, H. and Rozelle, S. (2003) 'Privatizing rural China: insider privatization, innovative contracts and the performance of township enterprises', *The China Quarterly*, 176, December: 981–1005.

Li, Y. and Sheldon, P. (2011) 'Skill shortages: where labour supply problems meet employee poaching', in P. Sheldon, S. Kim, Y. Li and M. Warner (eds) *China's Changing Workplace: Dynamism, Diversity and Disparity*, London: Routledge, pp. 129–43.

Lin, J.Y. (2011) *Demystifying the Chinese Economy*, Cambridge: Cambridge University Press.

Linz, J.J. and Stepan, A. (1996) *Problems of Democratic Transition and Consolidation*, Baltimore MD: The Johns Hopkins University Press.

Liu, Y. (1992) 'Reform from below: the private economy and local politics in the rural industrialization of Wenzhou', *China Quarterly* 130, June: 292–316.

Lokanathan, P.S. (1935) *Industrial Organization in India*, London: George Allen and Unwin Ltd.

Luethje, B. (2012) 'Diverging trajectories: economic rebalancing and labor policies in China', East-West Center Working Papers, Politics, Governance, and Security Series, no. 23, April, www.eastwestcenter.org/sites/default/files/private/pswp023.pdf (accessed 10 February 2013).

Luethje, B., Luo, S. and Zhang, H. (2011) 'Socio-economic transformation and industrial relations in China', final research report, unpublished manuscript, Frankfurt/Düsseldorf: Hans Böckler Stiftung.

Luzan, S. (2009) 'Nazionalisaziya poslednikh let', in V. Tambovtsev (ed.) *Prava Sobstvennosti, Privatisaziya i Nationalisaziya v Rossii*, Moskva: Novoye Literaturnoje Obozrenije pp. 277–290.

MacFarlane, N. (2006) 'The "R" in BRICs: is Russia an emerging power?' *International Affairs* 82(1): 41–57.

MacKinnon, R. (2011) 'China's "networked authoritarianism"', *Journal of Democracy* 22(2): 32–46.

Madison, A. (2001) *The World Economy. A Millennial Perspective*, Paris: Organisation for Economic Co-operation and Development.

Mahoney, J. and Thelen, K. (eds) (2009) *Explaining Institutional Change, Ambiguity, Agency and Power*, Cambridge: Cambridge University Press.

Makarov, S. (2011) 'Rating korrumpirovannosti ministerstv i vedomstv Rossii ot *Novoj Gazeti*', in *Novaja Gazeta*, 28 June, novayagazeta-nn.ru/2011/191/reiting-korrumpirovannosti-ministerstv-i-vedomstv-rossii-ot-novoi-gazety.html (accessed 10 December 2012).

Mancuso, W.P. (2004) 'O *lobby* da indústria no Congresso Nacional: empresariado e política no Brasil contemporâneo', *Dados* 47(3): 505–47.

——(2007) 'O empresariado como ator político no Brasil: balanço da literatura e agenda de pesquisa', *Revista de Sociologia e Política* 28: 131–46.

Mani, S. (2009) 'Is India becoming more innovative since 1991? Some disquieting features', *Economic and Political Weekly* 44(46): 41–51.

Marques-Pereira, J. and Théret, B. (2009) 'Mediations Institutionnelles de la Regulation Sociale et Dynamiques Macro-Economiques', *Ponto de Vista*, 9 September.

Marx, K. (1970) *Das Kapital I. Zur Kritik der politischen Ökonomie*, Berlin: Dietz Verlag.

Marx, K. and Engels, F. (1966) 'Manifest der kommunistischen Partei', in I. Fetscher (ed.) *Marx-Engels Studienausgabe. Bd. 3. Politische Ökonomie*, Frankfurt/M.: Fischer Bücherei, pp. 59–82.

Mazumdar, S. (2008a) 'The corporate sector and Indian industrialization: a historical perspective', in S.R. Hashim, K.S. Chalapati Rao, K.V.K. Ranganathan and M.R. Murthy (eds) *Industrial Development and Globalisation*, New Delhi: Academic Foundation, pp. 193–236.

——(2008b) 'Investment and growth in India under liberalization: asymmetries and instabilities', *Economic and Political Weekly* 43(49): 68–77.

——(2008c) 'Crony capitalism and India: before and after liberalization', Institute for Studies in Industrial Development, Working Paper No: 2008/04.

——(2010) 'Industry and services in growth and structural change in India', Working Paper No: 2010/02, New Delhi: Institute for Studies in industrial Development.

Mboweni, T. (2012) 'Jordan Wrong on ANC policy choice', *Sunday Independent*, 18 November.

McCarthy, D.J., Puffer, S.M. and Naumov, A.I. (2000) 'Russia's retreat to statization and the implications for business', *Journal of World Business* 35(3): 256–74.

McKinley, D. (1997) *The ANC and the Liberation Struggle: A Critical Political Biography*, London: Pluto Press.

McNally, C.A. (2002) 'Strange bedfellows: communist party institutions in the corporate governance of Chinese state holding corporations', *Business and Politics* 4(1): 91–115.

——(2008a) 'Introduction: the China impact', in C.A. McNally (ed.) *China's Emergent Political Economy – Capitalism in the Dragon's Lair*, New York and London: Routledge, 3–16.

——(2008b) 'The institutional contours of China's emergent capitalism', in C.A. McNally (ed.) *China's Emergent Political Economy – Capitalism in the Dragon's Lair*, New York and London: Routledge, pp. 107–25.

——(2011) 'China's changing *Guanxi* capitalism – private entrepreneurs between Leninist control and relentless accumulation', *Business and Politics* 13(3): 1–28.

——(2012) 'Sino-capitalism. China's re-emergence and the international political economy', *World Politics* 64(4): 741–76.

——(n.d., forthcoming) 'The challenge of refurbished state capitalism: implications for the global political economic order', *Der Moderne Staat* (The Modern State).

McNally, C.A. and Lee, P.N.S. (1998) 'Is big beautiful? Restructuring China's state sector under the policy of *Zhuada*', *Issues and Studies* 34(9): 22–48.

MDIF (2012) *Brazilian Trade Balance*, Brasilia: Ministry of Development, Industry and Foreign Trade.

Mearsheimer, J.J. (2010) 'The gathering storm: China's challenge to U.S. power in Asia', The Fourth Annual Michael Hintze Lecture in International Security, University of Sydney, 4 August.

Mello, B. (2010) 'Communists and compromisers: explaining divergences within Turkish labor activism, 1960–80', *European Journal of Turkish Studies* (October).

MERG (1993) *Making Democracy Work: A Framework for Macroeconomic Policy in South Africa*, Macroeconomic Research Group, Cape Town: Oxford University Press.

Michelson, E. (2007) 'Lawyers, political embeddedness, and institutional continuity in China's transition from socialism', *American Journal of Sociology* 113(2): 352–414.

Miller, B.D. (1997) *The Endangered Sex: Neglect of Female Children in Rural North India*, Oxford: Oxford University Press.

Ministry of Labor and Social Security (2012) *Çalışma Hayatı İstatistikler'* (Labour Statistics), Ankara: Ministry of Labor and Social Security, www.csgb.gov.tr/csgbPortal/ShowProperty/WLP%20Repository/sgb/dosyalar/istatistik (accessed 3 November 2012).

Ministry of Planning (2009) *A mão visível do governo*, Brasilia: Ministério do Planejamento, jbonline.terra.com.br/pextra/2009/09/02/e020927895.asp (accessed June 2012).

Mizobata, S. (2008) 'Introduction: economic transformation from the varieties of capitalism', in S. Mizobata (ed.) *Varieties of Capitalism and Transformation*, Kyoto: CAEA, pp. 2–42.

Moll, P. (1996) 'Compulsory centralisation of collective bargaining in South Africa', *American Economic Review* 82(2): 326–29.

Moraes, W.S. (2010) 'Capitalismo Sindicalista de Conciliação e Capitalismo de las Calles: Brasil e Venezuela no Pós-Neoliberalism', in R. Boschi (ed.) *Variedades de Capitalismo, Política e Desenvolvimento na América Latina*, Belo Horizonte: UFMG.

Morgan, G. (2005) 'Introduction: changing capitalisms? internationalism, institutional change, and systems of economic organisation', in G. Morgan, R. Whitley and E. Moen (eds) *Changing Capitalisms? Internationalism, Institutional Change, and Systems of Economic Organisation*, Oxford: Oxford University Press, pp. 1–18.

Mozur, P. and Orlik, T. (2013) 'China laborers linger in cities', *The Wall Street Journal Asia* (Hong Kong), 2 January: 4.

Müftüler-Baç, M. (2005) 'Turkey's political reforms and the impact of the European Union', *South European Society and Politics* 10(1): 17–31.

Myant, M. and Drahokoupil, J. (2010) *Transition Economies. Political Economy in Russia, Eastern Europe and Central Asia*, Hoboken NJ: Wiley-Blackwell.

Mykhnenko, V. (2007) 'Strengths and weaknesses of "weak" coordination: economic institutions, revealed comparative advantages, and socio-economic performance of mixed market economies in Poland and Ukraine', in B. Hancke, M. Rhodes and M. Thatcher (eds) *Beyond Varieties of Capitalism: Contradictions, Complementarities & Change*, Oxford: Oxford University Press, pp. 351–78.

Nathan, A.J. (2009) 'Authoritarian impermanence', *Journal of Democracy* 20(3): 37–40.

——(2013) 'Foreseeing the unforeseeable', *Journal of Democracy* 28(1): 20–25.

Nattrass, N. (1994) 'Politics and economics in ANC economic policy', *African Affairs* 93(372): 343–59.

——(1995) 'The crisis in South African gold mining', *World Development* 23(5): 857–68.

——(1996) 'Gambling on investment: competing economic strategies in South Africa', *Transformation*, 31 December.

——(1997a) 'Collective action problems and the role of South African business in national and regional accords', *South African Journal of Business Management* 28(3): 105–12.

——(1997b) *Business and Employer Organisations in South Africa*, International Labour Office, Employment and Training Department, Occasional Report no.5, Geneva.

——(1999) 'Globalisation and social accords: a comparative analysis of Sweden, Australia and South Africa', *Labour, Capital and Society* 32(2): 158–90.

——(2000) 'Inequality, unemployment and wage-setting institutions in South Africa', *Studies in Economics and Econometrics* 24(3): 129–42.

——(2001) 'High productivity now: a critique of South Africa's growth strategy', *Transformation* 45: 1–24.

——(2011) 'The new growth path: game changing vision or cop out?' *The South African Journal of Science* 107(3/4): 1–8.

Nattrass, N. and Seekings, J. (2012) *Differentiation within the South African Clothing Industry: Implications for Wage-Setting and Employment*, Centre for Social Science Research, Working Paper no. 307, University of Cape Town.

Naughton, B. (1992) 'Implications of the state monopoly over industry and its relaxation', *Modern China* 18(1): 14–41.

——(1995) *Growing Out of the Plan: Chinese Economic Reform, 1978–1990*, Cambridge: Cambridge University Press.

——(2007) *The Chinese Economy. Transitions and Growth*, Cambridge, Massachusetts: MIT Press.

——(2008) 'SOE policy – profiting the SASAC way', *China Economic Quarterly* 12(2): 19–26.

Nayyar, D. (ed.) (1994) *Industrial Growth and Stagnation: The Debate in India*, Bombay: Oxford University Press for Sameeksha Trust.

——(1998) 'Economic development and political democracy: interaction of economics and politics in independent India', *Economic and Political Weekly* 33(49): 3121–31.

——(2008) 'The internationalization of firms from India: investment, mergers and acquisitions', *Oxford Development Studies* 36(1): 111–31.

Nee, V. and Opper, S. (2007) 'On politicized capitalism', in V. Nee and R. Swedberg (eds) *On Capitalism*, Stanford CA: Stanford University Press, pp. 93–127.

——(2012) *Capitalism from Below. Markets and Institutional Change in China*, Cambridge, Massachusetts: Harvard University Press.

Nemtsov, B. and Milov, V. (2010) 'Putin: what 10 years of Putin have brought', www.putin-itogi.ru/putin-what-10-years-of-putin-have-brought/#2 (accessed 10 December 2012).

Nölke, A. and Vliegenthart, A. (2009) 'Enlarging the varieties of capitalism: the emergence of dependent market economies in East Central Europe', *World Politics* 61(4): 671–702.

NSSO (2006) *Employment and Unemployment Situation in India 2004–05*, New Delhi: National Sample Survey Office.

——(2011) *Key Indicators of Employment and Unemployment in India 2009–10*, New Delhi: National Sample Survey Office.

O'Donnell, G. and Schmitter, P.C. (1986) *Transitions from Authoritarian Rule: Tentative Conclusions About Uncertain Democracies*, Baltimore MD: Johns Hopkins University Press.

OECD (1999) 'Labour Market Performance and the OECD Jobs Strategy', *Economic Outlook* 65, June: 142–61.

——(2008a) *Environmental Outlook to 2030*, Paris: Organisation for Economic Co-operation and Development.

——(2008b) *Growing Unequal*, Paris: Organisation for Economic Co-operation and Development.

——(2009) *OECD in Figures 2009*, Paris: Organisation for Economic Co-operation and Development.

——(2010a) 'Going for growth in Brazil, China, India, Indonesia and South Africa', *General Economics & Future Studies*, 1, Paris: Organisation for Economic Co-operation and Development.

——(2010b) *Tackling Inequalities in Brazil, China, India and South Africa. The Role of Labour Market and Social Policies*, Paris: Organisation for Economic Co-operation and Development.

——(2010c) *OECD Economic Surveys: China*, Paris: Organisation for Economic Co-operation and Development.

——(2010d) 'Population Growth Rates', *OECD Factbook 2010*, Paris: Organisation for Economic Co-operation and Development.

——(2011a) *Employment Outlook 2011*, Paris: Organisation for Economic Co-operation and Development.

——(2011b) *Society at a Glance*, Paris: Organisation for Economic Co-operation and Development.

——(2011c) *Reviews of Labour Market and Social Policy: Russian Federation*, Paris: Organisation for Economic Co-operation and Development.

——(2011d) *OECD Economic Surveys: Russian Federation 2011*, Paris: Organisation for Economic Co-operation and Development.

——(2011e) *State-Owned Enterprise Governance Reform: An Inventory of Recent Change*, Paris: Organisation for Economic Co-operation and Development.

——(2012a) *Economic Outlook 2012, 1*, Paris: Organisation for Economic Co-operation and Development.

——(2012b) *Economic Outlook 2012, 2*, Paris: Organisation for Economic Co-operation and Development.

OECD Library (n.d.) *Employment and Labour Market Statistics: Employment Protection Legislation*, Paris: Organisation for Economic Co-operation and Development, www.oecd-ilibrary.org/employment/data/employment-protection-legislation_lfs-epl-data-en (accessed April 2012).

OECD Statistics Portal (n.d.) *Indicators of Product Market Regulation (PMR). Integrate PRM Indicators*, Paris: Organisation for Economic Co-operation and Development, www.oecd.org/document/36/0,3746,en_2825_495698_35790244_1_1_1_1,00.html (accessed April 2012).

Oi, J.C. (1992) 'Fiscal reform and the economic foundations of local state corporatism in China', *World Politics* 45(1): 99–126.

Oi, J.C. and Walder, A. (eds) (1999) *Property Rights and Economic Reform in China*, Stanford CA: Stanford University Press.

Ökten, Ç. (2006) 'Privatization in Turkey, what has been achieved?', in S. Altug and A. Filiztekin (eds) *The Turkish Economy: The Real Economy, Corporate Governance and Reform*, London: Routledge-Curzon, pp. 227–51.

Önder, N. (1999) *The Political Economy of the State and Social Forces: Changing Forms of State-Labour Relations in Turkey*, PhD thesis, Canada: York University.

Öniş, Z. (2007) 'Conservative globalists versus defensive nationalists: political parties and paradoxes of europeanization in Turkey', *Journal of Southern Europe and the Balkans* 9(3): 247–62.

——(2010) 'Crises and transformations in Turkish political economy', *Turkish Policy Quarterly* 9(3): 45–61.

——(2012) 'The triumph of conservative globalism: the political economy of the AKP era', *Turkish Studies* 13(2): 135–52.

Öniş, Z. and Şenses, F. (eds) (2009) *Turkey and the Global Economy, Neo-liberal Restructuring and Integration in the Post-Crisis Era*, London: Routledge.

OYAK (2012) *Corporate History*, Ankara: OYAK, www.oyak.com.tr/EN/corporate/oyak-in-brief.html (accessed 19 November 2012).

Özbudun, E. (1991) 'The post-1980 legal framework for interest groups associations', in M. Heper (ed.) *Strong State and Economic Interest Groups: The Post-1980 Turkish Experience*, Berlin, New York: Walter de Gruyter, pp. 41–53.

Özel, I. (2003) 'Beyond the orthodox paradox: the break-up of state-business coalitions in Turkey in the 1980s', *Journal of International Affairs* 57(1): 97–112.

——(2010) 'Islamic capital and political Islam in Turkey', in J. Haynes (ed.) *Religion and Politics in Europe, the Middle East and North Africa*, London: Routledge, pp. 139–61.

——(2012a) 'The politics of de-delegation: regulatory (in)dependence in Turkey', *Regulation and Governance* 6(1): 119–29.

——(2012b) 'Is it none of their business? Business and democratization, the case of Turkey', *Democratization*: 1–36.

——(2013) 'Differential Europe within a nation: europeanization of regulation across policy areas', *Journal of European Public Policy*, pp. 741–59.

——(2014) *State-Business Coalitions and Economic Development – Comparative Perspectives from Turkey and Mexico*, London: Routledge, forthcoming.

Pamuk, Ş. (2008) 'Economic change in twentieth-century Turkey: is the glass more than half full?' in R. Kasaba (ed.) *The Cambridge History of Modern Turkey, Turkey in the Modern World*, New York: Cambridge University Press, pp. 266–300.

Papola, T.S. and Sharma, A.N. (2004) 'Labour: down and out?' *Seminar* 537, Special Issue on India Shining, May.

Pappe, Y. and Galukhina, Y. (2009) *Rossijskij Krupnij Biznes. Perviye 15 let*, Moskva: Visshaia Shkola Economiki.

Parsons, R. (2007) 'The emergence of institutionalised social dialogue in South Africa', *South African Journal of Economics* 75(1): 1–21.

Parthasarathi, P. (2011) *Why Europe Grew Rich and Asia Did Not: Global Economic Divergence, 1600–1850*, Oxford: Oxford University Press.

Patnaik, U. (1994) 'India's agricultural development in the light of historical experience', in T.J. Byres (ed.) *The State and Development Planning in India*, Delhi: Oxford University Press, pp. 265–90.

——(1999) *The Long Transition: Essays on Political Economy*, New Delhi: Tulika.

——(2003) 'Food stocks and hunger: the causes of agrarian distress', *Social Scientist* 31(7/8): 15–41.

——(2007) 'Neoliberalism and rural poverty in India', *Economic and Political Weekly* 42(30): 3132–50.

Peck, J. and Nik, T. (2007) 'Variegated capitalism', *Progress in Human Geography* 31(6): 731–72.

Pedersen, J.D. (2008) *Globalization, Development and the State the Performance of India and Brazil since 1990*, Basingstoke: Palgrave Macmillan.

Pei, M. (2006) *China's Trapped Transition: The Limits of Developmental Autocracy*, Cambridge MA: Harvard University Press.

——(2012) 'Is the CCP fragile or resilient?' *Journal of Democracy* 23(1): 27–41.

Perlez, J. (2012) 'Chinese insider offers rare glimpse of U.S.-China frictions', *The New York Times*, 2 April.

Petrov, N. (2011) 'Obilije slabogo gosudarstva', *Pro et Contra*, September–October.

PEW (2012) *Russians Back Protests, Political Freedoms and Putin, Too*, Washington DC: PEW Research Center, 23 May.

Pierson, P. (2004) *Politics in Time. History, Institutions, and Social Analysis*, Princeton NJ: Princeton University Press.

Pleines, H. (2001) 'Korruption und organisierte Kriminalität', in H.-H. Höhmann and H.-H. Schröder (eds) *Russland unter neuer Führung*, Münster: Agenda-Verlag.

PMT (2011) *Privatization: Implementation by Years*, Ankara: Prime Ministry of Turkey, www. oib.gov.tr/program/uygulamalar/1985-2004_years_table.htm (accessed 26 September 2011).

Polanyi, K. (1957) *The Great Transformation. The Political and Economic Origins of Our Time*, Boston MA: Beacon Press.

Politkovskaya, A. (2007) *A Russian Diary*, London: Vintage Books.

Pontusson, J. (2005) 'Varieties and commonalities of capitalism', in D. Coates (ed.) *Varieties of Capitalism, Varieties of Approaches*, Basingstoke: Palgrave Macmillan, pp. 163–88.

Porter, M. (1990) *The Competitive Advantage of Nations*, New York: The Free Press.

Power, T.J. and Taylor, M.M. (2011) 'Introduction', in T.J. Power and M.M. Tayler (eds) *Corruption and Democracy in Brazil. The Struggle for Accountability*, Notre Dame IN: University of Notre Dame Press.

Pro Inno Europe (2011) *Innovation Scoreboard 2010*, Brussels: European Commission.

Qiang, X. (2011) 'The battle for the Chinese internet', *Journal of Democracy* 22(2): 47–61.

Rao, J.M. (1994) 'Agricultural development under state planning', in T.J. Byres (ed.) *The State and Development Planning in India*, Delhi: Oxford University Press, pp. 220–64.

Ray, R.K. (1985) *Industrialisation in India, Growth and Conflict in the Private Corporate Sector: 1914–47*, paperback edition, 2nd impression, Delhi: Oxford University Press.

——(1994) 'Introduction', in R.K. Ray (ed.) *Entrepreneurship and Industry in India, 1800– 1947*, Delhi: Oxford University Press.

Redding, S.G. (1990) *The Spirit of Chinese Capitalism*, Berlin: Walter de Gruyter.

Reddy, D.N. and Mishra, S. (2008) 'Crisis in agriculture and rural distress in post-reform India', in R. Radhakrishna (ed.) *India Development Report 2008*, New Delhi: Oxford University Press, pp. 40–53.

Robinson, V. and Brummer, S. (2006) 'SA democracy incorporated: corporate fronts and political party funding', *Institute for Security Studies*, ISS Paper 129, November: 1–40.

Rodrik, D. (1991) 'Premature liberalization, incomplete stabilization: the Özal debate in Turkey', in M. Bruno, S. Fischer, E. Helpman and N. Leviatan (eds) *Lessons of Economic Stabilization and its Aftermath*, Cambridge MA: The MIT Press.

Roett, R. (2010) *The New Brazil*, Washington, DC: Brookings Institution.

Rogoza, J. (2011) 'In Putin's shadow. Dmitri Medvedev's presidency', *Punkt Widzenia* 11, Warsaw: Center for Eastern Studies: 1–31.

RoyChowdhury, S. (2005) 'Labour and economic reforms: disjointed critiques', in J. Mooij (ed.) *Politics of Economic Reforms in India*, New Delhi: Sage, pp. 264–90.

Rumney, R. (2004) 'Who owns South Africa?: an analysis of state and private ownership patterns', in J. Daniel, R. Southall and J. Lutchman (eds) *State of the Nation, 2004–2005*, Pretoria: HSRC Press, pp. 401–22.

Rungta, R.S. (1970) *The Rise of Business Corporations in India, 1851–1900*, Cambridge: Cambridge University Press.

Runov, A. (2009) 'Tradicii vlasti-sobstvennosti, sistema dolzhnostnikh prav i privatizacia v Rossii', in V. Tambovtsev (ed.) *Prava sobstvennosti, privatizatcia i nationalisacia v Rossii*, Moskva: Novoje Literaturnoje Obozrenije, pp. 90–144.

Runov, A. and Tambovtsev, V. (2009) 'Vlast-sobstvennost ili dolzhnostnije obiazannosti?' in V. Tambovtsev (ed.) *Prava Sobstvennosti, Privatizatcia i Nationalisacia v Rossii*, Moskva: Novoje Literaturnoje Obozrenije, pp. 145–52.

Rutland, P. (2008a) 'Putin's economic record: is the oil boom sustainable?' *Europe-Asia Studies* 60(6): 1051–72.

——(2008b) 'Democracy in Russia: a Tocquevillian perspective', in A. Craiutu and S. Gellar (eds) *Conversations with Tocqueville. The Global Democratic Revolution in the 21st Century*, Lanham MD: Rowman and Littlefield Publishers.

——(2010) 'The oligarchs and economic development', in S.K. Wegren and D.R. Herspring (eds) *After Putin's Russia. Past Imperfect, Future Uncertain*, Lanham MD: Rowman and Littlefield Publishers, pp. 159–82.

SACP (2006) 'Class struggles and the post-1994 state in South Africa', part 2 of South African Communist Party (SACP) Central Committee Discussion Document, published in Bua Komanisi 5(1), May.

Sandschneider, E. (2001) 'Das innenpolitische "System" Putin', *SWP-Studie*, Berlin: Stiftung Wissenschaft und Politik.

Santana, C.H.V. (2008a) 'BNDES e fundos de pensão à procura do estado da arte', *Custo Brasil* 12, Janeiro.

——(2008b) 'BNDES e Fundos de Pensão: Inserção Externa das Empresas Brasileiras e Graus de Coordenação', *Ponto de Vista* 1, Agosto.

——(2011) 'Conjuntura crítica, legados institucionais e comunidades epistêmicas: limites e possibilidades de uma agenda de desenvolvimento no Brasil', in R. Boschi (ed.) *Variedades de Capitalismo, Política e Desenvolvimento na América Latina*, Belo Horizonte: UFMG.

Santos, F. and Pogrebinschi, T. (2009) 'Conferências Nacionais e Processo Legislativo: participação, deliberação e representação na política brasileira', unpublished article, presented at ANPOCS Annual Meeting, Caxambu.

SARB (2002) *Annual Economic Report, 2002*, Pretoria: South African Reserve Bank.

Satarov, G.A., Levin, M.I. and Cirik, M.L. (1998) 'Rossija i korrupcija: kto kogo', Moskva: INDEM Foundation, www.indem.ru (accessed 10 December 2012).

Sayarı, S. (2011) 'Clientelism and patronage in Turkish politics and society', in F. Birtek and B. Toprak (eds) *The Post-Modern Abyss and the New Politics of Islam: Assabiyah Revisited–Essays in Honor of Şerif Mardin*, Istanbul: Bilgi University Press, pp. 81–94.

Schmidt, V.A. (2002) *The Futures of European Capitalism*, Oxford: Oxford University Press.

——(2008) 'Discursive institutionalism: the explanatory power of ideas and discourse', *American Review of Political Science* 11: 303–26.

——(2009) 'Putting the political back into political economy by bringing the state back in yet again', *World Politics* 61(3): 516–46.

Schmitter, P.C. (2012) 'Varieties of capitalism and types of democracy', in M. Ido (ed.) *Varieties of Capitalism, Types of Democracy and Globalization*, London and New York: Routledge, pp. 17–51.

Schneider, B.R. (2004) *Business Politics and the State in Twentieth Century Latin America*, Cambridge: Cambridge University Press.

——(2008) 'Comparing capitalisms: liberal, coordinated, network, and hierarchical varieties', unpublished article, Evanston IL: Northwestern University.

——(2009) 'Hierarchical market economies and varieties of capitalism in Latin America', *Journal of Latin American Studies* 41(3): 553–75.

Schröder, H.-H. (1999) 'El'tsin and the oligarchs: the role of financial groups in Russian politics between 1993 and July 1998', *Europe-Asia Studies* 51(6): 957–88.

——(2008) 'What kind of political regime does Russia have?' in S. White (ed.) *Politics and the Ruling Group in Putin's Russia*, Basingstoke: Palgrave Macmillan.

Schrooten, M. (2011) 'Brazil, Russia, India, China and South Africa: strong economic growth – major challenges', *DWI Economic Bulletin* 4: 18–22.

Seekings, J. and Nattrass, N. (2005) *Class, Race and Inequality in South Africa*, New Haven CT: Yale University Press.

——(2011) 'State-business relations and pro-poor growth in South Africa', *Journal of International Development* 23(3): 338–57.

Sen, Sukomal (1997) *Working Class of India: History of Emergence and Movement 1830–1990*, second revised edn, Calcutta: K.P. Bagchi & Co.

Sengupta, A, Kannan, K.P. and Raveendran, G. (2008) 'India's common people: who are they, how many are they and how do they live?' *Economic and Political Weekly* 43(11): 49–63.

Sengupta, N.K. (1983) *Changing Patterns of Corporate Management*, Delhi: Vikas.

Shambaugh, D. (2008) *China's Communist Party: Atrophy and Adaptation*, Berkeley and Los Angeles: University of California Press.

Shapiro, J. (2012) *China's Environmental Challenges*, Cambridge: Polity Press.

Shevtsova, L. (2007) *Russia – Lost in Transition. The Yeltsin and Putin Legacies*, Washington, DC: Carnegie Endowment for International Peace.

——(2010) 'What's the matter with Russia?' *Journal of Democracy* 21(1): 152–59.

——(2013) 'Russia and China: is the world ready for their decline?' *The American Interest*, 11 February.

Shi, T. and Lui, J. (2010) 'The shadow of confucianism', *Journal of Democracy* 21(4): 123–30.

Shirk, S.L. (1993) *The Political Logic of Economic Reform in China*, Berkeley and Los Angeles: University of California Press.

Siaroff, A. (1999) 'Corporatism in 24 industrial democracies: meaning and measurement', *European Journal of Political Research* 36(2): 175–205.

Sicsú, J., de Paula, L.F. and Michel, R. (eds) (2005) *Novo-Desenvolvimentismo: Um Projeto Nacional de Crescimento com Equidade Social*, São Paulo: Manole, Konrad Adenauer Stiftung.

Sil, R. (2005) 'The puzzle of the post-communist proletariat: Russian labor in comparative-historical perspective', draft paper prepared for Talk sponsored by CDATS/CERES, Georgetown University, February.

Simmons, B.A., Dobbin, F. and Garrett, G. (2006) 'Introduction: the international diffusion of liberalism', *International Organisation* 60(4): 781–810.

Simmons, C. (1985) '"De-industrialization", industrialization and the Indian economy, c. 1850–1947', *Modern Asian Studies* 19(3): 593–622.

SIPRI (2012) *SIPRI Yearbook 2012*, Stockholm: Stockholm International Peace Research Institute.

Sivasubramonian, S. (2000) *The National Income of India in the Twentieth Century*, New Delhi: Oxford University Press.

Slovo, J. (1990) 'Has socialism failed?' Discussion document (online), www.sacp.org.za/docs/history/failed.html (accessed June 2012).

Sobolev, E.N. (2010) 'Regulirovaniye socialno-trudovikh otnoshenij v Rossii: genesis, mekhanismi, napravlenija transformacii', thesis, Russian Academy of Science, www.vak.ed.gov.ru (accessed 10 December 2012).

Solinger, D.J. (1989) 'Capitalist measures with Chinese characteristics', *Problems of Communism* 38(1): 19–33.

——(1991) *From Lathes to Looms – China's Industrial Policy in Comparative Perspective, 1979–1982*, Stanford, CA: Stanford University Press.

South African Reserve Bank (2011) 'Statistics', Pretoria: SARB (online), www.resbank.co.za (accessed 31 March 2011).

Souza, C. (2011) 'Modernização do Estado e Construção de Capacidade Burocrática no Governo Federal', unpublished article, presented at workshop 'Capacidades Estatais para o Desenvolvimento: Vantagens Institucionais Comparativas em Países Emergentes (BRICS, Turquia e Argentina)', IPEA, November.

SSI (2011) *SSI Statistical Yearbook*, Ankara: Social Security Institution, www.sgk.gov.tr/wps/
portal/en?CSRT=11511896528340930569 (accessed 5 May 2012).

State Statistical Bureau (1997) *Zhongguo tongji nianjin* (Statistical Yearbook of China), Beijing:
Zhongguo tongji chubanshi.

——(2001) *Zhongguo tongji nianjin* (Statistical Yearbook of China), Beijing: Zhongguo tongji
chubanshi.

Steinfeld, E.S. (2010) *Playing our Game: Why China's Economic Rise Doesn't Threaten the West*,
Oxford: Oxford University Press.

Steinmo, S., Thelen, K. and Longstreth, F. (eds) (1992) *Structuring Politics: Historical Institutionalism in Comparative Analysis*, Cambridge: Cambridge University Press.

Stoner-Weiss, K. (2006) 'Russia: authoritarianism without authority', *Journal of Democracy*
17(1): 104–18.

Streeck, W. (1992) *Social Institutions and Economic Performance*, Beverly Hills CA: Sage.

——(2004) 'Taking uncertainty seriously. complementarity as a moving target', Österrei-
chische Nationalbank, *OeNB Workshops*, no. 1: 100–15.

——(2008) *Re-Forming Capitalism: Institutional Change in the German Political Economy*,
Oxford: Oxford University Press.

Streeck, W. and Thelen, K. (2005) 'Introduction: institutional change in advanced political
economies', in W. Streeck and K. Thelen (eds) *Beyond Continuities. Institutional Change in
Advanced Political Economies*, Oxford: Oxford University Press, pp. 1–39.

Streeck, W. and Yamamura, K. (eds) (2001) *The Origins of Nonliberal Capitalism: Germany and
Japan in Comparison*, Ithaca NY: Cornell University Press.

Stubbs, R. (1999) 'War and economic development: export-oriented industrialization in East
and Southeast Asia', *Comparative Politics* 31(3): 337–55.

Su, Z., Hui, Z. and He, J. (2013) 'Authoritarianism and contestation', *Journal of Democracy* 28
(1): 26–40.

ten Brink, T. (2011) 'Institutional change in market-liberal state capitalism: an integrative
perspective on the development of the private business sector in China', MPIfG Discussion Paper 11/2, Cologne: Max-Planck-Institut für Gesellschaftsforschung.

Thelen, K. (2004) *How Institutions Evolve. The Political Economy of Skills in Germany, Britain,
the United States and Japan*, Cambridge: Cambridge University Press.

——(2009) 'Institutional change in advanced political economies', *British Journal of Industrial
Relations* 47(3): 471–98.

Thompson, M, Ellis, R.J. and Wildavsky, A. (1990) *Cultural Theory*, Boulder CO: Westview Press.

Thorner, D. (1956) *The Agrarian Prospect in India: Five Lectures on Land Reform Delivered in
1955 at the Delhi School of Economics*, Delhi: University Press.

Tonin, M. (2009) 'Employment protection legislation in Central and East European countries',
South-East Europe Review 4: 477–91.

Transparency International (2011) *Corruption Perceptions Index 2010*, Berlin: Transparency
International.

Treisman, D. (2007) 'Putin's silovarchs', *Orbis* 51(1): 141–53.

Tsai, K. (2007) *Capitalism without Democracy. The Private Sector in Contemporary China*, Ithaca
NY: Cornell University Press.

Tucker, A. (2010) 'Restoration and convergence: Russia and China since 1989', in G.
Lawson, C. Armbruster and M. Cox (eds) *The Global 1989. Continuity and Change in
World Politics*, Cambridge: Cambridge University Press, pp. 157–78.

Turam, B. (2012) 'Are rights and liberties safe?' *Journal of Democracy* 23(1): 109–18.

Turkish Republic Undersecretariat of Treasury (2004) *Treasury Statistics, 1980–2003*, Ankara:
General Directorate of Economic Research.

Turkish Statistical Institute (2013a) *Foreign Trade by Months and Years*, Ankara: Turkish Statistical Institute, www.tuik.gov.tr/PreHaberBultenleri.do?id=10827 (accessed 17 January 2013).

——(2013b) *Statistical Tables*, Ankara: Turkish Statistical Institute, www.turkstat.gov.tr/VeriBilgi.do?alt_id=61 (accessed 19 January 2013).

——(2013c) *Price Statistics*, Ankara: Turkish Statistical Institute, www.turkstat.gov.tr/PreTablo.do?alt_id=19 (accessed 19 January 2013).

Turok, B. (2008) *From the Freedom Charter to Polokwane: The Evolution of ANC Economic Policy*, Cape Town: New Agenda.

Tyabji, N. (2000) *Industrialisation and Innovation: The Indian Experience*, New Delhi: Sage Publications.

UNCTAD (2010) *World Investment Report*, New York: United Nations Conference on Trade and Development.

——(2011) *World Investment Report*, New York: United Nations Conference on Trade and Development.

Vakulabharanam, V. (2010) 'Does class matter? Class structure and worsening inequality in India', *Economic and Political Weekly* 45(29): 67–76.

van Wyk, J. (2009) 'Cadres, capitalists and coalitions: the ANC, business and development in South Africa, leaders, elites and coalitions', *Discussion Paper* 46: 1104–8417, Uppsala: Nordiska Afrikainstitutet.

Vavi, Z. (2008a) 'Walking through the door', *Mail and Guardian*, 5–11 September: 35.

——(2008b) 'Ten steps to a new economy', *Mail and Guardian*, 19–25 September: 30.

Veblen, T. (1915) *Imperial Germany and the Industrial Revolution*, London: MacMillan.

Virmani, A. (2004) 'India's economic growth: from socialist rate of growth to Bharatiya rate of growth', Working Paper No. 122, Indian Council for Research on International Economic Relations (ICRIER).

——(2011) *Global Economic Governance: IMF Quota Reform*, Washington, DC: International Monetary Fund; IMF Working Paper, July, WP/11/208.

Vis, B. (2008) *Biting the Bullet or Steering Clear? Politics of (Not-) Unpopular Welfare State Reform in Advanced Capitalist Democracies*, Academic Dissertation, Amsterdam: Free University of Amsterdam.

Volkov, V. (2002) *Violent Entrepreneurs: The Use of Force in the Making of Russian Capitalism*, Ithaca NY: Cornell University Press.

Vromen, A. (2010) 'Debating methods: rediscovering qualitative approaches', in D. Marsh and G. Stocker (eds) *Theory and Methods in Political Science*, Basingstoke: Palgrave Macmillan.

Wade, R. (1990) *Governing the Market: Economic Theory and the Role of Government in East Asian Industrialisation*, Princeton, NJ: Princeton University Press.

Wai-Chung Yeung, H. (2004) *Chinese Capitalism in a Global Era: Towards Hybrid Capitalism*, London: Routledge.

Waldmeir, P. (1994) *Anatomy of a Miracle: The End of Apartheid and the Birth of the New South Africa*, London: Penguin.

Waldner, D. (1999) *State-Building and Late Development*, Ithaca, NY: Cornell University Press.

Wang, T. (2013) 'Goodbye to gradualism', *Journal of Democracy* 28(1): 49–56.

Wank, D. (1999) *Commodifying Communism: Business, Trust and Politics in a Chinese City*, Cambridge: Cambridge University Press.

Watson, M. (2003) 'Ricardian political economy and the "varieties of capitalism" approach: specialization, trade and comparative institutional advantage', *Comparative European Politics* 1(2): 227–40.

Wedeman, A. (2012) *Double Paradox. Rapid Growth and Rising Corruption in China*, Ithaca NY: Cornell University Press.

White, G. (1993) *Riding the Tiger – The Politics of Economic Reform in Post-Mao China*, Stanford CA: Stanford University Press.

Wikipedia (n.d.) *Sex-selective Abortion* (accessed June 2012).

——(n.d.) *Sexual Violence in South Africa* (accessed June 2012).

——(n.d.) *Administrative Provinces in the People's Republic of China* (accessed June 2012).

——(n.d.) *Environmental Issues in Brazil* (accessed June 2012).

——(n.d.) *Environmental Issues in India* (accessed June 2012).

——(n.d.) *Environmental Issues in Russia* (accessed June 2012).

——(n.d.) *Environmental Issues in Turkey* (accessed June 2012).

——(n.d.) *Pollution in China* (accessed June 2012).

——(n.d.) *Indian Economy* (accessed June 2012).

Williamson, P.J. and Zheng, M. (2008) 'The global impact of China's emerging multinationals', in C.A. McNally (ed.) *China's Emergent Political Economy – Capitalism in the Dragon's Lair*, New York and London: Routledge, pp. 83–101.

Wolf, A., Wagner, J., Röhn, O. and Nicoletti, G. (2010) *Product Market Regulation. Extending the Analysis Beyond OECD Countries*, OECD Economics Department, Working Paper 799, Paris: Organisation for Economic Co-operation and Development.

World Bank (1992) *China: Reform and the Role of the Plain in the 1990's*, Washington, DC: The World Bank.

——(2003) *The Little Green Book 2003*, Washington, DC: The World Bank.

——(2011) *Worldwide Governance Indicators*, Washington, DC: The World Bank, www. info. worldbank.org/governance/wgi/sc (accessed June 2012).

——(2012a) *The Little Green Book 2012*, Washington, DC: The World Bank.

——(2012b) *World Development Indicators*, Washington, DC: The World Bank.

——(2012c) *China 2030: Building a Modern, Harmonious, and Creative High-Income Society*, Washington DC: The World Bank.

——(2013a) *World Development Indicators: Country Data, Turkey*, Washington, DC: The World Bank, data.worldbank.org/country/turkey (accessed 19 January 2013).

——(2013b) *Worldwide Governance Indicators: Country Data Report for Turkey, 1996–2011*, Washington, DC: The World Bank, info.worldbank.org/governance/wgi/pdf/c221.pdf (accessed 15 January 2013).

WTO (2000–11) *International Trade Statistics* (annual issues), Washington DC: World Trade Organization.

Yakovlev, A. (2006) 'The evolution of business-state interaction in Russia: from state capture to business capture?' *Europe-Asia Studies* 58(7): 1033–56.

Yang, D. (2004) *Remaking the Chinese Leviathan: Market Transition and the Politics of Governance in China*, Stanford CA: Stanford University Press.

Yeldan, E. (2006) 'Neoliberal global remedies: from speculative-led growth to IMF-led crisis in Turkey', *Review of Radical Economics* 38(2): 193–213.

Yurtoğlu, B. (2000) 'Ownership, control and performance of Turkish listed firms', *Empirica* 27: 193–222.

Zaznaev, O. (2008) 'The presidentialization of a semi-presidential regime: the case of Russia', in S. White (ed.) *Politics and the Ruling Group in Putin's Russia*, Basingstoke: Palgrave Macmillan, pp. 27–41.

Zemin, J. (2002) *Build a Well-off Society in an All-Round Way and Create a New Situation in Building Socialism with Chinese Characteristics*, speech at the 16th CPC Party Congress, Beijing, 9 November.

Zheng, Y. (2004) *Globalization and State Transformation in China*, Cambridge: Cambridge University Press.

Zudin, A. (2006) 'Gosudarstvo i biznes v Rossii: evolucija modeli vzaimootnoshenij', *Neprikosnovenniy Zapas*, 6(50) www. magazines.russ.ru/nz/2006/50/zu18.html (accessed 10 December 2012).

Zweig, D. (2002) *Internationalizing China: Domestic Interests and Global Linkages*, Ithaca NY: Cornell University Press.

Index